Hamlyn DIY &
DECORATING

Hamlyn DIY &
DECORATING

HAMLYN

First published in Great Britain in 1996 by
HAMLYN an imprint of
REED CONSUMER BOOKS LIMITED
Michelin House, 81 Fulham Road, London SW3 6RB
and Auckland, Melbourne, Singapore and Toronto

ISBN 0-600-59452-1

A CIP catalogue record for this book is available from the British Library

Publishing Director: **Laura Bamford**
Executive Editor: **Simon Tuite**
Art Editor: **Mark Stevens**
Managing Editor: **Lucinda Pearce-Higgins**
Editor: **Jonathan Hilton**
Contributors: **Ned Halley, Judith Devons and Jackie Matthews**
Jacket Design: **Ben Barrett**
Jacket Photography: **Laura Wickenden**
Photography: **Paul Forrester and Colin Bowling**
Illustrators: **Kevin Hart, Kevin Jones Associates and Paul Webb**
Picture Researchers: **Liz Fowler and Emily Hedges**
Indexer: **Jackie Matthews**
Consultant: **Ned Halley**

Designed by Town Group Consultancy Ltd.
Produced by Pica Colour Separation, Singapore.
Produced by Mandarin Book Production
Printed in China
Reprinted 1997

We would like to thank Parry Tyzack, 329 Old Street, London, EC1 for
their assistance with tools and equipment.

In describing all the projects in this book, every care has been taken
to recommend the safest methods of working. Before starting any task,
you should be confident that you know what you are doing, and that you
know how to use all tools and equipment safely. The Publishers cannot
accept any legal responsibility or liability for accidents or damage
arising from the use of any items mentioned, or in the carrying out
of any of the projects described.

Contents

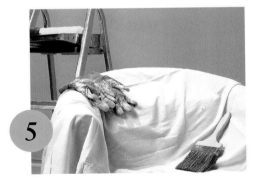

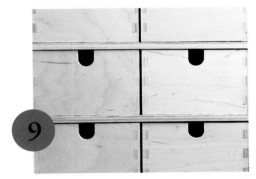

Introduction

Today, the materials and equipment that go into making and maintaining a comfortable and attractive home are within everyone's reach. Choosing do-it-yourself and decorating items, in the day of the hardware superstore, has never been easier, or more enjoyable.

The do-it-yourself industry's success is due to the recognition by manufacturers and retailers that a "professional" standard of work, when it comes to home maintenance and improvement, is no longer the preserve of the full-time craftsman. Tools and materials that were once the preserve of builders, carpenters, and other trades now have no more mystique than a paint brush or a roll of wallpaper.

But of course there is more to decorating than mere merchandise. Paints and wallcoverings may be easier to use than they've ever been, but how do you choose the right colors, patterns and finishes for the effects you want to create? Is there a set technique for papering around a doorway? Which do you paint first, the walls or the ceiling? And while power tools might make light of a job such as preparing wood for a shelving system, what arrangement will best suit your needs, and what methods of construction is most appropriate to your type of home?

In other words, while good materials are a big part of the story, bright ideas and basic skills are no less important. And that is what this book is all about. In plain words and clear illustrations, The *Hamlyn Home Decorating Book* explains the principles of interior decorating and home maintenance, giving guidance on tools and materials, techniques and tricks-of-the-trade, to working efficiently and safely – all with that vital objective, the professional finish, in prospect.

Whether you are a complete novice or a more experienced handyperson intent on more ambitious decorative effects, this book will serve to excite your interest, and to bring new tasks within your scope. Sections of the book range from using color and pattern to repairing and preparing surfaces, creating all kinds of decorative finishes, improving flooring, lighting, storage – even the shapes of your rooms.

In every case, the sections take a step-by-step approach, offering ideas, outlining the items you will need, illustrating the methods by which you can achieve the best possible results. This is a book to inspire as well as to inform, to read at leisure as well as to follow project by project. Whatever type of jobs around the house you are contemplating, if the appropriate section gives you the confidence as well as the practical advice you need to tackle it, then this book will have achieved its purpose.

1

Color

Choosing colors

Adding color, pattern, and texture can be one of the most exciting aspects of decorating your home. Through the use of color, you can express aspects of your personality. Color also allows you to create precisely the mood and atmosphere that you want, and so, as a result, make your home uniquely yours.

The visible spectrum is huge and the color possibilities almost limitless. For example, a red scheme can vary from crimson to scarlet, peach to shocking pink, and it can be adapted to very different living areas. In a formal dining room, lit for evening entertaining, rich crimson tones can be very romantic – suffusing the entire decor from tablecloth to patterned fabrics and carpet. In a sunny family kitchen, the scarlet tones of terracotta tiles, patterned blinds, and a range of accessories can appear to be friendly and inviting. In a bedroom, combining deep and pale tones of rose and peach in the wallpaper, bedspread, and curtains can produce a country-style atmosphere. For something different in the bathroom, consider shocking pink carpeting set against wallpaper decorated with a riot of enormous roses.

Color inspirations

You can build an entire color scheme around a single item such as a rug, or a piece of furniture. For example, your imagination may be inspired by a wooden hutch painted a rough apple green color. This color contrasts wonderfully with brown, and so it is ideally suited to a room with a natural wood floor, unpainted brick walls and pine furniture. The effect you are trying for can be further heightened with additional touches of the same green – for example, in cushion covers, painted window frames, and perhaps a few accessories.

Green is the color we associate with living things, so it is an easy hue to live with and a popular choice for decorating schemes. Particularly if you live in a city, it makes sense to bring the colors of

Above *Soft pink tones and patterned fabrics look perfect in the context of this charming bedroom, offset by the solidity of dark-stained furniture.*

Right *Careful color planning, using bold pattern in checks and colored stripes are united by a continuous color theme. The result is a range of geometric patterns which look part of an integrated theme.*

Left *Highlights of color and pattern from a floor rug are picked up in the furnishings in the room.*

nature indoors; the varieties of green range from earth green to olive green, emerald to turquoise. Consider enhancing a range of greens with a flush of deep purple for a rich, almost regal effect.

For a color scheme that is strikingly different, consider decorating areas of your home in bold blocks of primary colors. A spacious and sparsely furnished sunny hallway or living room can look warm and welcoming with a daffodil-yellow ceiling, bleached wood floors, orange curtains, and turquoise cushions and accessories set against deep blue-grey walls. This, however, is only one possible color scheme from the myriad available from which you can choose.

Another way to add bold splashes of color is to hand-paint or stencil lively motifs on walls and furniture – an ideal treatment for an informal entrance way or kitchen, bedroom or bathroom. The subject of the motif can vary from room to room – to reflect changing uses and activities – or stay consistent throughout, and so act as a unifying decorative element. In this way, you can begin to build bridges between the decorative approaches in different areas of your home.

As you will see in more detail further on, your choice of colors can make a room seem smaller or larger, cramped or spacious, warmer or cooler, brighter or more subdued. Knowing which colors to select to achieve the precise effect you want is not always an easy task. The secret of success lies in the skill with which the fabrics, furniture, wallpaper, and decorative objects are selected and mixed. So it is vital to look and learn as much as you can before actually buying anything.

Developing a color sense

Everyone can develop an eye for harmonious color combinations, and so become aware of how colors and patterns work together. To explore your own taste and style, observe color combinations in window displays, color magazines, and advertising brochures. Make notes of what you like and and what you don't, and even cut out interesting pictures and glue them onto a large sheet of paper. You will soon begin to develop your own personal preferences and discover the combinations you find most pleasing.

There are some broad guidelines to help you choose color combinations for your home. For example, to emphasize spaciousness, choose a limited range of white, pale pastels, or shades of blue. To give a feeling of intimacy, use plenty of deeper tones and bold colors in the warm red range; and include lots of colorful patterns and textures.

Decorating in rich, bright colors will help to enliven a dull, predominantly shady room, while subtle colors and darker tones will subdue a sunny room. Warm bold colors and strong contrasts create a lively and inviting atmosphere, while cool tones and subtle contrasts create more of a calm and relaxed environment.

Despite all these "rules," using color is a very personal matter. Color – like music – varies enormously in the mood and atmosphere it creates, and we all have our own taste. So allow your own style and taste to develop as you plan; have confidence in whatever colors appeal to you, and have fun!

1

COLOR

Above *Bold blocks of primary color have been successfully employed here to create an unusual and striking decor for this children's room.*

Below *Green is a popular choice for a decorating scheme. This unusual variation on the theme incorporates a suffusion of turquoise.*

Bright or dark

When thinking about colors for a decorative scheme, consider what tones they should be to complement the mood and atmosphere of each room. In fact, the tones of a color can have a greater influence on decor than the basic color, making a room appear larger or smaller, brighter or duller. This may seem confusing, but by following a few guidelines you can incorporate a variety of tones in your decorating scheme to achieve very precise effects. First, make a list of factors to consider, such as the dimensions of the room to be decorated. If the room is small, using pale tones will make it appear more spacious; if it is large, dark tones will create a feeling of warmth and intimacy.

If you have a sunless room, you may wish to enliven it with light tones, while a sunny room can tolerate a range of darker tones. Consider, too, the major items of furniture, and the carpets and curtains, that the decor must complement. If you already possess a dark-colored set of furniture and want to create a bright, spacious atmosphere in your living room, consider light tones for the rest of the decor. If, however, you have pale carpets, the room will appear warmer with the addition of deep-toned, rich-colored furnishings.

Below *The warm tones of this shade of pink create an intimate atmosphere, ideal for a bedroom, without closing the room in to any significant degree.*

Right *The pale muted tones in this bathroom provide the perfect atmosphere for long, luxurious bathtimes. Pale tones also maximize the impact of any available natural light.*

White

Decorating in white has many advantages. Since white reflects light, it makes poorly lit areas seem brighter, and it increases the apparent size of a room – ideal for creating an illusion of spaciousness in a relatively small room. White walls are like a bare canvas, complementing pale-toned furnishings and providing a strong backdrop for dark items without making the room seem cluttered. You can easily and quite dramatically alter the mood of a predominantly white room simply by integrating colorful cushions, pictures, and other accessories, all of which can be easily changed.

One drawback to choosing a completely white decor is that it can make a room appear rather cold and clinical. To offset this, include a few touches of warm tones and textured surfaces.

Pastel shades

Decorating a room in pastel shades allows you a great deal of flexibility when it comes to choosing accessories to match. Pastel shades by themselves can help to create an atmosphere that is bright and spacious – useful for small and well-lit areas. At the same time, pastel shades can impart a feeling of tranquillity and restfulness; this may be ideal in

Left *Large rooms allow you more flexibility when it comes to selecting bright or dark tones as part of your decorative scheme. The almost strident contrast between the purple of the chair and sofa coverings and the red of the cushions does not look overpowering in this large, bright, sun-filled room.*

Below *Rich, deep tones of red create a warm, lively atmosphere – ideal for this dining area. The decor does not appear dingy, however, because there is plenty of natural and artificial light to compensate.*

a bedroom or quiet living room where you like to settle down with a good book. Pastel tones from the blue end of the spectrum give a cool effect; those tinged with red, orange, or yellow add warmth.

An easy way to create color harmony with pastel shades is to choose a couple of basic colors – perhaps a pale blue and a beige, for example – and only add tones that are very slightly lighter and darker versions of them.

Dark tones

Decorating with dark tones is a definite design statement. If you are not used to working with color, this decision takes a degree of courage. For a start, it can be difficult to visualize the effect beforehand, and if you are not happy with the result, it will take several coats of paint to restore a light-toned base to work on.

Dark tones can be very effective in the right environment. They are ideal for creating a cozy atmosphere in a large, well-proportioned room, one that either has lots of natural light or else relies on well-placed artificial lighting.

Alternatively, painting one wall of a room, or an alcove within a room, in darker tones can be a useful technique for accentuating certain features or adding a sense of depth. However, you need to exercise caution in small or poorly lit areas. Hallways, especially, need to be bright and inviting.

ILLUSIONS WITH TONES

- For an illusion of both spaciousness and intimacy, use very pale tones for the ceiling and floor, darker hues for the walls, and fill the room with light-colored furniture and accessories.

- Special features and shapes in a room can be highlighted by juxtaposing complementary contrasts of light and dark tones.

- Offset the coldness of very pale tones with textured surfaces and touches of red or orange. Blue tones and smooth surfaces accentuate coolness.

Combining colors

When planning color combinations, you need to consider how bright or dark a decor should be and what range and intensity of color to use. For lively color harmony, it helps to know a few basic principles of color theory and to understand how different colors influence one another when used in interiors.

Above *Color juxtapositions designed to challenge convention have been employed in this imaginatively decorated room. The predominant color here is primary red, which has an enclosing effect on the space. This effect is enhanced by the canopied ceiling, also in red with a smaller panel of blue.*

Right *Although this room looks to be full of color, it is rather illusory, since apart from various shades of pink the only other "color" used is white.*

The color wheel

Color designing is based on the spectrum of visible light, which can be visualized as a color wheel, like that illustrated below. At three equidistant points on the wheel are found the primary colors – red, blue, and yellow – from which all other colors are derived. Mixing two primary colors in equal proportion results in the formation of the secondary colors – orange, violet, and green. When a primary color is mixed with an adjacent secondary color, a tertiary color – such as red-violet or blue-green – is produced. Seeing colors as spokes of a wheel enables you to see how one color relates to another.

Color contrasts

Colors that are on opposite sides of the color wheel, such as blue-green and red, are highly contrasting. Known as complementaries, they will fight for dominance and tend to clash if used in their "pure" intensities. However, you can incorporate them in your decorating scheme either by using them in extremely unequal proportions or by muting one or both of the colors as lighter or darker tones. You can then enliven the overall color scheme by introducing just a few hints of strong contrasting color.

Tonal variations

The pure forms of each of the primary, secondary, and tertiary colors can be modified to create an enormous range of tonal variations simply by adding differing amounts of white or black. However, it is the subtle variations in tone that are most likely to produce color combinations that blend together successfully in a room's

color scheme. For example, a range of pale blue-greens and blues will combine happily together.

If you want the striking contrasts of colors on either side of the color wheel, use lighter or darker tones of one or both colors. As a general rule, lighter tones produce subtle harmonies; darker tones give bolder and more dramatic results.

Warm and cool colors

On one side of the color wheel are the "warm" colors – red-violet, red, red-orange, orange, yellow-orange, and orange. On the other side are the "cool" colors – yellow-green, green, blue-green, blue, blue-violet, and violet.

Colors from the same side of the color wheel tend to blend most effectively, whereas a mixture of warm and cool tones may produce jarring results.

Whether you opt for a warm or a cool color range depends on the mood you wish to create. Warm colors tend to be lively and exciting. Cool colors tend to suggest a relaxed, calm atmosphere. The degree to which you achieve these atmospheric effects depends on the intensity of the colors you choose, and whether you use them pure or mixed.

Right *The brightness of the yellow used on the armchairs and rug is effectively balanced by the white walls and sofa.*

Above centre *With white as the background color, decorative themes can be established by the accessories used within the room. As fashions change, so, too, can the accessories without major upheaval.*

Above *Colors from the red/yellow part of the color wheel produce a warm decorative theme.*

Match or mix

Unless you are starting from scratch with an empty room, you will probably have certain basic elements to match with your color scheme. Do you already have a fitted carpet, a set of curtains, or a suite of furniture to be incorporated? Will you paint the walls in a tone that contrasts or complements the existing colors? Will you introduce more colors and, if so, which ones? The question is, what to match and what to mix?

Left *To create a thoughtful color scheme for a room, determine which color is to be your starting point, or source color. It may, for example, be the dominant color of the sofa fabric. Next, make a test card of paint colors that you can use either to harmonize or contrast with it.*

Above *A predominantly white color scheme produces a decor that feels bright and spacious, which is ideal in a small room.*

Matching a scheme

As a basic rule, choose one color of an existing item and use it as the cornerstone of your color scheme. To match, extend tonal variations of this color – lighter and darker tones – onto the walls and other features.

Alternatively, pick two colors that are very close on the color wheel (*see p. 14*), such as blue and blue-violet, and then use varying proportions of each. As long as you make sure that there is sufficient continuity of color to create a consistent atmosphere, you can then introduce touches of black, white or some other colors to avoid a bland result.

MATCHING COLORS

- Carry fabric swatches with you when shopping for new decorative materials. It is surprisingly difficult to remember exactly how light or dark a color is.

- Colors look different according to the light, so it helps to examine all colors under the same lighting conditions.

- Large expanses of a single color can look dull. Instead, match a variety of closely related tones with an occasional splash of contrasting color to create a more lively harmony.

- For successful color schemes, incorporate a balanced mixture of primary colors, darker tones, and lighter tones.

Below *Softer pastel shades can be used to good effect as a foil for smaller areas of more vivid hues, seen here in the paintwork, fabric cover, cushions, and window shade.*

Experimenting with mixing

You can mix strongly contrasting colors to create a pleasing effect as long as you follow a few basic guidelines. Pure primary colors are lively and vibrant, but they can also be overpowering and garish. To avoid problems, use them in unequal proportions and introduce lighter or darker variations of each. For example, rather than introduce equal amounts of red and yellow in the same color scheme, select varying proportions of paler and darker red-oranges and yellow-oranges.

Complementary colors – those on opposite sides of the color wheel – can be mixed successfully, too. Although such combinations usually clash, they can work if they are less "pure." For example, juxtaposing tones of warm reddish green alongside dark, slightly greenish red creates very pleasing harmonies.

Another way to mix contrasting colors is to start with just a few closely related

Above *In a children's play area, the use of bright primary colors creates the right type of atmosphere and can be visually stimulating as well.*

Center left *The starting point for the decorative scheme in this room was the mellow brown of the ceiling and wall beams, the color of which has been picked up in the curtains, cushion covers, and furniture.*

Bottom left *In a large room, you can be bold in your use of color and pattern. A restrained color palette usually works best, however.*

warm or cool colors and then set them against the opposite cool or warm colors from the color wheel.

Using black and white

White mixes well with almost any color scheme. Interspersed with pale colors, it can create subtle harmonies. White can serve as a backdrop for strong colors or as a way of brightening up dark ones. Black contrasts well with white, yellow and pale tints – ideal for bold and dramatic effects.

Small rooms

Color influences mood. Whatever main color you choose for your decorating scheme, it will have greater dramatic impact on a small space than on a large one. In a small room the focus will be on combining simplicity with rich textures, tones and special features.

   With this in mind, choosing the decor for a small room can seem slightly daunting. However, if you abide by a few basic principles, color can really work to your advantage. Since you can decorate a small room relatively quickly and inexpensively, why not take the chance to experiment? You can try more unusual color combinations and explore different textures and effects.

1

COLOR

LIGHTING AND MIRRORS

- If you use dark colors in a small room, make sure the lighting is adequate so that they don't look dull and gloomy.

- Experiment with indirect lighting. It influences subtle colors and gives an extra dimension to small spaces, particularly in alcoves and corners.

- Since mirrors reflect both light and space, they can dramatically transform a room. They are particularly effective in small spaces, where they can be angled to catch interesting features.

Illusion of spaciousness

When you are not very experienced, the simplest way to ensure an uncluttered and restful effect in a small room is to limit the basic decor to white. Very pale colors make surfaces recede and seem less noticeable, thus creating the impression of spaciousness. Conversely, dark colors emphasize surfaces, making them appear to advance toward you.

Incorporating color

Although white is a good choice for small rooms, if used in its pure form it can be stark and boring. By using just a hint of color, you can begin to make more of a statement. For a start, walls can be painted in one of an enormous range of almost-whites – from warm peach to soft, cool blue. Texture, too, can add interest and warmth to a predominantly white scheme.

   If bright-toned colors are important to you, incorporate curtains, cushions, small prints, or rugs as a way of introducing colors in occasional splashes. When the time comes for a new look, all you need to do is change the accessories. However, if you have a lot of furniture and accessories, it may be better to select plain fabrics and muted tones to avoid a cluttered feeling.

   But don't feel limited to white and the off-whites just because you are decorating

Left *A basic light-toned decor provides an uncluttered background for a small, crowded room.*

in a small room. Why not start with a strong color, such as yellow or violet? There is no basic problem here, as long as you bear one principle in mind – limit your color scheme to different shades of a single color. You can even incorporate dark-toned colors in a small room as long as you avoid creating too many color contrasts or combining them with bright, richly colored furnishings. If you include too many colors, a small room may end up looking cramped and cluttered.

Illusion of height

In a small room with a low ceiling, you can use color to give an illusion of height and space. If the room has no decorative features, simply paint the ceiling white and the walls a single almost-white tone from baseboards to ceiling. If the room has traditional moldings, such as dado or picture rails and cornicing, you can "shade up" by painting each horizontal "band" of the wall a subtle tonal variation of white. As an example, start by painting the ceiling white, the cornice an almost-white tone, then the area above the dado with a touch more color. Continue like this down to the baseboard. The floor will be the deepest color, but avoid very dark floor tones, as this will make the room look even smaller than it is.

Left In a small room, color-coordinated furnishings add interest to a plain, pale background. The mood can be changed quickly and without great cost simply by changing accessories, furnishings, cushions, and blinds.

Below In a small kitchen, built-in units, such as floor and eye-level cupboards and cabinets, make more effective use of the available space than freestanding furniture.

Bottom Using bright-colored furnishings and accessories is a good way of introducing visual interest when space is tight.

Rooms within rooms

Many modern houses, as well as older-style traditional houses, have deep alcoves, recesses, or even a storeroom, that can be modified to make a room within a room. If the area is reasonably large, then a private bathroom (*see below*) may be a possibility. If the space is smaller, however, it could be ideal as a walk-in closet. Natural light will probably be restricted, if not absent altogether, so you need to pay particular attention to the colors used and the way they are affected by different types of artificial lighting.

Large rooms

Making a small room feel spacious is a familiar decorative challenge. Less frequent, perhaps, but equally challenging is the task of making a large, high-ceilinged room feel warm, intimate, and friendly. In both of these situations, color is a vital tool for producing the particular effect you want to achieve.

Warm-toned surfaces in reds, oranges, and yellows give the illusion of appearing to advance toward the viewer, so they are an ideal choice when you want to make distant walls seem nearer and the room cozier. In contrast, cool blue and green tones give a feeling of movement away from the viewer, so they are better avoided in this situation.

Deep, rich colors emphasize surfaces, making them appear to advance toward the viewer, and so are another good choice for large rooms. Conversely, pale tones are less conspicuous and have the effect of making surfaces blend into the background. This makes them more suitable for decorating small rooms.

A large room can withstand – and even benefit from – strong, pure colors. In fact, decorating it in a variety of colors, tones, and textures is another way of making it appear intimate. All the vivid contrasts break up large expanses of space, creating interest and a feeling of warmth. It is a good idea to link these strong colors with their very pale equivalents – or neutral colors, such as tones of grey – to avoid garish results.

CREATING AREAS OF INTEREST

- If you decorate a room in predominantly warm, dark tones, introduce furnishings in pale tones of the same warm colors for harmony and brightness.

- Create two well-defined but linked areas in a large room by decorating one area in subtle warm tones and the other in similarly subtle cool tones.

- Try painting just one wall of a large room in a dark tone to create an area of intimacy.

- Experiment with lighting to create different areas of interest in a large space – recessed lights for soft background effects, spotlights for work surfaces, and display lights for focal points.

Creating zones

In a very large, open-plan room, one way to achieve a feeling of intimacy is to create several clearly marked zones. Each zone can be defined both by its color scheme and by its furniture. For example, to break up an expansive living room, choose four complementary tones for each of, say, four areas – perhaps one for a dining corner, another for studying, another by the windows for daytime work, and another for evening relaxation and socializing. Be sure to choose colors that are different enough to provide the desired contrast, but not so far apart in the spectrum that they clash and compete for attention. Link the colors together by interspersing some neutral tones, such as beige or grey.

Left *The use of different areas of bright color, tone, and pattern attracts the eye and, thus, helps to prevent this large, long room from appearing impersonal. The structural beams also act as visual "resting points," so you don't immediately look to the far end of the space.*

Opposite top *Open shelves and doorless cupboards make a feature of the wide range of objects, ornaments, and utensils in this large kitchen – an effect that would be overpowering in a smaller room.*

Opposite right *Large expanses of strong, pure color help to break up the areas of pale-toned decor in this living room. The effect is eye-catching without being garish.*

Lowering a high ceiling

There are some simple decorating tricks you can try in order to reduce the apparent height of a high-ceilinged room. One method is to paint the ceiling in a dark, rich tone such as a brick red, possibly matching the floor covering. Then paint the walls in a complementary pale shade. This will add intimacy and, at the same time, avoid a drab or dull atmosphere.

If the walls of the room have dados or other interesting features, paint these in a contrasting lighter tone to create another focal point and further break up the expanse of wall surface. Alternatively, paint both the ceiling and the top of the walls down to the dado in one dark tone, the dado in the contrasting pale tone, and the lower walls in a medium tone that complements the ceiling and upper walls. This will give the illusion of a much more compact room with a lower ceiling height.

Purpose and mood

Choice of colors in decorating your home is partly determined by the size and shape of each of the rooms, the existing furnishings, the furniture and the lighting. However, most important of all, your decorating scheme will reflect the mood that you wish to create; and this in turn will be influenced by the function of each of the different areas of your home.

When you are choosing a color scheme, consider the purpose of each room and how much it is used. For example, do you have a busy living room with a lot of activity in a small space? If so, lots of strong colors may add to the confusion. Instead, plan color schemes that provide a fairly simple, neutral background. Perhaps you have a clinical-looking bathroom that could benefit from a lively color treatment, or a room that needs to serve more than one function at different times of the day.

Whatever your color scheme, think about how frequently you may need to redecorate and how much you may want to spend. If you want to be able to create an entirely different atmosphere at minimal cost, keep the room's basic color scheme fairly light and simple. Then you can introduce strong colors with curtains, blinds, painted woodwork, prints, plants, accessories, and lighting – all of which can be changed with minimal disruption.

Kitchen

Although kitchens vary enormously in basic design, they are working spaces that need to be bright and fresh. Rich yellows, oranges, and reds often work well. Cool blues and greens tend to be effective in rooms with lots of early-morning sunlight. Since most kitchens are cluttered places, choose a color scheme that is easy on the eyes – such as pale, soft tones – and add color with accessories. If you have a broad expanse of plain-colored laminate or wood, created by the doors and drawers of built-in units, you will have lots of scope for using a contrasting color on the walls and floor.

Above *The kitchen is often regarded as the heart of the home. This is where meals are prepared and, in a large kitchen, where the family gathers to eat and, often, just to socialize. The colors and patterns in this kitchen radiate a feeling of warmth, and the general clutter is welcoming and relaxed.*

Left *The Shaker influence is evident here, with a row of high-level pegs used to keep utensils and other kitchen requisites handy but out of the way. Although this is essentially a hardworking space, color has been used to create a sunny atmosphere, while the single concession to comfort is a wicker easy chair.*

Right *A plain, yet colorful, decorative scheme is perfectly in keeping with the simple, adobe-style plastered walls and ceiling of this family room.*

Living room

The living room is the area of the house for relaxing in, enjoying leisure activities, getting together with the family, and entertaining. And so the ideal color scheme should reflect all the moods and atmospheres required of this multipurpose space. Personal tastes vary greatly, but one approach would be to decorate a busy living room with plain, pastel walls or small-patterned wallpaper. In a sparsely furnished room, splash out with bold, contrasting colors and patterns to enliven the decoration and perhaps create two or more color zones.

Home office/work area

The working environment at home should be decorated in clean, simple tones that offer the least excuse for eyes to wander. Typical schemes are black and white or one using wood and neutral browns.

Bedroom

Although most people aim for an atmosphere that is peaceful, relaxing, and comfortable for the bedroom, the choice of color is a highly subjective one. Some people like the romantic atmosphere of warm pastel shades, for example, while others prefer the cool tranquillity of blues and blue-grey. If you are uncertain, then consider a range of pale harmonies in tones of beige and brown. These are warm yet fairly neutral, and they respond well to small touches of color.

Child's room

When you plan a child's room, take account of changing needs and tastes over the years – from nursery to play room to teenage study area. If you want to keep

redecorating costs down to a minimum, consider using a basically neutral decor for walls, ceiling, and any built-in furniture, while making changes with new accessories as necessary.

Bathroom

The bathroom tends to be a cool room – made colder by the unyielding enamel, chrome, glass, and ceramic surfaces. Unless you are starting from scratch, you will want to work your decorative scheme around the color of the existing bathtub, sink, tiles, and other fixtures. Warm-toned, off-white walls, brightly colored accessories, and lots of green plants are a straightforward choice for softening the bathroom environment. But since the bathroom is used only briefly and infrequently, you could take the opportunity to experiment with more colorful and adventurous options.

Hall

The hall is the first thing visitors see when they enter your home, so it sets the mood for the rest of the house. If the entrance is spacious, consider using vivid colors and large-patterned decorations. However, follow a basic decorating guideline and stick to simple patterns, pale colors, and small designs if you want to make a narrow entrance hall seem wider and more inviting. You can also use subtly contrasting colors and textures to add interest to a hallway that is long or narrow.

Top left *A home office needs to have as few distractions as possible, so a simple black and white scheme is a practical choice.*

Middle left *Decorating in tones of blue and white provides a streamlined yet elegant decor for this study/bedroom. The beige carpet lends warmth to what would otherwise be a cool color scheme.*

Left *A ship's lantern, a model sailboat, and a frieze of frolicking dolphins creates the perfect mood for this country-style bathroom.*

Collecting samples

Collect samples of existing and proposed wallcoverings, carpets, upholstery, curtain fabrics, and any other major decorative elements. Take them with you when you shop for each item, and lay them on a flat surface to see how they look next to one another, keeping in mind the expanse of space to be covered by each color and the type of illumination they will be seen by.

Color
impact

In our everyday lives, brilliant colors are available at every turn. Part of the experience of visiting other countries is in viewing the colors of the landscape and buildings that we see there. These colors define a nation, and can differentiate the south of France from the south of the United States.

When visiting New England, no one can fail to be charmed by the array of brown-red barns and pale blue, grey and ocher painted houses, In Mexico, the colors are lively and extrovert combinations of vivid earth reds and yellows juxtaposed with brilliant greens and vibrant pinks and blues.

On European soil, the stunning, dusty, earthy pinks of Italy have long been an inspiration to many, while in Greece, Spain and Portugal, there are dazzling buildings painted in limewash white, often with a touch of clear blue.

All countries use earth colors, especially oxide reds and yellow ochers, which have always been cheap and plentiful. These color tones differ slightly from one country to the next – sometimes being warmer or deeper.

Today, the interest in historical color has been revived, with the help of historians, conservationists, and artists who advocate and realize the need to understand the authentic colors of the past world.

Left *Cushions, rugs, and fabric in rich tones and patterns of blues and purples are beautifully set off by the soft yellow of the paintwork. Lengths of cream fabric fall from a crown heading in soft folds around the sofa-bed. Casual combinations of cushions, pillows and accessories are ideal for creating intimate and relaxing corners of the home in which to rest and to enjoy a quiet time.*

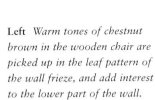

Above *The contrasting colors, patterns and textures of this rug and cushion show how easy it is to add interest to any arrangement.*

Left *Warm tones of chestnut brown in the wooden chair are picked up in the leaf pattern of the wall frieze, and add interest to the lower part of the wall.*

Left *This stencilled ivy leaf motif trails delightfully around the handle and frame of the door and is continued along the tops of the walls, bringing the vibrant shades of yellow and blue into contact with one another.*

Color in your home is created by a variety of elements which include paints, wallcoverings, furnishings, textured fabrics, furniture, floor coverings, and works of art of all kinds. These elements can work together, resonate in tone, or vibrate with their difference. Whether you select one style or create a happy mix, every single element that you place in a room relates to each other and interacts. These choices create an atmosphere that is uniquely your own.

Below *The paintwork of this hand-detailed baseboard and door frame creates a strong country feel to this room.*

Below *Bold patterns in fabrics and furnishings are used, to dramatic effect, in this vibrant color range.*

Above *This distinctive floor painting is influenced by the strong patterns and colors of the fabric furnishings in the room.*

Right *Velvet cushions piled high and trimmed with tasseled fringe serve as an attractive small table. The luxurious textures and deep colors of the cushions create a stylish contrast to the natural materials of the basket holding them.*

Left *This traditional polished wood chair compliments the simplicity of the neutral tones of the walls and the richer color scheme of the furnishings in this basement room.*

Right *A calm and tranquil environment is created through this imaginative and inventive exploration of the full range of shades and tones available when using a simple color scheme of just one or two colors. This effective combination of varieties of brown and neutral color creates an atmosphere of spaciousness, warmth and harmony. The strength of the natural light adds a lightness and vitality to what is already a stylishly sumptuous room setting.*

Choosing patterns

Like color, pattern can serve many functions. Patterned wallcoverings can be a focal point or a backdrop, or they can alter the apparent dimensions of a room. In addition, patterns are more effective than plain surfaces in disguising an odd-shaped room or covering uneven walls. Patterned fabrics can give a new lease of life to old upholstery, and patterned rugs and curtains can be stylish and sophisticated. When choosing, you need to consider how effectively a large area of pattern will complement or contrast with your existing color schemes.

Patterns influence the mood of a room, much like colors do, so start by considering the function of the room. Large, bold patterns – like deep, rich colors – are intense and active, and work best as focal points in large living areas. Small, subtle patterns – like pale, neutral colors – offer a less-challenging backdrop.

You will also need to consider the basic color scheme with which the pattern will contrast or harmonize. If the pattern is fairly small, it will take on the appearance of a single tone when seen from a distance. You can then use the principles of color matching to decide if it works with the rest of the decor.

A common mistake is to choose a pattern that is either too dark or too fussy. Be sure to consider both the lighting and the size of the area you are decorating. If you are not certain what pattern to choose, opt for one with an off-white background and colors subtly contrasting or complementing the colors in the room.

Balance is all important. Too little variety of color, tone, pattern, or texture can make the room seem lifeless. Too much, and it can look chaotic. If you already have a neutral color scheme, then you have the scope to balance it with a variety of rich patterns. But if you have heavily patterned, richly colored curtains, consider a plain wallcovering in a muted tone of the predominant color in the pattern.

Right *A limited range of colors – predominantly blue and red – prevent the pattern in this room from becoming overpowering. The stark plainness of the upper walls and ceiling is an effective balance.*

COLLECTING IDEAS

- To collect ideas for color and pattern combinations, keep a file of samples from magazines and swatches of color and pattern of your existing and proposed decor. Pay attention to any bold-colored items that need to match, and take all the samples with you when shopping for fabrics and wallpaper.

- Remember that the predominant colors in a pattern influence mood. Reds have a warm, welcoming quality; blues are restful and calming; browns and oranges are warm; yellows are bright and reflective; greens have a natural, cool, and spacious feel. Patterns in pale, neutral tones of these colors act like texture to add depth and interest rather than explicit mood.

Size and scale

1

COLOR

The scale of patterns that you incorporate into your decorating scheme can vary from enormous repeats that dominate a room to minuscule mini-prints that are hardly visible from a distance. Generally, large patterns have much the same effects and uses as vivid colors, while small patterns function like muted colors. It is easier to have a great variety of color and pattern if the patterns are detailed and of a fairly similar small size.

Large patterns

Large-scale patterns require careful planning. If the design contrasts highly with its background, it will create a basic color scheme around which the rest of the decor must revolve. Usually, large, bold patterns emphasize form and movement. They look most attractive when used on large areas such as a stairway, where the design can be seen in its entirety without the interruption of furnishings. Like dark colors, they can also be effective on a single wall of a large room, as a focal point

Below left *Big areas of large-scale patterns, such as the ones in this living room, in vivid primary colors dominate a room. The effect will be overpowering unless the room is well proportioned and balanced with more muted decorative elements, such as a comparatively plain carpet and ceiling.*

Below *A very limited range of colors has been used here, from the blue-purple part of the spectrum. Note that although the patterning is bold, it is all of a consistent size and the background is plain.*

Right *Apart from the full-length drapes, this dining room is totally without pattern. The expanse of red of the walls, ceiling, and carpet is effectively alleviated by the high-gloss white woodwork.*

PATTERN FOR EFFECT

- Bold, vertically striped wallpaper increases the apparent height of either small or larger rooms.

- Horizontal stripes make the walls appear longer and lower.

- One way to incorporate a large-scale design into a fairly small room is to choose a pattern with muted colors on a background that does not form too vivid a contrast.

or backdrop to plain furnishings. Large patterns tend to make a small room look smaller, and are less suitable for rooms with lots of windows, doors, or alcoves, since the motifs will be constantly interrupted. However, you can emphasize the intensity of a small space by using a large pattern in a small room.

Small patterns

Small patterns – like pale, neutral colors – suit smaller spaces. They are particularly effective in rooms with lots of surfaces at different angles, such as an attic room. Here, miniature designs, such as small floral patterns, can give the illusion of a larger, cohesive space.

Tiny patterns take on a single color and tone when viewed from a distance, making them the easiest to match to a color scheme. Whether you allow a small-scale pattern to function as a single tone throughout a room, or coordinate it with areas of plain color, is a personal decision. In general, however, a balance of plain color and patterned areas tends to be easy on the eyes. Avoid using small designs in large rooms, since they can look spotty.

Above right *The blue check chair was the starting point for this room's decorative theme. The blue color, contrasted with white, is repeated in the curtains and wall lamps and, using paler tones, in the wallpaper, too. The yellow background color of the sofa finds expression in the pot of flowers, and is reflected in the wall frieze.*

Right *It is easier to change from one pattern to another if you mark the transition by making it a feature. The change from the airy pattern of the upper walls to the busier lower walls is accomplished by using a frieze with a large, repeating pattern.*

Pattern harmony

Contrasting a single pattern with a limited number of solid colors requires thought and planning. The size, style, and colors of the pattern all need to be selected carefully so they harmonize with the rest of the decor. When it comes to combining two or more patterns that match or contrast with one another, the challenge is that much greater. However, by following a few guidelines, you will quickly see how to use a variety of patterns to create a strikingly successful decorative scheme.

MAKING DECISIONS

- Making a sample board is both useful and fun. Collect samples of the materials you propose to use and see how they look when laid out next to one another on a board. Include colors from paint charts, swatches of fabrics, pieces of wallcoverings, samples of carpet and scraps of any other materials. Cut out the samples into their correct proportion in relation to the scheme and paste them onto the board.

- If you are using a variety of patterns, create visual continuity by relating their predominant colors throughout the house.

- Link areas of the home by limiting the wallcoverings in the halls and stairways to a single pattern and color, or by having fitted carpets in a single color and texture throughout the house.

Size, shape and color

There are many ways to create a decorative scheme with patterns. So much color mixing and matching is a matter of personal taste! For example, patterns can be the same size and form but have different colors, such as varied floral designs. Or they can have the same form and color but be different sizes, such as different types of stripe. Or they can have the same color and size but have varied forms, such as a mixture of geometrics and florals.

Perhaps the easiest way to match patterns is to pick ones that have the same size and design and differ only in color. In this context, you then really only have to choose colors that contrast or blend well together, following the guidelines established earlier.

If you want to combine small, regular patterns with large, bold ones, make sure that the two patterns are linked by color. If the overall colors of each pattern are close to one another on the color wheel (see p. 14), the effect will be successful.

Above *In this bedroom, a clever mix of patterns creates a striking yet restful decor. The patterns, varying from plaid and star-shaped to floral, are linked through a limited number of colors close in tonal range.*

Below *Two different patterns – one large and geometric, the other small and floral – have been linked through color. Yellow and white are repeated in the wallpaper, tablecloth, and cushions, as well as in the bedposts, chair, and table lamp. Even the framed prints are color-coordinated.*

Right *In this kitchen, two different styles of pattern have been connected through the use of color.*

Below *Although initially looking discordant, all the various colors making up the patterns in this child's room have been thoughtfully coordinated to produce overall harmony.*

Bottom *The same plant motif has been carried through comprehensively in this room – in the chair and table coverings, curtains, wallpaper, and frieze.*

Successful contrasts

When you match or mix your pattern, if their main colors are complementary they will work well together – if they are lightened or darkened in tone, and used in unequal amounts. Common examples of complementary colors that contrast successfully are rust red with dark green and dark blue with orange.

Very different patterns – such as florals and geometrics – can also work together, if their main colors are linked. As a general rule, the more complex the patterns, the simpler the colors should be, to avoid clashes. For good results, choose patterns with a single main color and small amounts of contrasting accent colors; or patterns with two main colors that are very close in tone; or mix complementaries and link them with neutral tones.

Pleasing results can also be obtained by matching large, bold patterns with small-scale versions of the same or similar designs in the same color scheme. This can be very effective in a child's bedroom.

Pattern
and texture

Like pattern, texture is often used for decorative effect – adding interesting focal points, and variety to a room. Textured surfaces, whether on walls, furnishings, or flooring, are also useful as a device for concealing underlying imperfections. Since the texture of a surface has a significant effect on how the final color looks, it is an important element to consider when planning a scheme.

The same color appears quite different depending on whether it is applied to a rough or smooth surface. Rough surfaces scatter light and make colors appear darker and duller. They can, in some situations, create interesting shadows. By contrast, smooth surfaces reflect light and make colors look lighter and livelier. Even black or very dark walls reflect some light if decorated with gloss paint.

Texture and lighting

Imagine a well-lit room with ceramic-tiled floors, shiny plastic furniture, venetian blinds, and gloss walls. Painted in primary colors, these smooth, shiny surfaces would reflect all the light, and the resulting glare would be overbearing. Yet in a poorly lit area, such colors and textures could serve a valuable function. Now imagine the same room with thick-pile carpets, wood furniture, lace curtains, and burlap wall-covering. In strong light, these textures would modify even the palest colors and prevent glare. Yet in poor light, even a white color scheme could look drab.

Creating a mood

Smooth surfaces create a cold, clean, sparse mood – especially when combined with black or white. Such a scheme may be ideal for the bathroom, and it could also work well for a business-like study. However, for a bedroom or candle-lit dining area, textured surfaces, such as brick, wood, cork, and coarse fabrics, can create a softer mood. When used with a combination of muted colors and tones, they imply warmth and intimacy.

Combining color, pattern and texture

Just as the predominance of a single color can be overwhelming or dull, so too can the use of a single texture or pattern. However, it is best to limit the variety of textures and patterns if you have a complicated color scheme. Otherwise, the effect can be cluttered and confusing. For example, if you have a range of textured surfaces in tones of, say, brown and beige, it is a good idea to limit the patterns and stick to smooth surfaces for the other colors in the room.

TRICKS WITH TEXTURES

- Create visual continuity by linking interconnecting rooms with the same carpet or by repeating a fabric.

- Break up large areas into more intimate areas by using textured hangings, drapes, and rugs.

- Create contrasts by interspersing textures and patterns with areas of plain, smooth color.

Above *Texture and pattern dominate in this child's bedroom, giving an enclosed and comforting, yet visually stimulating, effect.*

Opposite top *The pattern of a tiled floor, overlaid with a brightly patterned rug, anchors interest firmly at ground level in this lofty bedroom.*

Opposite bottom *Visual continuity has been assured here through the use of repeated color – the red, blue, and purple of the walls, ceiling, and furniture echoed in the patterning of the rugs and bedspread.*

Left *When only small areas of pattern are used, they immediately become a focal point for a room.*

Focal patterns

1

COLOR

If the room you are decorating has a special feature, you might like to emphasize it and treat it as a focal point. The most obvious focal points are fireplaces, large bay windows, and unusual recesses. Any of these could be accentuated by applying pattern to the surface. For example, to highlight a fireplace, use a wallcovering in a warm-toned complementary style, or turn an alcove or wall into a focal point with a splash of colorful pattern; offset these by keeping the adjacent walls plain. You could enhance a bay window with richly patterned floor-to-ceiling curtains.

The opposite can also work successfully. For example, you could decorate most of the room in subtle patterns, leaving an expanse of solid color in a featured alcove, as a backdrop to shelves of attractive ornaments or a display of framed pictures.

In general, select smaller and more subtle patterns for small areas; larger, bolder patterns work better in more spacious areas. Strong patterns tend to dominate and should be used thoughtfully. In a narrow room, horizontal stripes make the space look wider. Regular geometric patterns are more static and formal, while repetitive floral patterns give a sense of movement and flow.

PLANNING

- Warm, rich colors and hard, shiny surfaces appear to come toward you. Cool colors and soft flat textures give the appearance of receding more into the background. Bear this in mind when you want to alter the apparent size of a room.

- Draw a sketch of the room and indicate areas of contrasting color, texture, and pattern. When selecting a focal point, keep in mind a balance of activity in order to avoid making one area busy with pattern and color and another area relatively quiet and plain.

Above *This extremely white bathtub is set in a bathroom which is dominated by pastel colors. They work harmoniously together to give a very spring-like feel to a room which is both fresh and bright.*

Below *In this attic, attention is drawn toward the boldly colored, patterned rug. By limiting the range of colors and forms, the room looks more spacious than it really is.*

Planning the framework

At the planning stage, you will have lots of decorating ideas about incorporating light and dark tones, contrasting and harmonizing colors, and using textures and patterns. However, what seems like a good idea in theory may not be very appealing once you see the finished result. And what works for each room individually may be jarring as an overall scheme. In order to avoid disappointment, it is a good idea to think through a variety of decorating possibilities before starting.

Begin by listing the main colors, tones, patterns, and textures you are considering for each room. Draw a rough plan of the rooms involved and mark the existing features you do not intend to change. Make several copies, and color in different decorative schemes and color combinations. Attach samples of the wallcoverings and fabrics for both the new and the existing ones.

When looking at your plans, make sure there are some decorative elements that link different areas to create visual harmony. You could, for example, use the same carpet color throughout the house, or leave all doors as unpainted wood. With just a little careful planning, you will be able to achieve a harmonious decorative scheme and a balance of moods and styles for your own home.

Above *The simple device of using the same colors in the rugs leads the eye easily and naturally from one room to the other, creating a sense of unity.*

Left *The focus in the room is created by the fireplace. A play of color, tone and line is set up between the ceiling, beams and walls, the floor rugs, and the sofa.*

Basic eq

uipment

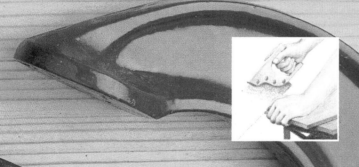

Tools you need

The right tools for the job greatly simplify the task in hand and ensure the best possible results. Some tools are expensive, but you must weigh their cost against the savings you will make by not paying someone else to do the work for you. Always buy the best tools you can afford; good, well-cared-for tools will last, so think of them as an investment.

Sharp scissors, chisels, and knives give a clean cut and are safer to use than blunt ones. For general use, do not buy a prepackaged tool kit. These often include a number of tools you will never use. Be selective and choose tools according to the work you plan to do.

Clean tools immediately after use. A wipe with an oily rag helps metal surfaces stay rust-free. Never let sharp tools rub against each other – this is the most common cause of blunted cutting edges.

A soft hold-all is best for carrying tools. Wooden, metal, or plastic tool boxes are heavy and cumbersome.

BE SAFE

- Keep hands away from the direction of any cut. Wherever possible, clamp work to free both hands to hold the tool correctly.

- Always unplug power tools when they are not in use, and store them out of reach of children. Wear protective clothing where recommended (*see p. 48*).

A basic tool kit

You will find many of the following tools useful for everyday household tasks. Specific tools for decorating and other special tasks are described in detail on later pages (*see p. 39-43*).

Portable workbench This provides a working surface and highly adaptable vise, and can be used as a step-up or as one of two trestles.

Steel ruler For use as an accurate cutting guide as well as for marking straight lines.

Yardstick Plastic rulers are lightweight and the folding wooden types are convenient.

Counterclockwise from top **1** *Heavy-duty craft knife* **2** *Saw*
3 *Backsaw* **4** *Mini hacksaw*
5 *Mole grips (self-grip wrench)*
6 *C-clamp* **7** *Adjustable wrench*
8 *Pincers* **9** *Pliers* **10** *Needle-nose pliers*

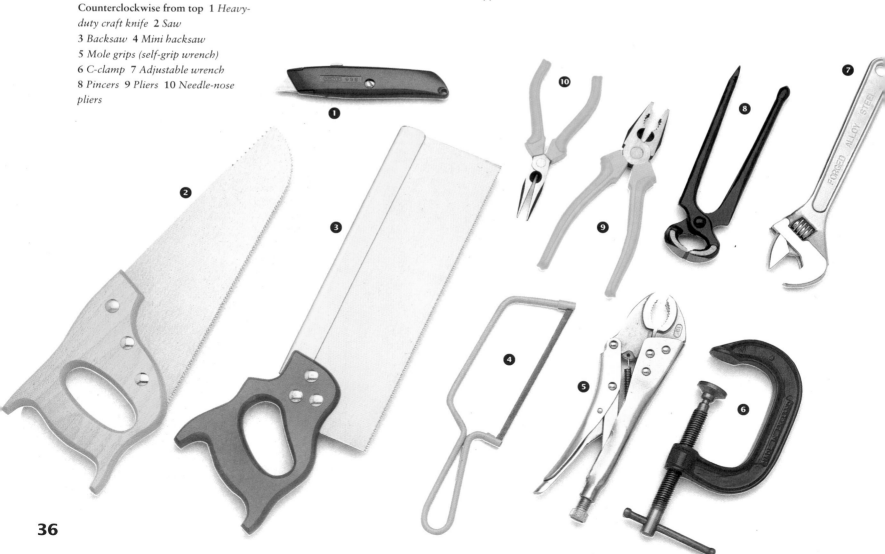

Carpenter's level For checking horizontal and vertical surfaces before fixing them in place.

Backsaw For fine cutting smaller wood sections, 10in (25cm), 13pt – the pt, or "point," refers to the number of teeth per inch (2.5cm) of blade.

Crosscut saw Used for cutting both metal and wood. Copes well with old and reclaimed wood that may contain nails or screws.

Mini hacksaw For cutting metal.

Crosscut handsaw Used for cutting larger wood sections, 22in (56cm), 10pt.

Cross-slot (Pozidriv/Supadriv) screwdriver Blade sizes differ for variously gauged crosshead screws.

Standard screwdriver Blade sizes differ according to screw sizes. Good-quality ratchet and spiral-ratchet screwdrivers are worthwhile labor-saving tools.

Electrician's screwdriver The handle is specially insulated to protect the user against accidentally touching a live wire.

C-clamps Used for holding work in position, 4in and 8in (10cm and 20cm).

Power drill With or without cord.

Set of twist drills and masonry drills Twist drills for wood and softer metals only. Not interchangeable.

Self-grip wrench (mole) Snap-locks onto objects, leaving your hands free.

Needle-nose pliers For gripping and manipulating small, hard-to-reach objects.

Pincers For pulling nails.

Craft knife With disposable blades.

Adjustable wrench With 1in (2.4cm) opening for routine plumbing tasks.

Chisels Choose the bevel-edged type. Sizes include ¼in, ½in, ¾in and 1in (6mm, 1.2cm, 1.8cm and 2.5cm.

Claw hammer The claw pulls out nails.

Soft-face mallet Used when it is important not to leave any mark on metal and wood surfaces.

Carpetner's square For marking right angles.

File For smoothing ½in (1.2cm) round.

Steel measuring tape Typically 12ft (3.5m) in length. Some types are clearly marked with both metric and imperial measurements.

Glue gun Filled with sticks of special adhesive and sealant for quick repair work.

Shaping tool Surform 9in (23cm).

Tool carrier Lightweight carrier for the tools needed for the job at hand.

Counterclockwise from top **1** *Soft-face mallet* **2** *Lump hammer* **3** *Claw hammer* **4** *Pin hammer* **5** *Cold chisels* **6** *Standard screwdrivers* **7** *Cross-slot screwdriver* **8** *Awl* **9** *Steel ruler* **10** *Carpenter's level* **11** *File* **12** *Steel tape measure* **13** *Chisels*

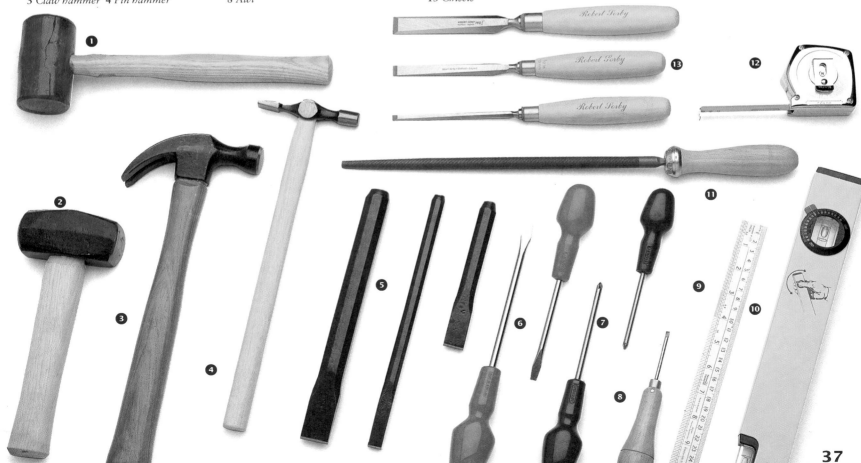

Painting tools

The way you apply paint is largely a matter of personal choice. You can use brushes in conjunction with a paint-roller – a tool developed for the amateur user of latex paint. The paint pad has its advantages, too.

There are also a few vital special items: triangular shave hooks and flexible scrapers for removing old paint; masking tape for protecting surfaces not to be painted; paint shield of metal or plastic to restrict paint to the area being painted; tack or tacky rag to pick up dust; clean, lint-free rags; paint stirrer (there is one usable with a power drill); paint buckets.

Use a bucket so the bulk of your paint stays free from contamination. It also makes carrying paint – especially up ladders – much easier, since not all paint cans have handles.

Brushes

For a good finish, choose brushes with genuine bristle or with the best-quality synthetic bristle. As a rule, costlier brushes do give the best results. Use inexpensive brushes for outside work, such as applying preservatives to wooden fencing or painting masonry.

Brushes that are well cared for improve with use. Loose bristles are shed and the tips become nicely rounded. Start a brush on primer and undercoat, then use it for fine finishing as it ages.

Useful brush sizes include an angled ¾in (1.8cm) cutting-in brush and ½in, 1in, 2in, and 4in or 5in (1.2cm, 2.5cm, 5cm, and 10cm or 12.5cm) brushes.

Radiator brush A brush with an elongated metal handle that can be bent to allow you to paint behind radiators.

Rollers

Used with a paint tray, the roller offers an easy way of applying paint to large, flat areas without leaving defined brush strokes. It is best for applying water-based paints, which you can easily clean off the roller. When using solid latex paint, lift the roller direct from the container. Roller types include:

Foam With easy-clean removable sleeve, but does not give the finest finish and will tear when used on rough surfaces.

Mohair Very close pile on a hard roller, giving fine finish to smooth surfaces. Not suitable for textured surfaces.

Shaggy pile Deep, floppy pile makes it suitable for textured surfaces. Can also be used to apply textured paint.

Radiator roller A thin, deep-pile roller on a long wire handle to reach behind radiators and into other awkward spots.

Texturing roller Specialized roller used to produce a rag-rolled effect.

Paint pads

These pads of fine mohair pile stuck to a layer of foam bonded to a metal or plastic handle are light and easy to use. Sizes range from 1in to 6in (2.5cm to 15cm), some with a hollow handle to hold the end of a broom for painting tops of walls or ceilings without a ladder. Suitable for smooth or textured but not rough surfaces.

Clean pads immediately after use, with water where water-based paints have been used. A pad does give a very fine finish when gloss-painting flush doors. Note that commercial cleaners can attack the adhesive holding the mohair to the foam.

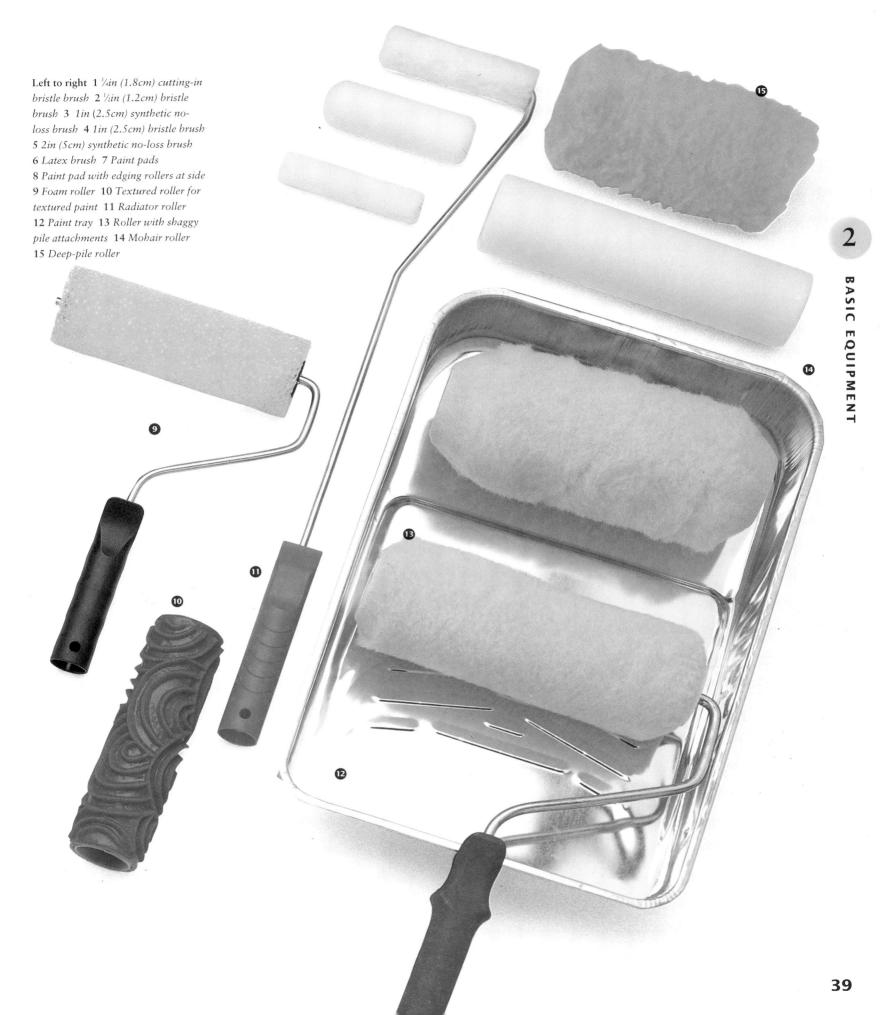

Left to right 1 ³⁄₄in (1.8cm) cutting-in bristle brush 2 ½in (1.2cm) bristle brush 3 1in (2.5cm) synthetic no-loss brush 4 1in (2.5cm) bristle brush 5 2in (5cm) synthetic no-loss brush 6 Latex brush 7 Paint pads 8 Paint pad with edging rollers at side 9 Foam roller 10 Textured roller for textured paint 11 Radiator roller 12 Paint tray 13 Roller with shaggy pile attachments 14 Mohair roller 15 Deep-pile roller

2

BASIC EQUIPMENT

Wallpapering tools

No expensive or specialized tools are required for hanging wall and ceiling coverings. A pasting table makes it easier to apply paste to long lengths of wallpaper or other material, and make sure that the scissors or knife you use to cut the wallpaper to length is sharp.

TIPS

- When hanging delicate wallpapers, you may find that a clean foam paint roller does a better job than a brush when it comes to smoothing the newly hung paper down. Apply only the lightest pressure to avoid marking the paper.

- When hanging paper from a platform, adjust its height so that you can stand comfortably without having to bend your neck or stretch your arms too far above your head.

Depending on the job, you may need a certain number of specialist tools for applying wallcoverings. The following is a checklist of the basic essentials:

Pasting table A sturdy, purpose-made pasting table is a wise investment. Easy to move, to store, and to put up, it provides a stable surface of ideal dimensions and makes pasting very much simpler. Alternatively you can use a flush door laid over trestles.

Bucket Use a clean plastic one for paste, with string tied across the top between the handle joints. You can then rest the pasting brush across the string when it is not in use.

Scissors You will need a pair of long decorating scissors, and a small pair for trimming.

Craft knife For use with a metal straight-edge or cutting guide to trim vinyls and heavy papers. Scissors are best with thin, wet paper.

Pasting brush Choose a brush at least 4in (10cm) wide, and keep it only for pasting.

Smoothing brush Also known as a paperhanger's brush, this has stiff but soft bristles and is used to brush trapped air out to the edge of paper and press the wallcovering into place. Always keep it clean and dry.

Sponge Essential for wiping away any surplus paste while it is still wet.

Seam roller Use this small wood or plastic roller to press down seams once the wallcovering is up. Don't use it on embossed papers or you risk making "tramlines."

Counterclockwise from left
1 *Smoothing brush* 2 *Steel tape measure* 3 *Scraper*
4 *Decorating scissors* 5 *Seam roller*
6 *Sponge*

Plumb line and weight This is used to produce true verticals. It is an essential piece of equipment for forming the starting point for every wallpapering job. A builder's line will hang better than ordinary string.

Pencil Use an HB or softer lead for marking the paper clearly. Sharp or hard leads can tear the more delicate papers.

Steel tape These measures are typically 12ft (3.5m) long, which should be adequate for measuring the height of normal walls.

Ruler It is important to have a ruler long enough to span the roll's width – normally about 21in (53cm). A retractable rule may tear the paper, so it is best not used.

Set square A large plastic square (or any improvised square) is useful for checking that your cuts are at a constant 90º angle.

Sanding pad Keep one to hand for sanding away any scraps of old wallpaper or lining paper you may find on a stripped wall just as you are about to hang the new paper. Likewise, a sharp scraper is a useful standby.

Clean rags Choose rags made of lint-free cloth, such as old sheets, for wiping the pasting table as the job progresses. Other material may leave fibers on the table.

Water trough For ready-pasted wallcoverings you need a water-resistant trough in which to soak the cut sections.

Stepladder You will need at least one stepladder in order to reach the tops of the walls or ceiling.

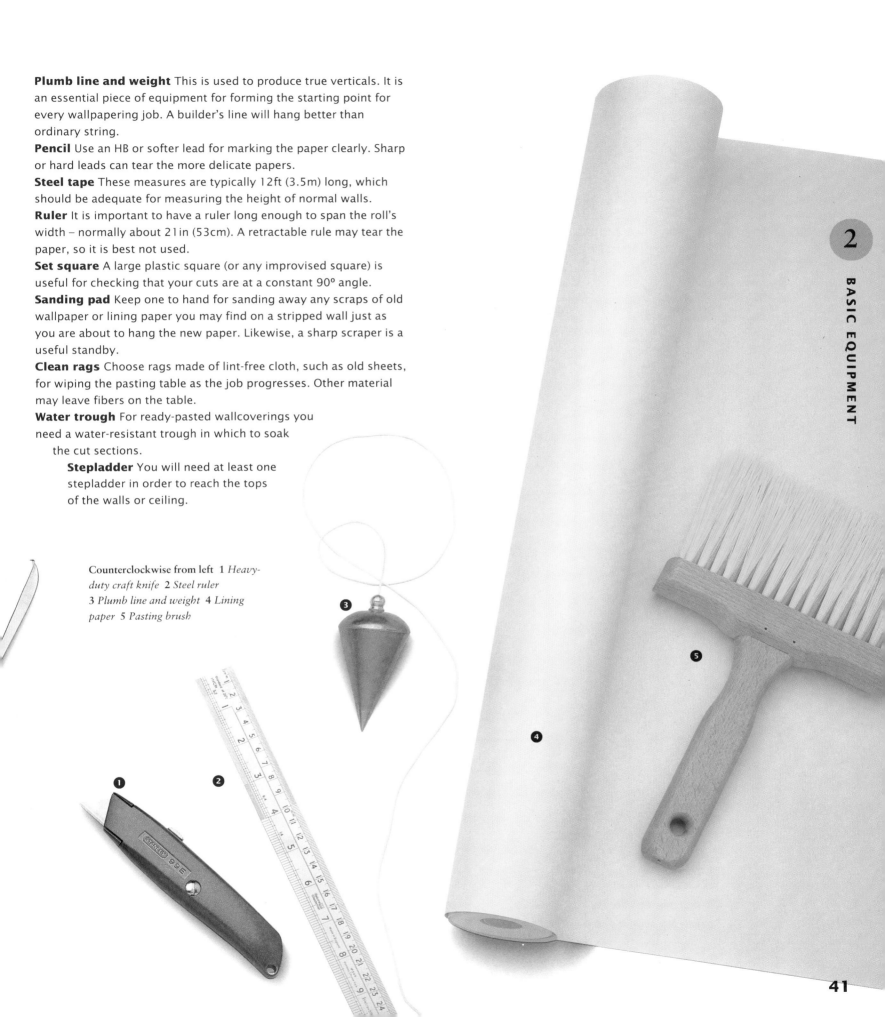

Counterclockwise from left **1** *Heavy-duty craft knife* **2** *Steel ruler* **3** *Plumb line and weight* **4** *Lining paper* **5** *Pasting brush*

Power tools

There seems to be a power tool for every imaginable maintenance task. Certainly the electric drill has become indispensable, and many other power tools are a great help in making work easier and results more accurate. Choose specific tools rather than just a basic drill to which lots of attachments can be added. Tools designed for the job will have the right range of speeds, and they will be well balanced and easy to use. For particular jobs, such as sanding floors, you may need to rent special equipment.

Safety

As a safety precaution when using any power tools, fit a circuit breaker. This device will cut off the power supply in microseconds in the event of a fault or accident involving a leakage of electricity to earth. After the fault is repaired, resetting the device is easy.

Electric drill

Many power drills have a "hammer" action, which allows them to penetrate dense masonry, wood, and softer metals. The action is one of pumping the drill bit back and forth to increase the "bite." It can be engaged or disengaged as necessary.

Simple drills are commonly geared to provide two speeds at the chuck, but the important feature to look out for is a variable-speed facility, usually operated by the trigger. As you squeeze the trigger in and out, the speed alters progressively between dead slow (important when starting a hole) and the maximum (which can be variably set on some models).

Another common option is a reverse gear, which is most useful for screwdriving. It means you can withdraw screws as well as drive them in.

As well as screwdriver blades, other useful drill options include circular sanding disks and wire brushes for cleaning and removing rust.

Electro-pneumatic drills, incorporating powerful hammer actions, are for tough masonry jobs. But they are large, single speed, and expensive. They are best rented when they are needed.

Cordless drills offer convenience and are easy and safe to use outdoors. But note that they are considerably less powerful than an ordinary tool.

Power drill chucks For longer life and easy working, tighten the key in each of the three holes in turn. To remove the chuck for adding accessories, insert the key normally and tap it sharply, but gently, with a light hammer or a piece of wood. If the chuck sticks, put the short end of a hexagonal Allen key in as it if was a drill, tighten up, and tap the key.

Electric saw

Jigsaws are invaluable for general cutting of wood and sheet materials. The best jigsaw will have a reciprocal blade and blowing action to clear the cutting line. Scroll action

1 *Power drill*
2 *Masonry bit*
3 *Twist bits*
4 *Radiator cleaning bit*
5 *Cordless drill/screwdriver*
6 *Screwdriver bits and extension*
7 *Countersink attachment*
8 *Polishing pad*
9 *Sanding sheets*
10 *Rotary sanding/polishing attachment*

is another refinement, enabling you to make tight curved cuts by turning the blade and not the whole tool.

Circular saws are useful for cutting sheet materials and wood in a straight line. These are not as versatile as jigsaws – and they are considerably less safe to use. Different blades are available for cutting a variety of materials.

Electric sander

Rotary sanders are attachments for power drills. Flint paper is fitted to a simple sanding disk or, for a better finish, a foam drum sander. A foam drum sander gives a good finish on both flat and shaped surfaces.

An orbital sander is a specific power tool, which drives a rectangular pad (to which the sandpaper is anchored) in small, rapid orbits. Use gentle pressure (always with both hands on the tool) to produce a smooth finish in quick time. Coarse, medium, and fine grades of sandpaper are available for orbital sanders. When you have completed sanding a floor with an industrial appliance, an orbital sander will give a smooth finish and is particularly useful for edges and corners of floors. Most sanders will work on wood, plastics, metals, or fillers, as long as the abrasive is suited to the top. A random orbital sander uses circular, grip-on pads and works in eccentric movements.

Hot air stripper

This is a convenient alternative to a blowlamp for softening and stripping old paint, particularly oil-based paint from woodwork. You can use a blowlamp which works off bottled gas, or a hot-air gun which is powered by electricity. This is more suitable near glass as there is less likelihood of damage. Beware of scorching and flames, caused by the heat of the blown air from the gun. Always remove anything from the work area that might catch fire and wear gloves to protect your hands from flakes of hot paint.

Special equipment

Many decorating and repair jobs can be made much easier with professional equipment, which you can rent for a reasonable charge based on the length of time you borrow the item. Charges for delivery and pick-up – which may be unavoidable for heavy equipment – need to be taken into consideration.

For large projects of long duration, it may make better sense to buy special equipment, such as a cement mixer or platform tower. Compare retail prices with rental rates. Bear in mind that you can always sell equipment in good condition after you have finished.

If you have never used an item of equipment before, get as much advice as possible before starting work – especially on safety aspects.

1 *Orbital sander*
2 *Random orbital sander*
3 *Jigsaw*
4 *Hot air stripper with scraper attachment*
5 *Paint scraper*

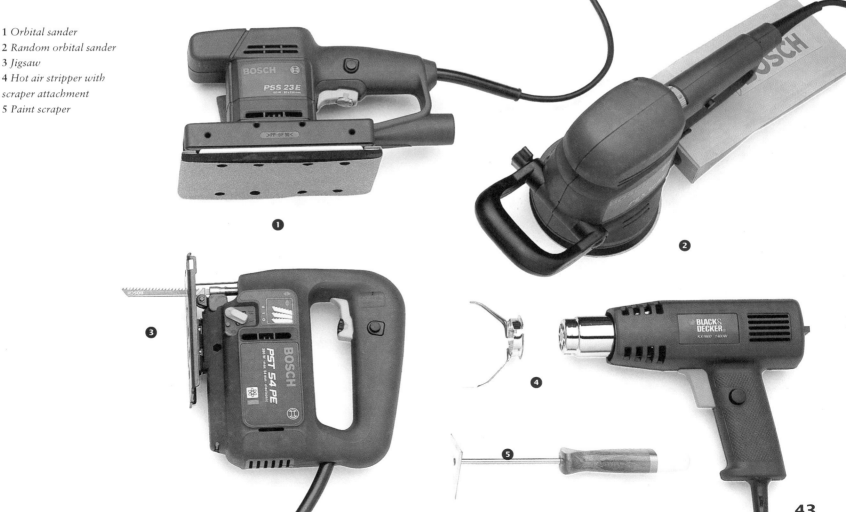

Steps and ladders

For all interior decorating work, having the right tools, observing basic, common-sense safety precautions, and making sure that you have easy access to the work to be done are all vital considerations. Many decorating accidents inside the home are completely avoidable and are due to simple carelessness about basic points of safety.

Comfort is another important consideration. Standing on the rungs of a ladder for lengthy periods of time, for example, will soon become hard on the instep, and may result in accidents as you move around. However, working from a solidly built, static platform surrounded by a safety rail is easy, safe, and more comfortable, and better-quality workmanship is likely to result.

USING LADDERS

- When decorating inside on steps, make sure that they are fully extended and stable. And if you are working from a ladder in, say, a high stairway, make sure the ladder is safely anchored and that the feet are at a distance from the wall equal to about a quarter of the height of the ladder itself.

- Always wear strong shoes (not boots) with grip soles. Standing on the rungs of a stepladder in gym shoes will soon cause your feet to ache. When you are climbing a ladder, hold onto the rungs, not the stiles, since this makes the ladder better balanced. Carry any tools and equipment in your overalls pockets, or wear a special tool-carrying belt, so that both your hands are free to grip the ladder.

- When you are painting on steps or a ladder, right-handed people should work from right to left; the opposite is the case for left-handed people. By adopting this working practice, you will always be moving the ladder away from the freshly painted area.

- Never go higher than the third rung from the top of a ladder or you will have nothing to hold on to. Do not stretch too far out to reach a work area – this is both dangerous and tiring. Only work within comfortable reach and move the ladder to new areas whenever necessary.

Stepladder It is wise to own at least stepladder. For indoor work, the ladder should have five treads or more, a platform, and a grab rail. Aluminum stepladders are much lighter than wooden ones, but are not as stable.

Working platform For comfortable ceiling work there should be about 3in (7.5cm) between the top of your head and the ceiling. Make a platform from two stepladders, or a stepladder and a strong box, with a scaffold board running between them. You can also rent trestles for the same purpose.

Staircase platform Designed to be used in confined spaces, you can rent a platform in sections for easy home assembly. Alternatively, improvise with a ladder section against the wall, and a stepladder (or a box) on the landing, with a scaffold board running between the two.

A dual-purpose adjustable ladder used with a scaffold board on stairs. Note: the ladder must be tied securely to the stairs.

An arrangement of ladders and scaffold board for decorating a stairway walls and ceiling. Two planks are needed for longer spans.

A continuous platform is needed when papering a ceiling.

Tie and nail boards and pad the ladder stiles for this arrangement on an L-shaped landing and stairs.

Scaffold tower

A scaffold tower is far safer and easier to work from than a ladder because it is more stable. It also provides access to a larger working area. Although a tower is used mainly for exterior jobs, it can prove just as useful inside tall rooms and, particularly, in stairways.

Scaffold poles in many different sizes can be bought or rented, and they come with very clear instructions on how they should be safely erected. Pay close attention to the details for locking sections together and double check that the frame is completely vertical. Use a carpenter's level and the adjustable feet to make sure the base frames are level. Some scaffolds for indoor use come with castor-like wheels, which you must lock securely once the tower has been pushed into its correct position to prevent it from moving.

A scaffold tower can be built straight up to a considerable height for exterior work, or indoors on a staircase.

Using tools

Buying the best tools you can afford and looking after them properly is common-sense advice. There is no doubt that good tools used well will produce top-quality work. However, it does not matter how much you pay for something if you fail to use it properly. You will not produce good work and, more important, you may endanger or harm yourself.

Cable and pipe detector

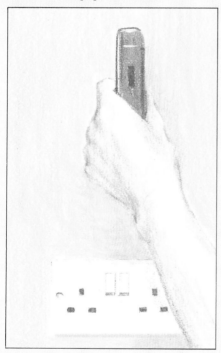

Concealing cables and pipes beneath the surface of plastered or partition walls is a neat solution. The safety rule when routing concealed cables and pipes is that they should always run either vertically or horizontally, never diagonally. This means that anybody attaching anything to the wall in the future knows where to expect them to be.

However, unless you know for a fact where pipes and cables are, using a cable and pipe detector will prevent any nasty surprises.

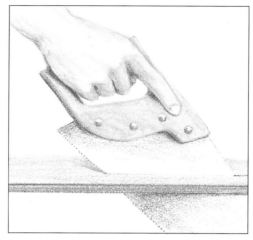

Hold the saw firmly with your index finger pointing in the direction of the cut.

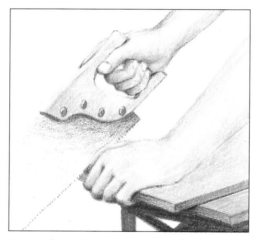

Keep a firm grip on the piece when starting, and saw gently to stop the blade jumping.

Hand tools

Keep all your tools sharp, clean, and in a good state of repair, and store them in dry conditions where there is no danger of rust forming on them. Bear in mind that a blunt or damaged tool, such as a saw or a chisel, is not only harder to use, and will not produce top-quality results, but it is also more dangerous – both to yourself and, potentially, to anybody else in the immediate vicinity.

Whenever you are going to use a saw, first firmly secure the piece of work to a workbench. Position the work so that the cutting line just overhangs the edge of the bench. This means that it has maximum support and also prevents the piece whipping about as you saw. Position

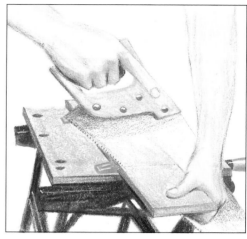

Support the end when close to finishing to prevent the saw from breaking clear.

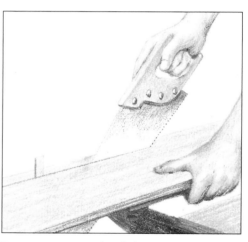

Supporting one side of the piece securely, always cut on the forward stroke.

yourself so that the saw becomes an extension of your arm, with your index finger pointing in the direction of the cut. Draw the saw gently and cleanly back and forth, cutting on the forward stroke only. Toward the end of the cut, support the cut piece to prevent the saw blade suddenly breaking clear and ripping the wood. If you have to put a lot of force behind the saw in order to get it to cut, then your saw needs to be sharpened.

A craft knife is an essential part of a tool kit. Make sure that the blade is sharp and that you use the correct type of blade for the material being cut – whether it is paper, floor tiles, or carpet. Remember to keep your fingers well away from the line of the cut, and do not exert too much pressure or the blade may slip sideways. Knives with retractable blades are the safest to use, and the types that feature snap-off blades mean that you always have a sharp edge to work with. Dispose of old blades safely.

Chisels can be very dangerous tools if they are blunt or misused. You should first secure the piece of work and then use a mallet to strike the handle of the chisel to take away the bulk of the wood. For the final paring away of the wood, it is best to use hand pressure only. Use the fingers of your other hand to steady and guide the blade to where you want it to cut.

Always make sure the piece you are working on is clamped firmly in position when using a power saw.

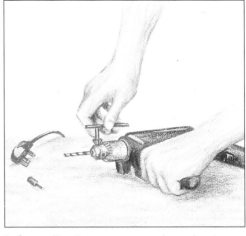

Before adjusting a power tool, unplug it. Make certain that blades and bits are correctly fitted before using it.

When chopping with a chisel, guide it between your thumb and index finger for accurate paring of the wood.

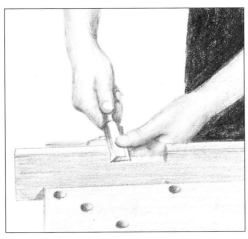

When using a chisel, make sure that the blade is sharp and clean. Keep your guiding hand behind the leading edge so that is it out of danger if the chisel slips.

Power tools

Electric tools add power to your elbow, bringing all kinds of jobs within the range of amateur enthusiasts. But beware – as well as making your life easier, they can also be lethal if not used properly.

Always keep young children and pets well away from the area in which you are operating power tools. When young children are in the house, unplug the tool if you leave the room, even if it is for only a minute or two. When carrying a power tool, never hold it by its cable – this can easily cause wiring problems resulting in an electric shock.

A few points to note especially are that you should always engage the safety guard when working on a power saw, and you must keep both of your hands and the power cable behind the saw's line of operation. Don't apply force to a power tool in order to speed up its operation. If you are drilling or sawing, then make sure that there is nothing underneath that may be damaged by the tool or cause damage to it.

In factories and workshops there are strict rules governing what people must wear while they are operating machinery and power tools. These are sensible guidelines designed to minimize the likelihood of accidents and injury, and you would do well to follow at home. The most basic rule is that you should never wear loose clothing or jewelry that could become tangled up in a moving part of a power tool. Long hair is equally dangerous, so tie it tightly back.

When changing a power-saw blade or drill bit, the first rule is always to unplug the tool. A distraction at the wrong moment, such as a knock at the front door, the telephone ringing, or the sound of someone or something falling over in another room, can all too easily divert your attention from the job at hand and you could inadvertently switch on while grasping a blade.

If you are using a power tool on an upper floor, make sure that the ladder or platform you are working from is solidly positioned. If possible, enlist the help of somebody below to switch on the power only when you are comfortably in your working position. Remember that the cord can become tangled up in your feet leading to a fall, so never let anyone stand below you as you work.

Always make sure that your work is well anchored down. If it is able to move, then you cannot be certain in which direction a power tool may go. To prevent this from happening, use workbench clamps or a vise to secure the work. In other situations where clamps or a vise cannot be used, such as when you are working on a door *in situ*, for example, either close the door tight or wedge it securely open underneath to prevent it from moving.

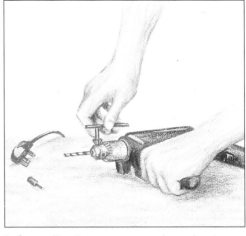

Safety at work

Using tools and materials correctly is vital not just to producing good results, but to your own safety. As well as taking common-sense precautions when doing electrical and plumbing jobs, always follow manufacturers' instructions when using power tools, or applying hazardous substances – and wear the recommended protective clothing. When using chemical products indoors, make sure that the room in which you are working is well ventilated. Once your work is finished, leave the windows open for a few hours to allow all the fumes to escape.

1 *Dust mask* 2 *Safety goggles*
3 *Respirator* 4 *Ear protectors*
5 *Heavy-duty rubber gloves*
6 *Leather gloves*

Wear heavy-duty gloves to protect against cuts when using dangerous tools and materials such as glass. Vinyl gloves give protection against chemicals and grease.

Ear protectors make noisy tools more comfortable to use, and protect against insidious damage to your hearing.

Protective clothing

The dangers may not always be as obvious as you might think. A spinning circular saw, a blowlamp, or a high ladder are self-evident hazards, but the effect of a dropped club hammer, or the fumes from a can of adhesive, or the fine dust thrown up when sanding paintwork may seem risks hardly worth considering.

But the danger from these items can be very real. A heavy hammer falling just a few feet can break bones in a foot that is inadequately protected. A flying particle of rust or paint is like a shard of glass and can damage your eyes. Inhaling fumes from some adhesives and corrosive liquids can have serious health effects.

Clothing Wearing appropriate clothes and, when necessary, safety clothes is essential. Loose clothing, scarves, necklaces, and ties are all potential hazards since they can become tangled in moving parts of machinery. If you have long hair, tie it back.

Footwear Wear safety boots with reinforced toe-caps when working with heavy building blocks or bricks – or hammers. Wear strong shoes when working from a ladder.

Gloves Wear heavy-duty industrial gloves in leather when working with dangerous tools or materials. Lighter vinyl gloves protect against oils, greases, and most chemicals, while natural rubber gloves – stronger than most kitchen gloves – withstand chemicals and resist tears and abrasions. Knitted gloves with latex-reinforced palm and back are good for carrying glass and metal.

Face masks To avoid inhaling airborne particles and fumes, a dust mask or respirator is vital. The simplest mask consists of a filter holder that molds to the shape of your face and takes a replaceable cotton gauze pad to cover the nose and mouth.

Respirators are robust, being made from molded rubber or plastic. They have an exhalation valve and a replaceable cartridge filter that resists organic vapor and paint spraying. You have to insert the appropriate filter for the substance being used.

Safety glasses Typical jobs requiring eye protection are sanding, painting a ceiling with a textured compound, spraying paint, and most metalwork tasks. Whenever you are using chemicals, make eye protection a priority.

In their simplest form, safety glasses are like standard ones, but with impact-resistant lenses. More sophisticated versions have ventilated side protection and non-fogging lenses. Safety goggles are the most robust, with safety lenses housed in a flexible plastic frame. Gas welding goggles have a shaded lens.

Ear protectors Foam earplugs with a connecting cord for easy removal are relatively cheap and give protection against noise levels above 80 decibels. More expensive – and more effective – are ear capsules or muffs, usually mounted on an adjustable headband, with interchangeable ear pads.

Safety helmets A safety helmet is generally needed only for a sizeable demolition or building project. You might prefer to rent a "hard hat" rather than buying one.

Overalls If you don't have old clothes to wear for painting and other work, a polypropylene suit is ideal. It protects your clothes, doesn't weigh you down, and is rip-resistant. Some styles have elasticated sleeve-cuffs and deep pockets for tools and materials.

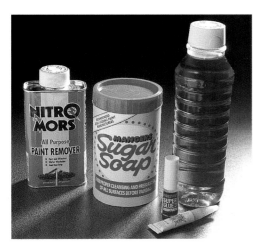

Carefully read and observe the manufacturers' safety instructions before using any product.

Chemical products

Adhesives, corrosives, and other chemical products used in maintenance work include many substances both harmful to the touch and capable of giving off fumes and causing dizziness and injury if inhaled. Most important of all, keep children away from these materials – which often come in bright and appealing containers and can all too easily be mistaken by a young child for something containing candy.

Always read the warnings, which, by law, appear on the packaging. Do this before you open the container, let alone start using it. Fumes arise immediately certain chemicals are exposed to the air – and if you are in a poorly ventilated space and have a particular sensitivity to any of the compounds involved, you could be putting yourself at risk.

Ventilation When ventilation is recommended, open wide all the windows in the room. It is probably best to close internal doors to prevent fumes carrying to other parts of the house. Leave windows open for a couple of hours after the work is complete to make sure fumes have dissipated.

Volatile fumes may ignite if exposed to a naked flame, so follow instructions to extinguish any pilot lights in boilers or stoves – and, of course, don't smoke.

Fumes permeate clothes so, when you have finished for the day, change into something clean and hang your working clothes out in the open for a couple of hours before washing them.

"Superglues" Cyanoacrylates, or superglues, are extremely powerful. A container can burst and squirt liquid into your face, so wear a mask and safety glasses. Familiarize yourself with the first-aid advice printed on the container in advance.

Any substance that gets on to your skin – adhesive, preservative, or paint-stripper – must be washed off immediately. Hold the affected part under running water. If the irritation or pain continues later, seek medical help.

Poisoning If swallowed, some liquids can cause severe sickness, permanent disablement, or even death. Store all chemicals in their original containers under lock and key and out of children's reach.

Never mix different household cleaners – a chemical reaction can result and cause poisonous fumes to be given off.

SAFE DISPOSAL

- Keep household and garden chemicals securely locked away.

- Store liquids below solids so that if a bottle leaks the liquid cannot flow onto the packs of solids.

- Check "best before" or expiry dates of materials you are using, and before throwing old ones away.

- Dispose of old materials through the appropriate local services.

- Do not throw old paint, chemicals, or noxious substances into household refuse, which may be returned to land-fills in the earth. These substances can contribute to contamination of land, ground water, rivers, and the sea through leakage or breakage. Contact your local government for advice.

Harmful
These substances are dangerous to the skin. Irritants give off vapors or gases that are dangerous to inhale.

Toxic
This covers solids, liquids, or gases that are dangerous if swallowed or inhaled, even in tiny quantities.

Highly flammable
Depends on a liquid's ability to form a vapor. Nail polish remover is very flammable.

Explosive
Explosive materials such as fireworks must be stored in a cool, dry place away from naked flames.

Corrosive
Both acids, such as vinegar, and alkalis, such as washing soda, are corrosive. Never mix the two together.

Oxidizing
Hydrogen peroxide and weed killer are common oxidizers. These release large amounts of oxygen to fuel fires.

paration

3

Stripping and cleaning

When preparing painted surfaces for re-painting – whether walls, woodwork, or floors – you don't need to remove the old paintwork if it is in good condition. It is sufficient to wash down the surface with a strong solution of sugar soap to break any glaze and remove grease to which the new coat will not adhere. Then simply rub over the surface with a flexible sanding pad to improve the "key," and dust it down before applying the new paint.

If the existing paintwork has been badly applied or consists of so many layers that it causes windows and doors to stick, then you should remove the paint. Surfaces that have been poorly painted, or overpainted several times, can take on a sticky appearance, robbing architraves and moldings of their fine detail. Decorative plaster looks particularly unattractive when it has been painted once or twice too often.

You may have to strip the paint in order to use one of the new microporous finishes that require direct contact with bare wood. Be cautious about stripping back wood in order to stain and varnish it, however. A great deal of sanding is necessary to remove all of the primer from the pores of the wood; if any remains, the stain will look patchy.

Stripping radiators

It is wise to strip paint from radiators before repainting them, since they will lose their heat efficiency if covered with too many paint layers. Special radiator paints are available that do not discolor when heated.

The quality of any redecoration depends on how well the room has been prepared. First, clear away all movable furniture that will only get in the way, and cover any surfaces, such as the floor, that you want to protect. If old wallpaper is involved, this may need to be stripped off. If painting on top of existing paint, make sure the surface is sound, free of dirt or grease, and that it has a good "key".

Chemical stripping

Chemical stripping can be expensive when large areas are involved. The secret is to be patient while the chemical works – otherwise you may have to apply more coats to get down to the bare wood or metal. Protect your eyes and hands, and keep the stripper away from plastic items.

There are two main types of chemical stripper. One is a liquid that you apply with a brush and scrape away when the paint bubbles and breaks up. The other type is a paste that you spread on and allow to set before lifting it away with the point of a trowel. The latter is best for moldings and textured surfaces, since it lifts paint out of hollows.

Be sure to neutralize the stripper after use, carefully following the manufacturer's instructions. This process involves washing the surface with plenty of water, probably with a little vinegar added.

Doors, unglazed sashes, and other large items can be taken to specialists for stripping, usually in a tank of caustic soda. However, this involves a risk of the discoloring wood, and the joints in woodwork may open up as any glue or filler dissolves.

Heat stripping

Most paints soften quickly when you apply heat, but take great care not to overdo it since the paint may ignite. Do not use newspaper on the floor to catch the hot, flaking paint because of the risk of fire. Have a bucket of water conveniently on hand just in case of emergencies. Hold the scraping tool so that the stripped paint cannot fall onto your hand. Cotton gloves provide adequate protection. Use a flame-proof deflector, such as panes of glass, to shield areas adjacent to where you are working.

Chemical stripping

1 Chemical strippers that are brushed onto old paintwork may take off several layers at a time.

2 Once the paint has bubbled, use a scraper to remove the old paint. If many layers of paint are involved, more than one application may be needed.

3 Once the surface has been stripped of all paint, it must be thoroughly cleaned with water to remove chemical residues.

Using a blowlamp

A blowlamp burns liquid gas either from a small container attached to the torch head or from a larger cylinder connected to the torch by a tube. The flame can be extremely hot, so keep it moving all the time to avoid scorching the wood or cracking glass.

Using a hot air gun

This tool resembles a powerful hair dryer, blowing a jet of air through a very hot electric element. Having no flame, it is safer than a blowlamp, but this can be deceptive since you don't see anything emerging from the gun. But it can become sufficiently hot to char wood and crack glass, so treat it like a blowlamp.

Stripping around door handles

You will achieve a neater finish if your remove door handles, and any other door furniture, prior to stripping. If for some reason a metal door handle cannot be removed, use a thin piece of plywood to shield it from the direct heat of a hot air gun or blowlamp. Chemical strippers may not affect the metal, but test them first on a

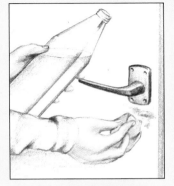

small area that cannot be readily seen – such as the inside surface of the handle.

Using a heat stripper

"Burning off" sounds rather alarming, but it is the professional's way of removing paint from woodwork; it is not suitable for use on painted plaster and metal.

The idea is to use heat to soften the paint so that it can be scraped off rather than actually setting fire to it. However, it does require care. To burn off a small area of defective paint you can use a hot air gun or a blowlamp with an attached container of butane gas. For larger areas, professional-sized equipment can be rented.

Hold the gun or blowlamp in one hand and a scraper in the other; keep the gun or lamp and scraper moving together. Use a shavehook for scraping moldings. Try not to scorch the wood or dig into it. If you are burning off window frames, keep the heat away from the glass. After you have removed the paint, sand the wood down with medium-grade sandpaper following the direction of the grain, paying particular attention to any moldings.

Wallcoverings

If you are planning to redecorate a papered wall or ceiling – whether with paint or a new wallcovering of some description – it is often essential to remove the existing paper first in order to achieve a smooth and professional-looking finish. However, some papers can be coated with latex paint and, provided that the surface is perfectly sound, all you need do is sponge it down with a mildly soapy water solution to remove the film of dirt and grease to which the new paint will not adhere, and redecorate on top.

Easy-strip wallcoverings, which consist of a decorative layer you can detach from the backing layer, must be removed entirely if you intend to paint the wall. The backing layer of these papers (including vinyls) is not suitable as a base for painting, although it may be fine to use as a lining paper for a new wallcovering.

Sometimes it is possible to paint over decorative wall-coverings, but it makes sense to experiment first by trying it on a small area and allowing the paint to dry thoroughly. The covering may be affected by the water content of the paint. If so, you will have to strip it all off.

Dealing with different coverings

If you have to soak a wall or ceiling covering before you can remove it – which is normally the case – you can save yourself a lot of time and effort by using a steam wallpaper stripper. Home-use models are available at a reasonable price. If only a small area of wall or ceiling covering needs to be removed, however, and you are not likely to use it again in the near future, it may be best to rent a steam stripper.

Standard wallpaper To remove most wallpapers, use a steam stripper or soak the paper with a mild mixture of warm water, liquid detergent, and a little wallpaper paste. The paste is used to hold the water on the paper. Leave the soaked area for 20 to 30 minutes before starting to lift the covering with a flexible scraper.

Duplex paper Treat this type of covering in the same way as you would standard wallpaper, but allow a longer soaking time.

Heavy paper Embossed and washable papers are, in particular, always difficult to strip. Roughing the surface with a coarse abrasive or scraper, such as a Skarsten, will help steam or water to penetrate the paper and loosen the paste beneath. Allow plenty of soaking time.

Painted paper You will have to break down the surface of the paper with a coarse abrasive pad soaked in water. It is best to avoid using a wire brush – this may leave tiny metal strands embedded in

---

Stripping standard wallpaper

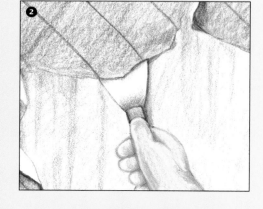
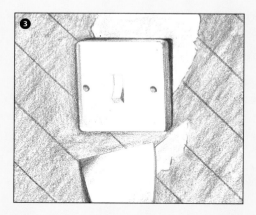

Look carefully at the condition of the wallpaper. If the surface is well stuck down and sound, you may not need to remove it before redecorating.

❶ Thoroughly wet the paper's surface. Use a sponge or a plant sprayer.

❷ Allow enough soaking time so that the paste starts to dissolve. Then work your scraper underneath the paper and lift it away from the plasterboard. If you wait too long, however, the paper will dry out and the paste will re-adhere.

❸ Water and electricity can be a fatal combination. As a precaution, turn off the power when stripping around a light switch or outlet and try to strip the paper dry.

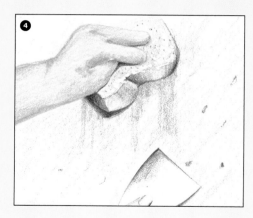

❹ Stubborn patches of paper and paste may require a second soaking.

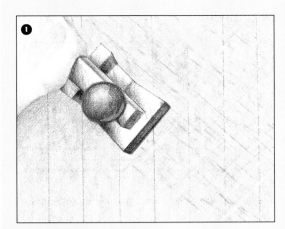

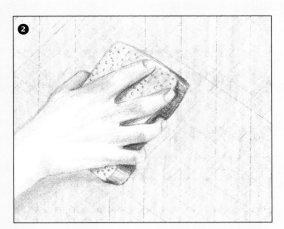

Washable wallpaper

Washable wallcoverings, other than those with separate backing papers, can be difficult to remove. Abrade the surface to allow water to penetrate and loosen the old paste. Use a serrated scraper to score the surface covering.

❶ To allow water to penetrate the washable plastic coating, first break up the surface using a serrated-edged scraper. A coarse grade of sandpaper is also suitable, although it may quickly clog.

❷ When the surface is roughed up, soak the paper liberally with a weak solution of warm water and liquid detergent. Use a sponge to force the water well into the wallcovering before you start to scrape.

Vinyl/easy strip

Many vinyl papers are easy to strip since the top layer pulls away intact, leaving the backing paper stuck to the wall. Loosen a corner of the vinyl at the foot, then pull the strip away, holding the vinyl out from the wall as you pull.

the plaster of the wall, leading to rust spots later on. Soak the abraded wall with water and then strip.

Easy strip You can strip this type of wallcovering simply by pulling the decorative layer away from its backing material, which, if thoroughly stuck down, you can paper – but not paint – over. If you do want to paint the surface, soak the backing paper with water and it should strip off relatively easily.

Vinyl Standard and blown vinyls have a backing layer and you can treat them in the same way as easy-strip papers.

Burlap Pull the layer of burlap away from the wall to separate it from its backing paper. Take care, however – burlap is popularly used as camouflage for badly flawed wall surfaces. If the plasterboard is in poor condition, the pulling action may make the situation worse by removing or loosening the plaster.

Lincrusta This type of covering is stuck in place using an extremely strong adhesive and it is, therefore, difficult to remove. Use hot water and a scraper to ease the sheet from the wall, taking care not to pull away the plasterboard. Soak and then remove any remaining adhesive.

Cork wall tiles Use a flexible scraper with force to lift away the tiles, then soak the exposed adhesive with water or use a hot air stripper to soften the remaining adhesive. Take care not to damage the wall plaster.

Styrofoam acoustic tiles Use a flexible scraper to ease the tiles away from the wall or ceiling, and then use a hot air stripper to soften the exposed adhesive before removing it with a flexible scraper or sharp shavehook. Be careful to protect your eyes, hands, and hair.

Stripping ceilings

Home-use steam strippers are perfectly safe to use because its water reservoir contains only cold water – the steam is produced at the faceplate of the stripper. Press the steam stripper against the paper using one hand and hold a scraper in the other. As the steam penetrates the paper, it will start to lift away from the sheet rock. Use your scraper to encourage this process. Get as close to the surface you are stripping as possible. Holding the steam stripper at arm's length soon becomes very tiring.

Repairing walls and ceilings

Above *For paint to be effective it needs to be applied to dry, sound plaster. Plaster that is damp is likely to result in the problems illustrated here.*

Once you have stripped and cleaned the walls and ceiling, you need to examine them for any defects, such as cracks and gaps in the surface. Most such problems should have become evident during the preparation stages; some others, however, may not initially be obvious. The most common of these is "blown" plaster, which occurs when patches of plaster lift away from the underlying wall. When rapped with your knuckle, blown plaster has a distinctive hollow sound. Ideally, you should hack out this defective area and patch with fresh material.

Although replastering an entire room is a major job – one that requires considerable skill and professional expertise – it is relatively easy to undertake minor repairs yourself.

Filling a small crack

1 Start by raking out any loose material from the crack, using the corner of your filling knife.

2 Using a small paintbrush, wet the crack with water. This stops the plaster from drying out the filler too quickly, causing it to crack or fall out.

3 Now fill the crack by drawing your loaded filling knife across it, at right angles to the crack.

4 Fill the crack slightly higher than the surrounding plaster. Leave it to set and, when it is hard, sand it back flush using a medium grit of sandpaper.

Repairing Walls

Small cracks If the cracks are small, fill them with a cellulose filler. Work the filler into the cracks with a flexible filling knife, leaving it just proud of the surface of the wall. When set, smooth the filler down with a medium-grit sandpaper and sanding block.

Large cracks With large cracks, your preparation must be thorough. Dig out all loose and crumbling material, right back to sound plaster. Damp the hole with a water spray and fill with a plaster repair filler. Take the filler just above the wall's surface and then sand it level when it has set. Be sure to use clean water to mix the plaster and clean the mixing platform or bucket after each mix. Any residues of set plaster will reduce the setting time of subsequent mixes and may weaken them.

If the cracks are particularly wide or deep, fill them in stages. Each layer should be no more than about ½in (12mm) deep. Score the surface to provide a key for the next layer, which you apply when the previous layer is set but not dry. With the final undercoat set (allow 1-2 hours) and scored, apply the finishing coat of plaster flush with the original wall surface. When smoothing the finish plaster, it may help to dampen the surface slightly, but don't overwet it or it will become dusty.

The filling material is likely to absorb more paint or wallpaper paste than the original plaster, so prime it with one or two coats of universal primer or latex before starting to redecorate.

Cracks at doors and windows Where the wall abuts door and window frames, cracks are commonly caused by the movement of the woodwork with temperature and humidity changes. Clear any loose material out of these cracks with the point of a small trowel. Then fill these cracks – and any gaps along the base boards – with an acrylic sealant, which grips better than a cellulose filler.

Filling a deep crack

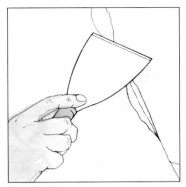

① Use a filling knife to widen the crack and then remove all loose debris. Dampen the crevice with water and fill it just higher than the surface of the wall or ceiling.

② When the filler is dry, sand it smooth. A deep crack may need a second application of filler. When it is dry, sand the surface flush with the surrounding plasterwork.

Patching plasterboard

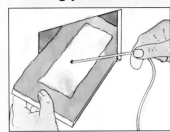

❶ Cut the plasterboard just larger than the hole. Tie string to a nail and feed it through a central hole. Dab edges of patch with plaster.

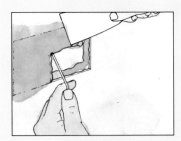

❷ With the plaster side facing you, pull the string tight while you add more plaster. When it is set, cut the string and finish filling.

❸ To repair a corner, pin a batten to one side flush with the corner. Fill the opposite side. When it is set, repeat on the other edge.

Types of plaster

Undercoat plaster For deep or wide cracks and holes, first apply an undercoat plaster. On absorbent surfaces, such as brick or lightweight block, choose a browning coat. If you are plastering over concrete or stone, use a bonding coat.

Finishing plaster For the final layer, apply a lightweight finishing plaster, such as a pre-mixed gypsum plaster to which you need only add water. This is more convenient than plasters that have to be mixed with sand.

Do-it-all plasters Special plasters have been developed for home use. They require no undercoat and you can apply them up to about 2in (5cm) thick, directly onto brickwork or similar walls without the sagging you would get with traditional plasters applied this way. These plasters are, however, more expensive than the traditional ones.

Some of these plasters have the advantage of staying workable for quite a long period, giving you plenty of time to bring your patch to a satisfactory finish. When the surface is completely dry, you can decorate it in the same way as conventional plaster.

One brand of ready-mixed plaster gives a skim finish that is ideal for levelling rough surfaces. You apply it either with a brush or a spreader (enclosed in the pack along with the plaster) to no more than a thickness of about ⅛in (3mm). You can skim this material onto plaster, plasterboard, bricks, or lightweight blocks, and its slow drying time gives you ample opportunity to bring it to a good finish.

An alternative sealant is expanding foam filler, which you inject down a fine tube into the gap, where it expands dramatically. Once set, it is easy to cut and shape to form a surface ready for sanding smooth and decorating. Expanding foam filler is particularly useful for packing awkward-shaped holes.

Deep holes If you have to fill a large cavity in a wall left by the removal of a drainage outlet, or perhaps a banister rail, it is not a good idea to pack it with filler. This is wasteful, and the filler may crack unless you apply it in a laborious series of layers. Instead, where possible, pack the hole with broken brick or stone and push cement in to fill the gaps and firm it all up – small bags of ready-mixed mortar are convenient for these minor jobs. Once you have packed the hole to within 2in (5cm) of the wall surface, you can apply an all-in-one plaster.

For plastering large areas, it is a good idea to nail temporary guide battens to the wall. These enable you to bring all the plastered surface to the same level. When the plaster has set, remove the battens and fill the grooves level with the rest of the job.

Weak spots Cracks between walls and ceilings rarely stay sealed, whatever material you use. This is a weak area where any slight movement of the building will re-open the cracks. An expanding foam filler is the easiest material to use, but the best solution to a very noticeable gap is to hide it with a decorative coving made of styrofoam or plaster.

Replastering Large expanses of wall in very poor repair, and areas of blown plaster, must be stripped back to the brickwork and replastered or re-covered.

Plastering

Unless you are skilled; it is unlikely that you would want to undertake replastering an entire room. You may, however, feel confident enough to tackle a large area of damaged or missing plaster where a window, door, or fireplace has been bricked up. For such a job, it is easier for the beginner to achieve a smooth, flat finish with either a ready-to-use plaster or a traditional type (see p. 57).

Your preparations for plastering must be thorough. Remove all loose and flaking plaster and if the reason for the original plaster failing is due to dampness then you must find the cause of the problem and cure it – otherwise the same fate awaits the new patch.

Once you have cleaned off all the loose material, wet the wall and apply the plaster. When you have applied about a ½in (12mm) undercoat, use a fairly wide straightedge to level it off. Work the straightedge up the wall using a sawing action.

The undercoat should finish about ⅛in (3mm) below the level of the surrounding plasterwork. This gap allows you to apply a fine finishing plaster flush with the surrounding surfaces. Use a little water with the top coat to give it a polished appearance.

Repairing a lath and plaster wall

1 Provided the laths are secure,you can fill holes in a lath and plaster wall as you would a solid wall. Reinforce broken laths using expanded metal mesh, stapled in place.

2 Dampen the laths and apply a plaster undercoat. Make sure that the plaster is forced between the laths for good adhesion. Key, allow the plaster to set, and then apply the finishing coat.

1 Use a wood or plastic float to apply the undercoat, working upward.

2 Draw a wood straightedge, spanning the patch, upward to level the surface.

3 Draw a scratcher over the drying undercoat to give the surface a good "key".

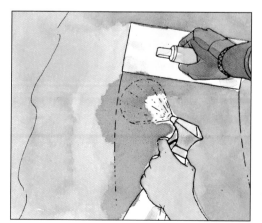

4 Use a steel float, aided by a light spraying of water, to give the top coat a fine, polished finish.

5 You will have to reinforce a large corner repair. Here angle bead is used, held in position by blobs of plaster.

6 Plaster the walls in turn, working away from the corner. Leave the nose of the bead exposed to form the corner's apex.

Ceilings

Once the ceiling has been stripped (*see p. 84-7*), fill any minor cracks with cellulose filler, as for walls (*see p. 88-9*). You may find that a large crack runs right across a ceiling, opening and shutting as the house moves slightly with the changing seasons. This type of crack is virtually impossible to seal and, unless you want to replace the ceiling, you may have to disguise it with ceiling tiles.

Plasterboard ceilings are particularly prone to forming cracks in the finishing coat along the joins between the boards. To minimize this, newly plasterboarded ceilings should be formed with small "lath" sections of board, and a plaster undercoat as well as a finishing coat applied. You can decorate the ceiling with a thick, textured paint to cover up these fine cracks. However, if you prefer a smooth finish, your best chance of a lasting repair is to work a fine-surface filler – or even a finely textured paint – into the cracks and smooth off with a dampened sponge.

Stains On a ceiling, stains will sometimes bleed through new decoration if they are not treated beforehand. Seal the stained area with either an aluminum primer-sealer or with a commercial stain block. Stain-sealers are now available in easy-to-use aerosol form.

Textured surfaces If you wish to remove a textured coating from a ceiling, beware: the coating may well have been applied by a previous occupant of your home – or for that matter by its builder – to conceal a ceiling in poor condition.

If you want to remove a textured coating, use a steam stripper to soften the compound, or apply one of the special stripping preparations that are now readily available. Either way, you will not find it to be an easy task, since you will have to scrape the compound away a little at a time and then wash the ceiling clean.

Plasterboard cracks

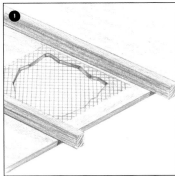
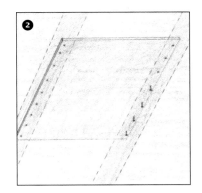
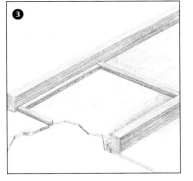

1 When you have to fill a large hole in a plasterboard ceiling, use expanded metal mesh stapled behind the hole. The mesh forms a backing to which the filler can adhere.

2 It is relatively easy to mend a hole that spans the ceiling joists. The resulting patch should make a neat, easily concealed repair that can simply be redecorated.

3 Where the old ceiling plaster thickness cannot be matched, fixing a framework of battens to the joists will help to compensate. Nail the side battens to the joists first, and then carefully tack cross battens on their ends.

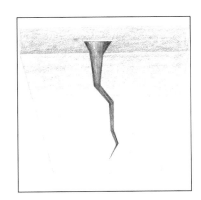
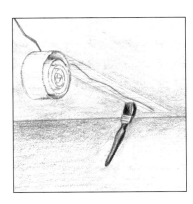
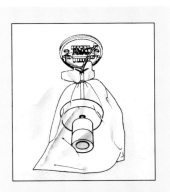

Hairline cracks
1 The first step in repairing a hairline crack is to widen it slightly using the corner of a stripping knife. Unless you do this, it will be impossible to work sufficient filler into the crevice to repair it.

2 After you have widened the crack and removed any loose debris, the crack should look like this detail in cross section – a slightly V-shaped crevice. The point of the V will be on the inner surface.

3 Work cellulose filler into the crack using a filling knife. When the filler has set, rub it smooth and flush with the surrounding plaster. To prevent the crack from reopening, fix a scrim mesh across the crack and cover it with lining paper.

Protecting a light fixture
To protect light fixtures, turn the power off and encase the cord and fixture in a plastic bag held in place with tape.

Floors

Whether you plan to lay a new floor covering or to make a decorative feature of an exposed floor, careful repair and preparation are vital. The floor should be as level as possible, clean, dry, and smooth. Smoothness is important, since any projections will quickly ruin a covering.

CHECKING THE FLOOR

- To help find small nails and tacks left in floorboards, slip an old nylon stocking over your hand and run it lightly over the boards.

- To check if the boards are uneven, lay a straight batten across the run of the boards. Pull the curtains or turn out the lights, then shine a flashlight behind the batten. Light will shine through where the boards undulate.

- Where the boards are badly worn, try lifting them and turning them over instead of buying new ones.

Solid floors

If a floor shows signs of dampness, it is important to deal with it. A minor case of rising damp might be cured by coating the floor with a special latex waterproofing compound, but a floor that is really damp will have to be dug up and replaced with a new concrete base, damp-proof membrane, and screed. If the damp is simply the result of moisture condensing on a cold surface, this usually clears up when the floor covering is laid.

Where the floor is just dusty, vacuum off the dust, then treat the floor with a coat of PVA glue, diluted one part glue to four parts clean water. This will seal the surface and prevent further dust from arising.

If the floor has projecting nibs of concrete, remove these with a bolster and club hammer. If the floor is uneven, it is best to use screeding compound to level it. You can buy this either as a powder that you mix with water, or ready-mixed in a tub.

Clean the floor thoroughly, then use a little of the compound to fill any holes and cracks. Allow these repairs to set before you apply the screeding compound over the whole area. Simply pour the compound out on to the floor, brush or trowel out, and leave it to find its own level.

Concrete or tiled floors

Bare concrete floors or securely fixed old quarry tiles can be painted with a special flooring paint designed to stand up to rough wear and tear. But do make certain that the floor is clean and dust free before starting. If it is dusty, treat it in the same way you would a solid floor, sealing it with a solution of one part PVA glue to four parts water. If the floor is in poor condition, however, coat it with a screeding compound to provide a new surface.

If you have an old property in which flagstones have been laid directly on the earth, and these are causing damp problems, you will need to seek professional advice. Lifting the stones to attend to the damp problem and then relaying the stones requires specialist skills and equipment. Flagstones that are dry but merely unsightly can be cleaned and their surface polished to a pleasing finish.

Wood floors

It is just as important for a wood floor to be smooth and sound as a solid one, so examine it carefully before laying any type of floorcovering. Remove any old tacks and unwanted nails and hammer down any floor nails that are standing proud of the boards.

If the floor is uneven, then you have two options. The first is to lay sheets of masonite, rough-side up, over the whole floor (lay board smooth-side up only if the floorcovering is recommended for laying that way). This seals any gaps and cracks between floorboards and improves the evenness overall. It also has the advantage

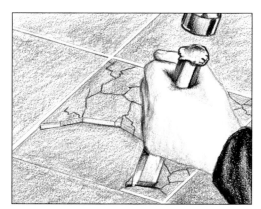

Repairing a ceramic floor
❶ Break up the damaged tile with a hammer and chisel and remove pieces with a small cold chisel. In case of splinters flying up, wear safety goggles at all times.

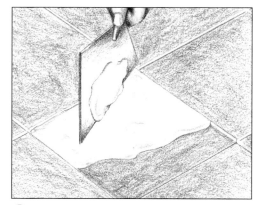

❷ Once you have removed all splinters of old tile, use a trowel to spread a layer of ceramic floor tiling adhesive in the hole you have created. Level the adhesive and make sure coverage is even.

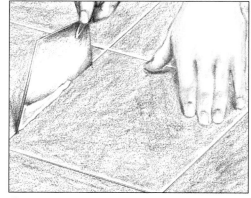

❸ Press the new tile into position and scrape off any excess adhesive with the trowel. Read the manufacturer's directions regarding drying time, and avoid walking on the tile until the adhesive has set.

Repairing and replacing floorboards

Good-condition floorboards are essential even if you intend to lay a floorcovering on top of them. Uneven boards will cause any surface covering to wear out that much quicker, and loose floorboards will squeak every time they are walked on.

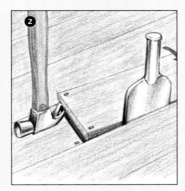

1 If you have tongue-and-groove type of floorboards, you will first have to saw through on each side of the board to free it from its neighbors and allow you to work on it.

2 To lift an ordinary floorboard, insert a floorboard bolster in the crack between the boards and lever upward with the help of a claw hammer.

3 Once the floorboard nails have come free from the joists, use a scrap of wood to hold the board while you work toward the other end with the bolster.

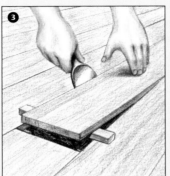

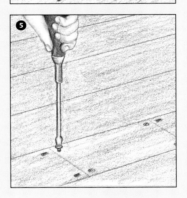

4 You will need to support a cut floorboard after it has been replaced. To do this, nail a small piece of scrap lumber to the side of the floor joist.

5 To allow access to pipework or wiring, screw the patch in place rather than using nails.

Laying masonite

Masonite gives an even surface and prevents dust rising up between the boards.

1 Before laying the sheets, condition them by brushing water onto the rough side.

2 Pin the sheets with their long sides parallel to the floorboards, staggering the joins in each row.

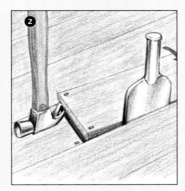

of adding to the floor's soundproofing quality. A disadvantage is that it makes it difficult to get under the floor at any future date if you need access to pipework or wiring.

The second option is to rent an industrial floor sander from a building supply store and sand the floor smooth (see pp.000-000). The sander will have a dust-collecting bag. Fine dust will escape, however, so you should wear a dust mask, eye protection, and old clothes or a boiler suit.

Before sanding, it is vital to punch all nails well below the surface of the floor. The machine is capable of grinding the floor down by a considerable depth, and any protruding nail will tear the paper belt.

Wherever possible, running the sanding machine in the direction of the wood grain will produce a better finish, and always progress from coarse to fine sanding belts. You may also need to hire a small belt sander to get into corners and close to the walls where the large sander won't fit. As an economic, if laborious, alternative, you can scrape the edge areas of the floor with a Skarsten scraper and then finish off with a sanding block.

Once sanding is complete, dust off the floor and vacuum it thoroughly before applying any finish. Using a damp cloth will help to settle fine dust.

If you plan to leave the floorboards exposed, you will need a good-quality finish. Apply the sealing coat as soon as possible, before the boards have a chance to become dirty, choosing a seal that is formulated to withstand heavy wear. Some sealing products are sold as floor seals, others as varnishes.

When applying the seal, work the first coat into the wood with a pad made up from an old handkerchief or sheeting material filled with cotton batting. This acts as a key for further coats (which you can apply with a brush) and it ensures that the seal does not flake away.

If you wish to stain – or paint – the floor, there are many methods involving separate stains or dyes and combined formulas that stain and seal.

Woodwork and metalwork

The care and attention you put into the preparation stages of treating wood and metal surfaces prior to decoration pay big dividends. Treating old or damaged wood or metal not only gives it a professional appearance, it also means less on-going maintenance and redecoration in the future.

Preparing bare wood

1 The first preparatory stage is to sand the wood, working along the grain with successively finer grades of abrasive paper.

2 If the abrasive paper clogs, clear it by drawing the uncoated side to and fro over the edge of a table or your work bench.

3 Treat sound knots with one or two coats of shellac knotting to seal in the resin and stop it from oozing through the paint film.

4 Fill any cracks or dents in the wood with cellulose filler if you intend to paint it. Use matching wood stopper prior to varnishing.

5 A coat of wood primer seals the surface and acts as a "key" for the subsequent coats of paint.

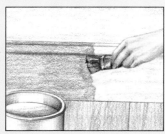

6 When the primer is dry, apply a layer of undercoat. Wait until this is dry and finish with a top coat.

Woodwork

Wooden doors and windows, and their frames, are subject to condensation – inside as well as outside. If you find areas of paintwork where there are hollows in the wood surface, or paint has flaked away, push into it with a sharp knife blade. If it sinks in with little resistance, the wood is rotten and there is no point redecorating until you have repaired it.

The first step is to lift out all the rotten material using a narrow chisel, cutting back to sound wood. If the gap left is large, cut and shape a new piece to fill. However, before you fit this, make sure the area is dry. If it feels damp, speed up the drying process with the aid of a hot air gun or blowlamp.

Hardening and filling When the area is dry, apply a commercial wood hardener to all the wood in the area of the repair. Be generous – allow it to soak right into the wood fibers and dab it in with a brush. For extra protection you can drill a number of holes, about ⅙in (4mm) in diameter, in the nearby wood and pour hardener into them. It will take about six hours to set, and will strengthen any soft fibers and prevent the ingress of more dampness.

Next, use a two-part wood repair paste to fill the hole. Check the instructions for the ratio of catalyst in one tube to repair paste in the other. Mix them together well, until they take on a uniform color, then fill the hole using a small trowel or filling knife. Leave the filler just higher than the surface and, when it is hard (in about 20 minutes at normal room temperature), smooth it flush with sandpaper. Always work in the direction of the grain of the wood to avoid ugly surface scratches.

Drying time of filler is about half if you are working outdoors in hot weather.

If you plan to paint the wood afterwards, then any two-part woodfiller will do the job. If, however, you intend to stain it and finish off with a seal or varnish, then make sure you choose a filler that will take stain. Some fillers will not, and you will end up with ugly blotches where the stain has been repelled.

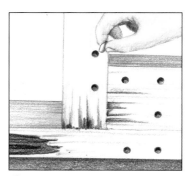

1 To protect wood around doors and windows, drill holes in the wood wide enough for wood-preserving tablets. If the wood subsequently becomes damp, the tablets release a fungicide that inhibits rot.

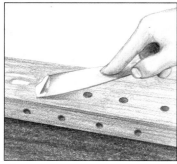

2 Fill the holes with an exterior-grade wood filler. Push the filler well into the holes, and clean up with a scraper or filling knife. Leave the filler just above the surface and sand it flush once it has hardened.

Surfaces and primers

Unpainted softwood (new or stripped), composite boards	Ordinary wood primers, all-purpose surface primers, or primer/undercoat
Resinous softwood and hardwood	Aluminum wood primer
Insulation board	Stabilizing primer
New plastering, plasterboard, rendering, or brickwork	All-surface primer under resin-based paints; no primer needed under latex
Porous or powdery plaster, rendering, or masonry	Stabilizing primer
Old wallpaper	Treat metallic inks with knotting
New iron and steel	Calcium plumbate primer outdoors; zinc chromate primate indoors
Bitumen-coated metal	Aluminum spirit-based sealer
Galvanized iron and metal	Calcium plumbate primer
Aluminum	Zinc chromate or zinc phosphate primer (*not* lead-based primers)
Copper and brass	No priming necessary
Lead	Allow to weather before painting; no priming necessary
Ceramic tiles	All-surface primer or zinc chromate metal primer
Plastic, glass fiber	All-surface primer

Preventing further damage To protect vulnerable areas of woodwork – such as sills, which are affected by condensation or rain – drill holes in the wood and insert and then seal in special wood-preserving tablets. These will dissolve and release a powerful fungicide should the wood become damp.

Having made good the damaged area, check carefully to see how it became damp in the first place. If condensation is the problem, ventilation may need improving. If dampness is rising, you may need to renew the damp-proof. If water is penetrating, you may need to replace window putty or re-seal around frames.

Replacing wood If the damaged area is greater than is practicable to fill, cut out and replace the damaged wood. Remove all the affected wood and shape the surrounding area so you can match it with new wood. Apply wood hardener to any remaining soft fibers.

Treat exposed wood with a clear wood preservative and, if you are planning to paint, use pretreated wood to fill the hole. Otherwise, treat your shaped piece with clear wood preservative before fitting it in place. It is best to cut the repair piece slightly too high

so you can plane or sand it flush with the surrounding wood.

Drill your repair wood to take rustless (zinc) screws, which you should countersink about ¼in (6mm) below the surface. Once you have drilled the repair wood, apply a liberal coating of waterproof wood glue – not forgetting the drilled holes – then screw the piece into place. Fill the screw holes with a two-part wood filler and leave it to harden.

Finishing off When the glue has set, smooth any projecting wood with sandpaper until it is flush with the surrounding areas. Unless you have been very accurate, you may find slight gaps in places between old and new wood. If so, fill the gaps with wood repair paste, allow it to set, and then smooth it back with sandpaper. You could use a wood stopping for this filling work, but if you do, be sure it is a weatherproof grade. Always use the correct mix: never use interior fillers for exterior repairs.

If damage is extensive, you may need a carpenter to carry out major repairs. And if you find that wood has dried out and crumbled and there are signs of whitish strands that give off a musty smell, suspect dry rot. Call in a treatment specialist at once.

Metalwork

Indoor metalwork, such as stair balusters and fireplace surrounds and inserts, can be unsightly if they have been painted and the surface is flaking. Paint that has been applied so thickly that it spoils the outline of decorative wrought iron is also unattractive. Remove excess or flaking paint manually with a wire brush or with a cup or wheel brush attachment on a power drill. Always wear face protection. If repainting, use a metal primer on the cleaned surface first.

Once metal has started to corrode, the process will continue and accelerate, unless it is properly treated. Where you find rust, indoors in bathrooms or on leaky radiators, or outdoors on decorative ironwork or gutters, use a wire brush to remove all traces of it. Finish off with steel wool to clear away any fine dust from the surface.

After that, paint over the whole affected area with a rust-neutralizing primer – or a decorative rust-resisting enamel paint of the type used for radiators, which does not need a primer coat – and allow it to dry completely before applying the top coat.

Neutralize rust by using a primer that reacts with the rust and forms a barrier between the metal and the moisture-laden air.

St

ructures. 4

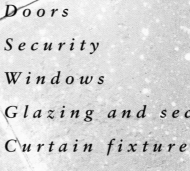

Walls

The different methods and materials used in the construction of walls often depend on the age of the building, when alterations or extensions (if any) were made and whether the walls are external or internal.

For the purposes of decorating it is not too important to know how walls are built, for they are usually covered internally with a layer of plaster or sheet rock, which presents a smooth surface for painting or papering. All types of wallcovering – from wallpaper and vinyl to burlap, cork, and ceramic tiles – can be mounted with special adhesives, as along as the plaster is firm and sound. But for attaching anything heavier, it is important to know what lies beneath the plaster so that you can make the right choice of mount (*see p. 68-69*).

Above *Stripping the interior surface of plaster off walls exposes the underlying brickwork. Once cleaned, repointed if necessary, and sealed, an exposed brick wall makes an attractive focal point for a room.*

External Walls

The outside walls of a house are usually built with a double thickness of bricks or blocks. Originally, walls would have been solid but, in the 1920s, cavity walls were first introduced and are now standard in houses built since that decade. These double walls improve insulation and reduce the risk of dampness. The inner leaf may be constructed of brick, block, or a 4 x 2in (5 x 10cm) wood frame. The inner side of brick and block walls are usually plastered, but a wooden frame is covered on the outside with exterior grade plywood and the inside with sheet rock.

Solid walls

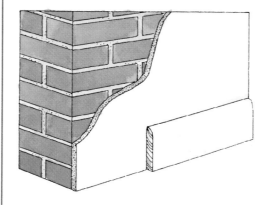

Plastered brick Normally found only in houses built pre-1920s.

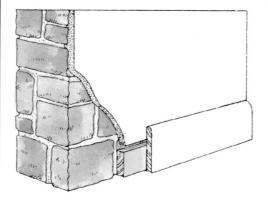

Plastered stone Normally found only in houses built pre-1920s.

Cavity walls

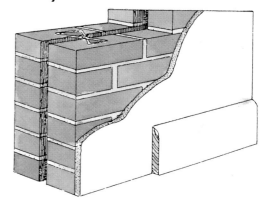

Plastered brick inner leaf Two leaves of brick separated by a 2in (5cm) gap.

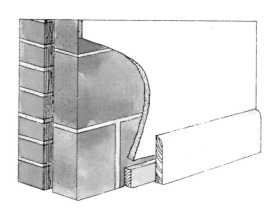

Plastered block inner leaf Two leaves of block separated by a 2in (5cm) gap.

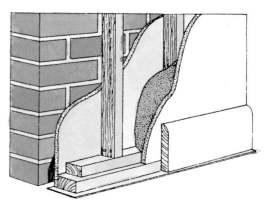

Wood frame inner leaf Outer leaf brick, or block, inner leaf of 2 x 4in (5 x 10cm) wooden frame clad on the outside with plywood, inside with sheet rock.

Internal walls

The walls within a building divide the interior space up into individual rooms, hallways, corridors, closets, and so on. These walls may be built from a number of different materials depending on the age of the building, and they may be either of solid or hollow construction. Some interior walls are also load-bearing. When struck with the heel of your hand, a solid wall sounds and feels solid, whereas a hollow wall makes more of an empty sound.

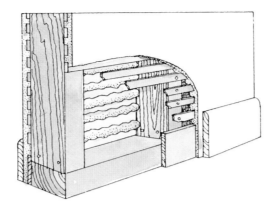

Lath and plaster stud Normally found in houses built pre-1920s. Plaster is pressed onto thin wooden laths, which are nailed across wooden uprights.

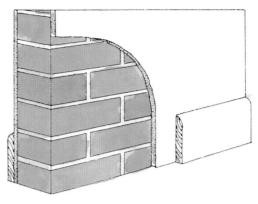

Plastered single skin of brick Ordinary bricks covered with about a ¾in (19mm) layer of plaster.

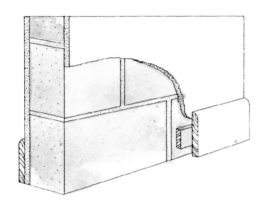

Plastered concrete block Lightweight building blocks covered with a ¾in (19mm) layer of plaster.

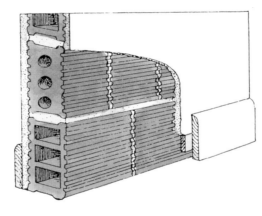

Plastered hollow clay block Lightweight building blocks covered with ¾in (19mm) layer of plaster.

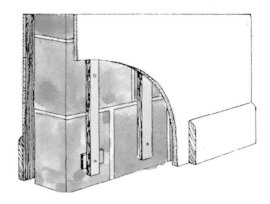

Plasterboard-lined block or brick Sheets of ⅜ or ½in (9.5 or 12.5mm) thick sheet rock anchored to the wall or 1 x 2in (2.5 x 5 cm) vertical wooden battens.

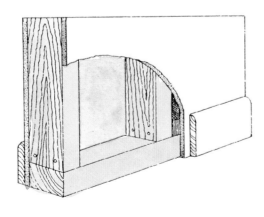

Plasterboard stud Sheets of ½in (12.5mm) thick plasterboard nailed onto wooden studs, usually 2 x 3in (5 x 7.5cm), and spaced at 16in (40cm) intervals.

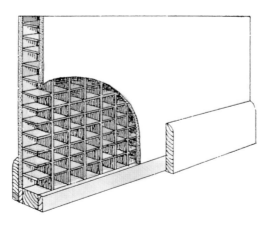

Cellular-core wallboard Cardboard honey-comb sandwiched between sheets of ¾in (19mm) sheet rock mounted between 1½in (3.8cm) wooden studs 16–24in (40–60cm).

Right (from top) *Cellular-core wallboard (useful for sound insulation); foil-coated plaster-board (if left exposed as a lining in an attic, for example, will help moderate temperature by reflecting the sun's rays); and sheet rock (used for partition walls and ceilings).*

Mountings

All walls appear to be "solid" to the person whose task it is to attach shelf brackets or other items to them with nails or screws. But in reality, when attaching anything more than a lightweight picture to a wall, for which a hook is usually adequate, it is necessary to find out what the wall behind the surface skin of plaster is composed of. If it is brick or stone, it will be too hard for you to be able simply to hammer ordinary nails into it, as you can with early forms of insulating block – known as breeze block. These insulating blocks have the texture of particles of ground coke. You can tell if you are working on a breeze block wall if the dust that comes out when you drill into it is dense black or dark grey in color.

Heavy objects, such as mirrors, shelving, kitchen cabinets, and wooden siding, must be securely anchored in place to the underlying structure with screws or nails; for plasterboard, special mounts have been devised that grip on to the board itself.

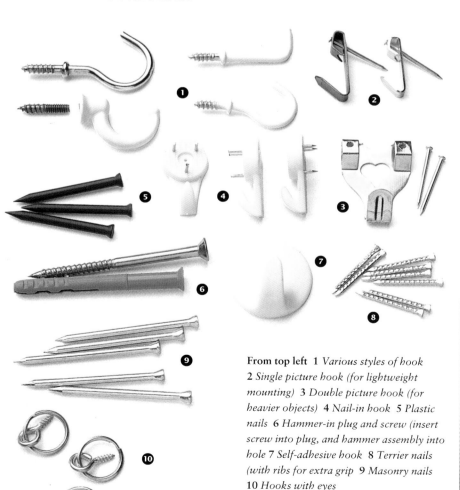

From top left 1 *Various styles of hook* 2 *Single picture hook (for lightweight mounting)* 3 *Double picture hook (for heavier objects)* 4 *Nail-in hook* 5 *Plastic nails* 6 *Hammer-in plug and screw (insert screw into plug, and hammer assembly into hole* 7 *Self-adhesive hook* 8 *Terrier nails (with ribs for extra grip* 9 *Masonry nails* 10 *Hooks with eyes*

Mounts for walls

Simple mounts may be made to wood and breeze block with ordinary nails. When faced with harder materials, however, you will need to drill a hole and plug it in order to make it firm and secure.

Bits designed for drilling into masonry are tipped with tungsten carbide. This can become sufficiently hot if the bit is blunt, if deep holes become choked with dust, or if the drill is used at too high a speed to remove the tip completely. Use a low drill speed if possible and withdraw the bit from the hole every $\frac{1}{2}$in (12.5mm), with the drill still running, to clear out the hole. Use a hammer action on brick or block walls.
Breeze block can be difficult to drill accurately because the irregularly sized particles tend to cause the bit to wander, making holes oversized and off-center. The only solution is to drill oversized holes, about $\frac{1}{2}$–$\frac{5}{8}$in (12.5–16mm), push in a length of dowel, and screw into that. If this is not tight enough, cement the dowel in first and let it set.

Steel reinforcement rods may be present near the surface of concrete blocks. If you encounter one of these, there is no alternative other than to re-site the mount or screw a wide batten to the wall and anchor into that.

Holes must be at least 1$\frac{1}{2}$in (3.8cm) deep in order to penetrate through the plaster and at least 1in (2.5cm) into the solid part of the wall. For a heavy-duty mounts, such as a bracket for a bookshelf, it will be necessary to have 2in (5cm) of the screw thread in the solid part of the wall.

Plugs Plugs are made from wood, fiber, or plastic. Plastic is the most common material and is generally satisfactory in brick, stone, and concrete. Many manufacturers make one-size plugs for any screw size between No. 6 and No. 12, which means that all the holes for these can be drilled with a single bit – a No. 12 or No. 14. If the plug is shorter than the hole, turn the screw once or twice into it, then tap the screw lightly into the wall before using the screwdriver.

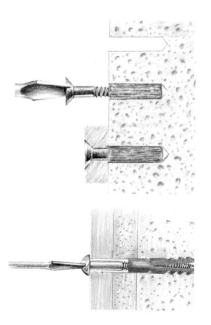

Expanding bolts For very heavy loads, such as those taken by pivoting support brackets, expanding bolts are your best choice. These have a soft iron plug around the stem, which expands to make a tight fit as the bolt is tightened in the hole.

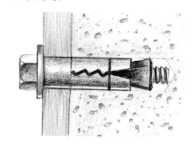

STRUCTURES

4

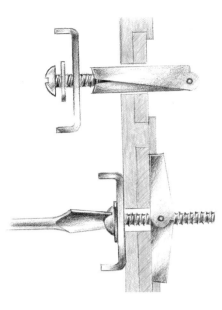

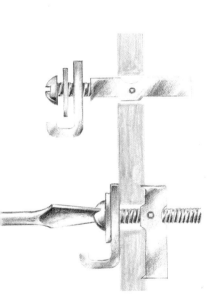

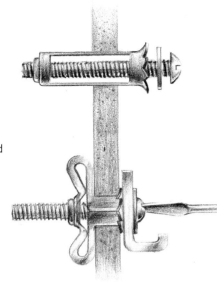

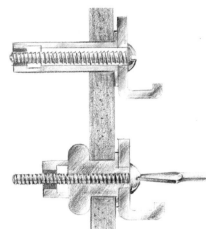

Hollow-wall mounts For hollow walls, those made of plasterboard or wallboard, there are two main types of mounts for heavy loads – gravity toggle fasteners and spring toggle fasteners. Both fasteners consist of a bolt with a specialized nut that folds down the shank as it is inserted through the object to be hung and the board. Once released, however, the nut opens out and grips onto the blind side of the board as the screw is tightened. These mounts are strong and spread the load over a wide area. Large toggle fasteners can even support the weight of radiators. These mounts are permanent, however, and once used they cannot be reclaimed.

Screw anchors Lighter mounts in hollow walls can be made with any of several types of plastic screw anchor. As the screw is tightened, the anchor opens and grips the blind side of the panel. Some screw anchors open like umbrellas and work on much the same principle. Yet others resemble masonry bolts, but are split in such a way that the plug around the stem collapses

as the screw is tightened to form a mushroom-shaped nut. These can be reclaimed and used again if necessary.
Battens Another way of mounting on a hollow wall is to screw battens to the framework behind and then mount on to this.

Glue

Although it is true that modern adhesives can perform miracles in certain situations, you should be at least a little cautious about using them instead of nails and screws. This is be-cause the strength of the bond more often than not depends on the adhesion of a layer of paint to the plaster. If you use adhesive over a broad expanse of wall, however, it is unlikely to let you down. Make sure you degrease the surface to which you are applying glue, using mineral spirit. You can also use a strong detergent, but then you must rinse and dry the surface. Neoprene-based adhesives, which can be squeezed from a tube or gun, are available for mounting thin wall panels. These take up minor irregularities in the wall surface, up to about ¼in (6mm).

HINTS AND TIPS

- If you have a large number of screws to plug into masonry walls, you can save a lot of time and trouble by using a tap-in screw/plug system.

- Screwing into a tightly fitting wall plug can sometimes be extremely difficult. If so, place a little soap, light grease, or a silicone lubricant on the screw ends before starting.

- No matter how much care you take when drilling, you often end up with oversized holes in masonry and breeze blocks. If the looseness is only slight, insert spills (splinters of wood or twists of paper) or matchsticks around the wall plug to take up the slack.

- When attaching objects to ceilings, it is important to discover where the joists are located. Once these have been found, you

can then drill directly into them and screw in woodscrews without having to use toggles or other types of mounts designed for hollow panels. If it is not obvious where the joists are located – paler strips on the paintwork or different notes in response to knocking are often tell-tale signs – drill a series of tiny holes through the plasterboard until you meet some resistance.

A partition wall

A room that is too large for its requirements often can be successfully partitioned to create two smaller, more manageable spaces that can be used for different activities. Constructing a partition wall yourself may seem like a major undertaking, however, one requiring considerable knowledge and skill. Happily, the task is much simpler and more straightforward than you might initially think – all that is required is a wooden framework covered with sheet rock. Bear in mind, though, that such a wall is simply a partition and is not load-bearing.

Below A large room may sometimes be put to better use if it is divided into different activity areas. In the example illustrated here, a partition wall – made up from sheets of plasterboard – has been built in order to create an attractive study/home office at the rear of a living room.

Materials and techniques

Making a frame of 2 x 3in (5 x 7.5cm) wood is straightforward. The framework must be anchored to the ceiling joists, which is not a problem where the partition is at right angles to them. If it runs parallel, it is best to locate it directly under a joist. Alternatively, noggings can be installed between the joists, but this will probably involve lifting carpets and floorboards in the room above. The tools required for building the frame are hammer, screwdriver, drill, level, and plumb line and bob. A footlifter, a rounded triangular section of wood cut from 2 x 10in (5 x 25cm) softwood is useful for lifting the sheet rock off the floor as you attach it.

Buy a ready-made door, if one is required, rather than try to construct it yourself. Match the door frame and architrave to others in your home.

Sheet rock is usually available in sheets 4 x 6 or 8ft (1.2 x 1.8 or 2.4m) long, in thicknesses of ½in (12.5mm) or ⅜in (9.5mm). The length of board needed depends on the height of the room. Thicker sheets are more expensive but require fewer supports.

Working with sheet rock requires few tools. A fine-toothed saw is needed to cut it, ivory-side up, although short lengths can be cut by scoring the ivory side deeply with a sharp knife and snapping the waste over a straightedge, cutting through the lining on the backing with the knife. Holes for light switches and sockets need to be marked on the board with a pencil and cut out with a padsaw or keyhole saw before being mounted. Attach the sheet rock to the framework with galvanized nails and hide the joins with joint tape and filler.

Constructing the framework

First, mark on the floor exactly where the wall and door, if required, are to be located. A continuous length of wood, the sole plate, broken only for the door opening, is mounted along the center line. It is nailed or screwed to the floor at 24in (60cm) intervals, two mounts at a time. The sole plate can be attached to floor-boards, but securing it through to joists will make the structure stronger.

Now attach the head plate to the ceiling. Using a level against a straight piece of wood or a plumb line, mark the ceiling directly above the sole plate. Attach a continuous length of wood to the ceiling, driving through into the joists. The head plate should be broken only if the ceiling is very low or the door exceptionally high.

Once the sole and head plates are in place, mount the vertical studs between them. Place at 16in (40cm) intervals for ⅜in (9.5mm) thick board or 24in (60cm) for ½in (12.5mm) thick board and at each side of any opening. Skewnail the studs, using two nails per mount.

For extra strength, attach noggings halfway up the studs, and where required for supporting heavy fixtures, such as a washbasin.

Mounting the sheet rock

Cut board 1in (2.5cm) short of the partition's height and hold it firmly against the ceiling while it is nailed to the framework. Anchor the boards with galvanized nails at 16in (40cm) intervals and ½in (12.5mm) from the edge. Drive each nail until the head dimples the board's surface but does not tear the paper lining.

1 Nail the sole plate to a concrete floor, or use nails or screws driven into the joists if you are anchoring it to a wooden floor.

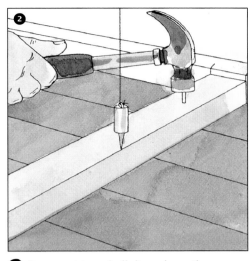

2 Snap a string chalk line along the ceiling as a guide for anchoring the head plate.

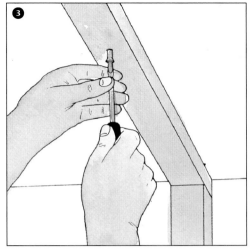

3 Use long screws to attach the head plate securely into the ceiling joists supporting the plaster.

4 Cut vertical studs precisely to length so that they are a tight fit when in place between the head and sole plates.

5 Tap each stud into place with a hammer and check with a carpenter's level to make sure that each is vertical.

Cutting sheet rock

Cut sheets of board with the paper lining face downward. Use a sharp, fine-toothed saw for long lengths of board. Alternatively, for short lengths you can use a sharp knife to score deep lines in the material and then snap off the waste over a straightedge. Cut out holes for switches with a padsaw or keyhole saw after first drilling a starting hole. Sand the cut edges lightly to remove any burrs.

6 Use a scrap of wood to support a stud so that it does not slip while you nail it to the sole plate.

9 Use fiberglass for sound and thermal insulation, especially between a bathroom and bedroom.

10 When mounting the sheet rock in place, slip a footlifter made of wood under the board to raise it to the correct height.

11 Nail the sheets of board to the battens using galvanized nails.

Locating joists

To locate the joists in a top-floor room, you need to climb up into the attic space and take a look. In a boarded attic or in an upstairs room, you need to note where the nails are that anchor the floorboards to the underlying joists. If the boards are covered, tap the ceiling in the room below with your knuckles. A "solid" sound and feel indicates the presence of a joist. Alternatively, you will have to make a series of small test holes with a drill to find the joists and then make good afterwards.

7 Supporting noggins can meet each other exactly or be slightly offset. Support it with a scrap while nailing.

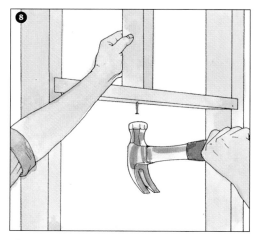

8 If a door frame is required, the top should be cut into the uprights so that it is firmly supported.

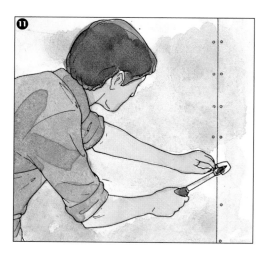

Disguising the joints

To hide the joints between the boards, to produce a smooth, professional surface that can then be painted or papered, the following materials are required:

- Jointing compound

- Jointing tape

- Steel float

- Filing knife

- Jointing sponge

1 To fill the joints between the plasterboards, first apply jointing compound to the tapered edges using a steel float.

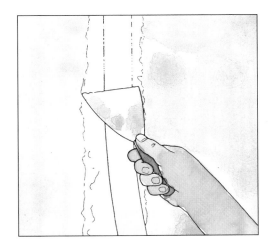

2 Next, apply jointing tape, pressing it down with a putty knife so that it is well embedded in the jointing compound.

3 Use the steel float once more to apply another band of jointing compound, 8in (20cm) wide.

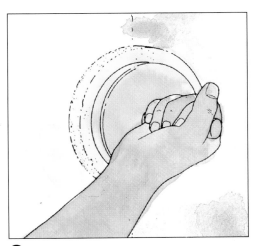

4 Feather the edges of the jointing compound with a moist sponge. Allow the compound to dry thoroughly.

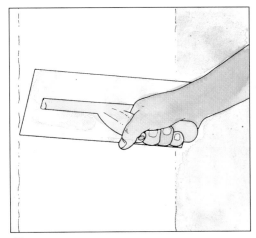

5 Finally, apply another band of jointing compound, this time 12in (30cm) wide.

Screen walls

Although they don't offer much benefit in terms of sound insulation and, often, they cannot be used as structural partitions, screen walls are a quick and relatively inexpensive method of dividing up a large space. In this way, different uses can be made of what was formerly a single-activity room.

As well as the traditional Japanese style of screen wall, freestanding "flats" can be used, or a wood and sheet rock partition can be constructed which is capable of supporting bookshelves and pictures.

Above *Here, a traditional Japanese type screen is made out of black wooden frame and textured glass.*

Below *Wood finish screen divides the space, and offers different ways of varying the arrangement of the room.*

Archways

An archway can be an elegant solution to softening what otherwise could be an inappropriately stark or boxy room feature. For example, where a wall that formerly divided two rooms has been removed to create a larger, more open space, a wider arch than is strictly necessary will transform the boring square opening framed by the supporting rolled-steel joist (RSJ) resting on its piers. On a smaller, more intimate scale, an arched opening can be used to link two related rooms, such as a kitchen and dining room or a bedroom and bathroom or dressing room. Arches can also be used to decorate alcoves, recesses, and other openings. Wherever they are placed, they sponsor a sense of spaciousness.

Right *An archway leading from the kitchen to a neighboring dining room is both convenient and helps to create an illusion of extra space.*

Below *A simple, unfussy arch lends a spacious feeling to a living room by linking it with the hallway beyond.*

Types and styles

Whether made to measure or bought as a preformed kit of lightweight galvanized steel mesh, an arch can be fitted into virtually any opening in the home. It is advisable to choose the style carefully, however, since the shape will affect the amount of headroom the opening ends up with, and it may not look right in certain situations. Elliptical, Spanish, and Tudor styles are ideal for wider openings, while Indian, Arabian and semicircular shapes are better suited to narrower doorways. Corner arches just round off the angle without greatly affecting the headroom anywhere, but the full, rounded shape of semicircular types eats into the headroom at the sides. Pointed arches are distinctive without taking any headroom from the middle of the opening.

Once the style of the arch has been decided, the unfinished opening needs to be measured to establish the size of arch required. In an already finished room, this may mean some hacking away to reveal the underlying construction.

Depending on its size the arch may be in two or more sections. If there are four sections, these are anchored individually to the wall, their beads being joined by lengths of connecting dowel. On a narrow wall, the two overlapping soffits (which form the underside of the arch) are fastened together with zinc-plated self-tapping screws or twists of galvanized binding wire. For a thicker wall – greater than 9in (23cm) – the additional width is made up with a strip of mesh known as a soffit strip, which is fastened in the same way.

Plastering

Once it is securely attached to the wall, the arch is ready for plastering. You can choose from a number of plasters: traditional two-coat lightweight plaster, one-coat plaster, or a number of premixed plasters. The latter tend to be more expensive if a large area is being covered, but they are more economical for small areas, involve less wastage, and – perhaps most importantly – are very easy to use.

With the two-coat method, a base coat of metal-lathing plaster is first applied to the frame. The plaster is smoothed on with a trowel, using the solid bead as a guide to plaster depth and for the trowel. When this coat is dry, a thin coat of finish plaster is applied in the same way. The result is a perfect shape and a professional finish. One-coat and premixed plaster also give good finishes.

No matter which type of plaster you use, you must allow it to dry out thoroughly before attempting to decorate.

Wallpaper patterns

Wallpapering an arch with lining paper is not complicated. The paper is applied to each face of the arch, sealing the edge by turning a margin of paper onto the underside of the arch. Then two strips of paper are applied to the underside of the arch to meet at the apex. Since large motifs and complicated patterns are difficult to match on the different faces of an arch, they are best avoided. Small random patterns or textured paper painted with latex are better choices.

Fibrous plaster arches

If you don't feel that your do-it-yourself skills are up to creating an ornate archway, then there are some easy and convincing "cheats" to fall back on, in the form of preformed, fibrous plaster arches. These arches, in various classic styles, are readily available, and are supplied in sections that you mount either directly to the opening, or to a light batten frame, using either screws or coving adhesive and tacks. Accessories, such as corbels and pillars, made from the same lightweight material, complete the effect.

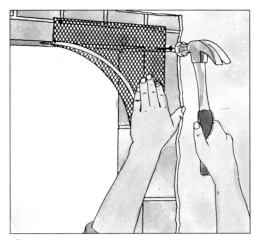

1 Mark the center of the opening, place one mesh archformer section on the wall, and lightly nail it in place.

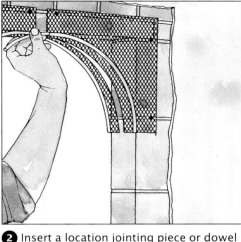

2 Insert a location jointing piece or dowel into the bead. Leave half protruding. Fit the other archformer. Repeat on the other side.

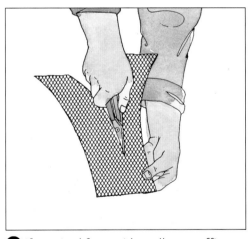

3 If required for a wide wall, cut soffit strips from mesh to cover the gap between the archformers.

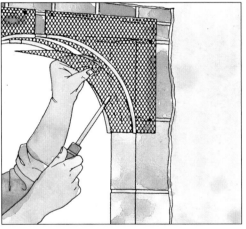

4 Attach the soffit strips to form a continuous infill on the underside of the arch using screws or ties.

5 Nail angle bead (for brickwork) or mini-mesh angle bead (for plasterboard) on all vertical corners below the arch.

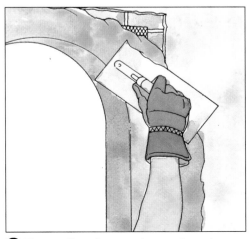

6 Plaster directly onto the steel mesh using either two-coat or one-coat plasters.

Ceilings

Although they are an integral part of a room's structure, ceilings tend to be ignored until they start to cause problems or they are in need of decoration. Fortunately, major problems are few and usually the most that is required before repainting or papering is for a few hairline cracks to be filled in. However, by simply adding molded decorative features to a ceiling, you can introduce a little style and distinction and perhaps bring harmony to a room.

Lowering a ceiling

There may be many good reasons for wanting to lower a ceiling, but the main ones are to make a room seem cozier and easier to heat, and also to hide a ceiling that may be cracked or have surface-mounted pipes. More than likely, the ceiling will be in a tall room and you will want to lower it by a significant amount. If, however, you want to lower it just a little, perhaps because it is in need of repair, you could construct a new one just a few inches below the existing one. If the original ceiling is old and sagging, make sure you remove any loose pieces that could eventually break away and fall, damaging the new ceiling below.

Problems with ceilings

Ceilings are constructed in one of two ways. Traditional lath-and-plaster ceilings are still found in many older houses and continue to do good service. These were made by nailing narrow strips of wood, known as laths, close together across the joists of the floor above to provide a key for the plaster, which often contained horsehair. Modern ceilings are more simply constructed – sheet rock is nailed directly to the joists. The joints between the sheets are then filled with plaster filler.

While plasterboard ceilings rarely cause any problems, the older lath-and-plaster ones tend to crack and sag as the house settles, and generally require more repair work.

Repairs are usually straightforward, consisting of cleaning out a crack or hole and making it good with cellulose filler. Large areas of damage will have to be patched with new material, however, and an old ceiling that is sagging excessively usually needs to be taken down and replaced with a plasterboard one. This is not difficult but extremely messy and dusty. If the room is tall, you could consider constructing a new ceiling just below the old one (*see left*).

Sometimes a large crack runs across the ceiling, stubbornly opening and shutting with the passing of the seasons and changes in the weather. Such a crack is virtually impossible to seal permanently and probably the best course of action is to cover the entire ceiling with tiles (*see opposite*).

Stains on a ceiling can sometimes "bleed" through new decoration. If this is the case, you will have to seal the ceiling with either aluminum prime-sealer or a commercial stain block.

Ceiling Types

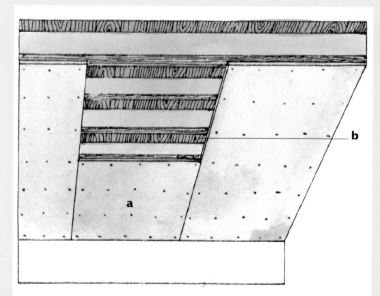

Sheet rock Sheets of plasterboard (**a**) are nailed to the undersides of the ceiling joists (**b**) and the joints between the boards are smoothed with plaster filler.

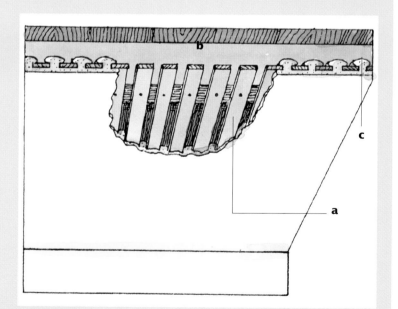

Lath and plaster Wooden strips known as laths (**a**) are nailed to the undersides of the joists (**b**). Plaster (**c**) can then be forced between the laths.

Far left *Tiles are useful for hiding a poor ceiling and for adding insulation. In the example here, the tiles are mounted in a lightweight frame.*

Left *A new ceiling has been added to this dining area to match the style of the built-in units, window frames, and furniture.*

Ceiling tiles

Ceiling tiles can be used to cover up a poor surface or to add insulation to a cold room. It is usually best to tile from the center of the ceiling toward the edges of the room. If, however, there is a straight wall near the room's entrance, you can use it as your starting point.

Styrofoam acoustic tiles are usually 12in (30cm) or 24in (60cm) square and have chamfered edges. They are glued on with a special tile adhesive that you spread over the entire ceiling. They are easy to trim and cut to size and shape using a sharp knife and straightedge.

Fibrous and gypsum plaster tiles are another option for covering a ceiling. These tiles are, however, much heavier than styrofoam types, so they have to be nailed to battens that are screwed at right angles to the ceiling joists and spaced so that the tiles meet at their centers.

Finding the joists may be a little difficult. If you cannot locate them by tapping, listening for a different sound in response, drill a series of small holes in the ceiling until you find one. Use 1¼ x ½in (3 x 1.5cm) battens. For tongued-and-groove tiles it is not necessary to install any cross-pieces, but some tiles may need them to give support along their edges. The tiles are nailed through their edges or installed with special clips, which are hidden by the adjoining tiles.

If the tiles are to be painted, it is easier to do this before they are attached to the ceiling. Use either latex or a fire-retardant paint – never use gloss paint, since it is highly flammable.

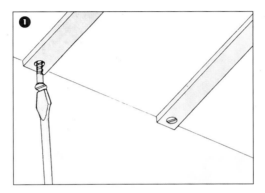

❶ Mark the ceiling where the joists run and also the center points for the battens. Cut, drill, and countersink the battens, and then screw them in place.

❷ Paint the tiles using a roller, and their chamfered edges with a narrow brush. Two coats may be necessary. Stipple-paint textured gypsum tiles using a brush.

❸ Mount the tiles on the battens, nailing them through their edges. With tongue-and-groove tiles, nail through the tongue or use special holding clips.

Moldings

Horizontal molding that separates a ceiling from the walls is often referred to as cornicing or coving. It has a dual role in that it decoratively disguises the right-angled seam between adjacent surfaces and successfully covers any cracks that may appear along it.

Many older houses are fortunate to have ornamental plasterwork on their ceilings, but prefabricated coving – available in many styles – can easily be installed to add a little sophistication to any room. Even plain rounded coving will go a long way to "finishing off" the ceiling perimeter of a fairly ordinary room. Rolls of decorative strip can be bought to add pattern and color to plain coving. Additionally, a ceiling "rose," a center piece of decorative plaster, can be mounted in the middle of a ceiling to set off the coving.

Styrofoam coving

Styrofoam coving is usually available, either plain or patterned, in 39in (1m) lengths, about 4in (10cm) wide. Internal and external corner pieces are also available with many types, avoiding the need for cutting complicated corner joints. The advantage of styrofoam is that it is very lightweight and needs only to be glued with a special adhesive. Plaster-coated styrofoam is also readily available in a range of styles.

Gypsum plaster coving

Gypsum plaster coving is normally available in 6½ft (2m) lengths, either 4in (10cm) or 5in (12.7cm) wide – although longer lengths can be specially ordered. Like styrofoam coving, plaster coving is also mounted with a special adhesive, but good wall and ceiling plaster surfaces are essential. Cutting miters for the corners can be tricky, but plaster coving is always supplied with a template. It is wise to practice cutting miters on scraps of wood before tackling the coving itself.

Right *Coving provides a decorative transition from wall to ceiling as well as hiding any unsightly cracks.*

Below *A range of different decorative moldings are available, made of plaster, plastic, resin, or styrofoam. Choose the style and depth of molding that best suits the architectural style and decorative theme of individual rooms.*

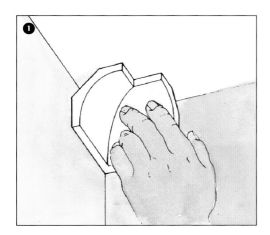

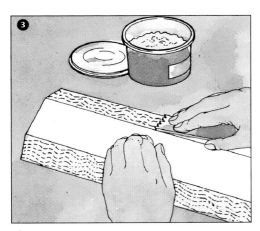

❶ Start by gluing on the corner pieces. Spread glue on the angled back of a corner piece and push it gently but firmly in place.

❷ Measure the distance between two corner pieces and cut a length of coving to fit with a trimming knife.

❸ Apply adhesive on the angled back of the coving and gently press and smooth the length in place. Remove any excess adhesive with a damp rag before it dries.

Center moldings, or "roses"

It was common for early 20th-century houses to have plaster centerpieces on the ceilings of one or more of the principal rooms used for entertaining. Although many of these have been removed due to modernization, they are, once again, finding favor among a new generation of home owners.

Reproduction ceiling "roses" can be installed to complement decorative coving. They are glued with adhesive in the same way as coving, but may need supporting until this has set. Large center pieces should be attached to the joists with brass screws driven through the plaster and their heads covered with filler. If a central light fixture is required, a hole may have to be drilled through the "rose" to accommodate the wire.

Right *Ornamental plaster roses of different styles are available in a variety of sizes to suit the proportions of any room. The inside of the rose center can be hollowed out to accommodate the wiring for a chandelier, and a hole has to be drilled through the middle to allow the wiring to hang down.*

Restoring old plasterwork

Much decorative plaster in older houses has suffered from decades of overpainting and sometimes neglect and physical damage as well. It is often surprising how sharp and attractive the original detail still is once the layers of paint have been cleaned off. Cleaning old plaster caked with distemper is a labor of love, however, requiring long patient hours wearing down the layers with an old toothbrush dipped in water and a pointed implement such as a skewer. Once the paint has been cleaned away, any cracks and chipped detail need to be filled. Before decorating, wash the molding and apply a stabilizing primer. A molding that has been overpainted with other types of water-thinned paints, such as limewash and cement paints, can simply be scraped and brushed with a stiff-bristled brush, and then wiped with mineral spirits. Any sections of excessively damaged plaster moldings can be repaired by specialist firms, who can also replace molding that may have been completely removed.

4

STRUCTURES

Floors

Floors, like ceilings, tend to be taken for granted until a problem occurs or a new surface is required. Then, knowing how the floor has been constructed will enable you to sort out any problems. Basically, there are just two types of floor – suspended wood and solid concrete – although some very old houses still have original stone or brick floors laid directly on soil or sand.

Little can go wrong with a well-constructed solid floor. Made from a concrete slab laid over a layer of rubble, such a floor is usually found on the ground level of modern houses and recently built extensions to older ones. The slab is topped by a damp-proof membrane, which blocks rising damp, and finished with a fine concrete layer. Solid floors rarely contain pipes or cables.

Wooden floors are commonly found in the upstairs rooms of houses of all ages and can be on the ground floor of older properties. Traditionally, they are wooden boards, plain or tongue-and-groove, nailed onto floor joists supported either by metal brackets, known as joist hangers, attached to the outside walls of the house or by low walls. Today, blockboard often replaces the floorboards of old. Electricity cables and pipework often run under wooden flooring.

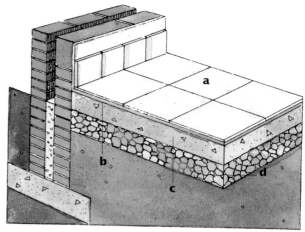

Solid floor Floor tiles (**a**) are here laid on the cement layer, which is protected from dampness by the damp-proof membrane (**b**). Beneath this is the concrete slab (**c**) on a layer of rubble (**d**).

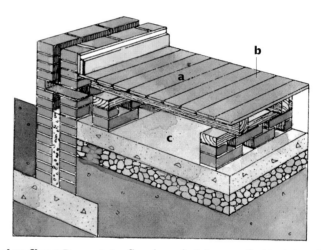

Wooden floor Downstairs floorboards (**a**) are nailed to joists (**b**), which, in turn, are supported by low walls; in some floors the joists are supported by joist hangers. The gap (**c**) is for air circulation to keep the wood dry.

Above *Floorboards, attractively laid and well sanded and sealed, can become a decorative room feature in their own right. Here, they also echo the use of wood in the beam above the fireplace.*

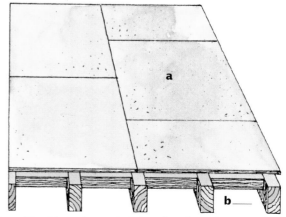

Upper floor Blockboard panels (**a**) or floorboards are nailed onto the joists (**b**), which may receive intermediate support from partition walls as well as from the outside walls of the house.

Preparing the floor

Before a covering can be put down, the floor must be clean, dry, and smooth.

Solid floors

If the floor is dry and smooth but dusty, vacuum and then seal it with one part PVA glue to four parts clean water.

Any dampness must be treated before a new covering is laid. Dampness coming up through the floor (test for this by laying a plastic sheet over it for a few days) will ruin any new covering. You may be able to treat damp with a bitumen paint, but if you are in any doubt seek specialist advice.

Remove projecting nibs of concrete with a steel chisel or bolster and club hammer. Small areas of damage can be patched with a cement-based filler or mortar, but if the surface is crumbling and dusty, the best solution is to cover it with a new layer using a self-levelling compound. Clean the floor and fill holes and cracks with a little of the compound made up following the manufacturer's instructions. Allow these to set, then apply the compound over the whole floor. Spread it with a trowel, then let it find its own level.

Wooden floors

Old tacks and nails must first be removed or hammered down below the surface using a nail set. Loose boards, which squeak and may warp, should be nailed down securely; use screws to force a warped edge back in place.

If the floorboards are uneven over the entire floor, there are two solutions. First, lay a sheet of masonite over the entire floor – smooth side up unless you are laying carpet tiles. This will seal gaps and cracks, but has the disadvantage of making any pipes or cables under the floor difficult to get to. Second, the floor can be sanded smooth using a rented industrial floor sander and small belt sander (*see right*).

Small holes can be filled with wooden plugs or wood putty, but saw out and re-place large areas of damage. To lift a board, punch the nails through and prize it up with a claw hammer and bolster. Tongue-and-groove board must be sawn along the seam with a padsaw to cut the tongue.

Sanding a wooden floor

Even quite badly damaged or neglected wooden floors can be brought back to a state where they enhance the appearance of a room. Mechanical sanders make this task considerably easier, although some hand finishing may be necessary.

- Hammer

- Nail set

- Mechanical sander

- Sanding belts and disks

- Disk sander

Re-screeding a concrete floor

The re-screeding compound used on concrete floors works on the principle that a liquid always finds its own level. The first stage of the process is to make make up the self-levelling compound following the manufacturer's instructions. If mixed correctly, it should have a stiff pouring consistency. Then all you need to do is pour it over the floor, where it will fill all gaps and cracks. Roughly trowel the compound over the whole surface and then leave it to level itself out and dry.

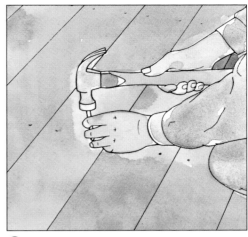

1 Punch all nail heads well below the surface of the floorboards before beginning to sand them.

2 Start by running the sander diagonally across the line of the floorboards. This will flatten down any warped boards.

3 Finish the main part of the floor by running the sander up and down the boards until the surface is even.

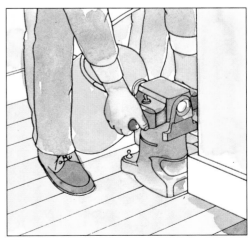

4 Use a heavy-duty disk sander in the inaccessible areas and then remove all traces of dust. The floor can now be sealed.

Doors

Doors can make a great contribution to the overall appearance of your home, and so their type and style need to be chosen with care. The front door, especially, needs to match the style of the house. Internal doors that harmonize with the mood and decoration of the interior make a substantial impact on the whole atmosphere. External doors should not only look good, however, they must also be solid enough to withstand inclement weather, providing an effective seal against wind and rain as well as heat loss. In addition, they must be sufficiently secure and well made and fitted to deter any opportunistic burglars.

Above *Painted in a color to match the rest of the paintwork, this door maintains the clean lines of the bathroom and its polished wooden floor.*

Top right *An elegant decorative glass panel, set into an old pine door; the flowers seem almost true-to-life and create an element of mystery.*

Top far right *A solid, old, studded wooden door provides a feature in the corner of this room.*

Flush doors

Flush doors consist of a cellular core arranged within a framework of solid wooden uprights, stiles, and a lock block sandwiched between two panels. Bonded together with resin adhesive, these materials make lightweight yet strong doors. The panels are usually flat, but are sometimes shaped to look like panelled doors. Some are inset with glass.

Fire-check flush doors have a core of fire-resistant material giving 30–60 minutes of fire resistance. These are required by law in certain places, say for access to an integral garage or where a house has been converted into apartments. It is also sensible to have a fire door in the kitchen.

High-security flush doors are designed to withstand heavy blows, even from a sledgehammer.

All types of flush door are available for exterior or interior use. Facings are either prepared for painting or in a wide choice of veneers for sanding and lacquering.

Panelled doors

Traditional panelled doors are now gaining in popularity, especially for exterior doors. The uprights and stiles are usually mortised and tenoned. Hardwood doors usually have four or more raised and fielded (sunken border) panels and are usually stained and sealed. The panels of softwood doors, which are designed to be painted, are normally exterior grade plywood.

Hanging a Door

When replacing a door, you will probably need help to hold the door in position as you check it for fit and attach the hinges to the frame.

The first task is to saw off the horns or remove the protective plywood covering the stiles. Then try the door in the opening to see where it has to be trimmed; it may be necessary to support it on wedges at the correct height and it must be perfectly level. Mark where the door is too big for the opening, allowing a maximum $\frac{1}{16}$in (2mm) gap all around and $\frac{1}{8}$in (4mm) at the bottom. Remove the door and saw off any major excess across the bottom, and plane the edges to fit. The hinges need to be recessed. Fit one screw in each hinge and then try the door. If necessary, adjust the depth of the hinge recesses.

If an external door frame has a water bar at the bottom, the door should close up against this, which might involve cutting a rabbet or step in the bottom of the door. This is best done with a circular power saw and the waste cleaned out with a chisel.

1 Ask a helper to hold the door in position against the frame while you mark in pencil where it needs to be trimmed.

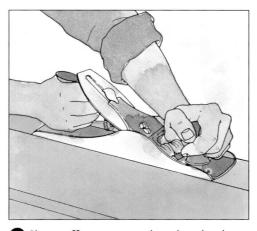

2 Shave off excess wood so that the door fits with a ¹⁄₁₂in (2mm) gap all around and ⅙in (4mm) at the bottom. Reposition the door in the frame to check the fit.

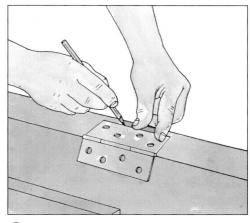

3 Mark positions for three 4in (10cm) butt hinges on the hanging side of the door, drawing around the hinges.

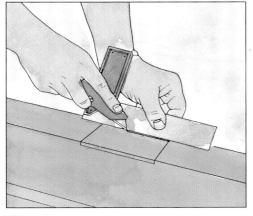

4 Use a sharp knife to score the outline of the hinges.

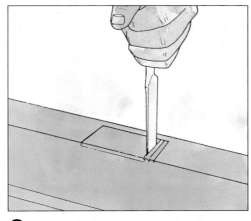

5 Cut out the hinge recesses by chopping across the grain at close intervals, using a wide chisel.

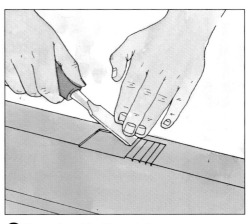

6 Turn the chisel bevel down to remove the chopped wood and level the base of the recess.

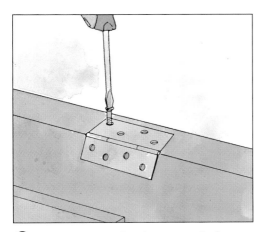

7 Drill pilot holes for the screws before driving them home.

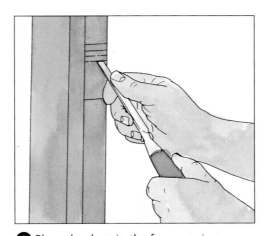

8 Place the door in the frame, using wedges if necessary to get the correct height. Mark the hinge positions on the frame and then cut the recesses.

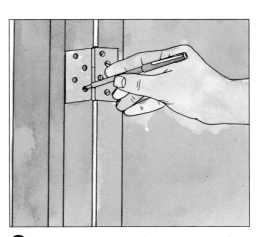

9 Mark the positions of the screws and drill pilot holes. Drive home only one screw in each hinge and try the door for fit before driving the remaining screws home.

Security

The openings through the outside walls of a house represented by the external doors are an obvious point of weakness, unless those doors are well made. But even the strongest of doors will offer little resistance to a hefty and determined kick if the frame on which it hangs is in poor condition or the hinge screws are rusty or have not been set deeply enough.

Top and above *The appearance of old doors in period houses can be spoiled by the addition of modern hardware. If you are lucky enough to have the original locks, it is worth the time and effort to refurbish them if they need repair.*

Making doors secure

Having checked that the frames are in good repair and well anchored to the wall, and that the hinge screws are robust enough, you can assess the type of locks your doors are equipped with. It is usually recommended that a front door is fitted with two deadlocking locks: one mortise and one rim. A mortise lock is housed in a mortise cut into the stile and incorporates a key-operated deadbolt. A rim lock, or rimlatch, is fitted in two parts, the body of the lock to the inside surface of the door and the key cylinder in a hole cut through the door. They are easier to put in than mortise locks, but are more obtrusive.

Security bolts are also a good idea. They are extremely effective against forced entry and are easy to install. Two bolts should be put in the top and bottom uprights of the back and any side doors, in addition to a mortise lock.

Some advisers suggest installing security or rack bolts on internal doors, with the proviso that they are used at night only once you have gone to bed. The theory is that intruders who get into a room from outside are then limited to that room unless they force an internal door, which would be noisy. It would be inadvisable to use these bolts during the day when you go out, since a burglar would know you were out and try to break the door down.

Hinge bolts, fitted to the hinge side of the door to strengthen it, are easy to install and very effective. The bolts are screwed into the edge of the door and fit into recesses drilled in the frame when the door is closed. Fit two bolts on each door.

A viewer installed in the front door at eye level allows you to see visitors before opening the door. A sturdy security chain fitted inside with strong screws is also recommended; it allows the door to be opened slightly without the risk of being pushed right open. Some chains have an alarm that sounds if the chain is forced.

Installing a cylinder rimlatch

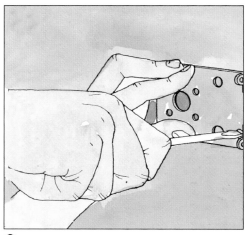

❶ Drill a hole through the door for the cylinder using a flat bit or hole cutter. Then set the lock mounting plate in position.

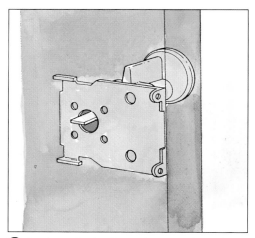

❷ Fit the cylinder from the outside and cut the connecting bar to the correct length with a hacksaw.

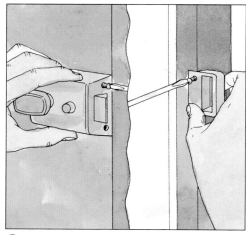

❸ Secure the lock to the mounting plate and screw the strike box to the frame.

Installing a rack bolt

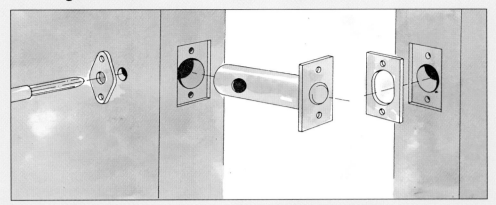

The lock is fitted into a hole drilled into the edge of the door and a recess is cut to take the plate. The keyhole is drilled from inside. Once the bolt is fitted, a mating hole can be marked on the frame and drilled.

Left *There is no reason why door hardware cannot be decorative and in keeping with the style of the door and house. There is a huge choice of mail slots, knockers, house numbers as well as decorative hinges, studs and escutcheon plates for keyholes. It is possible to find excellent reproduction brass hardware in many retail outlets. These examples would be perfect for using on doors dating from about the early 19th century to the present day.*

Right *With genuinely old doors, or if you just want to give your front door a period feel, there is a good choice of cast-iron door harware and elaborate hinges available.*

Installing a hinge bolt

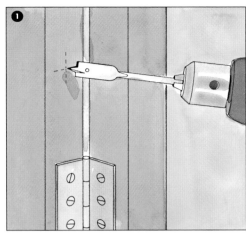

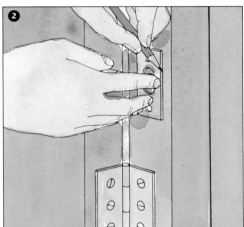

1 Drill a hole in the door edge to the correct depth and tap in the bolt.

2 Mark and drill a mating hole in the frame. Mark and cut a recess for the locking plate and screw it in place.

Windows

The principal functions of windows are to allow light into the house when shut and to provide ventilation when open. Cracks and crevices are integral to the design of windows, but when these are subjected to heat, cold, and moisture they become liable to drafts and rot. A regime of regular maintenance, such as filling cracks and abrasions, rubbing back and painting, will go a long way to ensuring that your windows give you long and trouble-free service.

Like doors (*see p.82-85*), windows represent the weak points in the solid structure of the walls of a building – they must move effortlessly, yet be capable of sealing a large opening. They are, therefore, vulnerable to forced entry and you need to make every effort to make them as secure as possible without spoiling their appearance.

Below *Windows are an integral part of the character of a building, and you should think long and hard before replacing them. Here you can see a traditional multi-paned sash window with a folding internal shutter.*

Types of window

A window consists of panes of glass set into a frame of wood, metal, or extruded aluminum, which may be coated in plastic for protection. The glass panes may be single or double glazed with sealed units that provide good insulation. They may also be in a variety of gauges, with the heavier gauges offering most resistance to breaking. Secondary glazing consists of additional panes added to the window recess after its construction to cut down on heat loss and drafts, or to minimize sound intrusion from, say, busy roads or children playing nearby.

Window design has changed through the ages and many older houses retain their original windows. Assuming that these are well and regularly maintained, they should continue to do good service indefinitely.

Modern windows are made in a variety of styles to suit various tastes, as well as in traditional styles to suit the architecture of earlier buildings. Each type of window has a different mechanism and serves a slightly different function.

Traditional windows

Older houses tend to have vertical-sliding sash windows, which were introduced to Europe in the 17th century and carried west with the colonists. These windows do not intrude into the room when opened and their design allows stale air to be drawn from the top while fresh air is sucked in through the bottom.

The drawback with sash windows is that their many moving parts require a fair amount of maintenance, and the sliding channels can become jammed if carelessly painted. The traditional wooden type has a deep box frame, while modern wooden or aluminum ones, which are fitted with spring-assisted spiral balances, are of slimmer construction.

Modern windows

Casement windows are the most common design installed in new houses. These consist of an opening sash, which is hung either on one side of the frame or from the top. Windows often incorporate a sash of each type as well as a stationery pane. Standard sashes close flush with the window frame, but storm-proof ones have projecting rabbeted sashes.

Another type of modern window design is the pivot window, so called because it turns about a central anchor point. This type of window is extremely useful for certain applications, particularly as skylights in attics. Louver windows are another form of pivot window. These consist of a series of unframed rectangles of glass held at each end in pivoting alloy carriers. The long edges of the glass panes are ground and polished. Often used as ventilators, they are difficult to draftproof and offer poor security.

Weather-resistant windows

Metal and plastic windows are generally more weather-resistant than wooden ones and, consequently, need less maintenance and repair. Unless they are galvanized or regularly painted, however, mild steel windows are vulnerable to rust.

Vertical sliding sash windows

Commonly referred to as sash windows or double-hung sash windows, this type of window was traditionally made with a box frame to house the pulleys, sash cords, and counterweights. The sashes are held in place by the outer lining of the box, a parting bead, and an inner staff bead; the beads are removed to service the sash mechanism. Pockets, removable pieces of wood set in the lower part of the stiles, give access to the weights. A window fastener is installed where the bottom rail of the outer sash and the top rail of the inner meet when the window is closed.

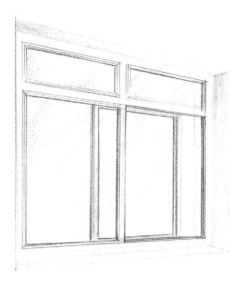

Aluminum and plastic windows

Aluminum and rigid plastic-framed windows are often installed to replace old wooden and metal-framed ones. Both types of material are extruded into complex sections that hold sealed double-glazed units and draftproofing material. They are set into wooden subframes, usually by specialist companies, and are virtually maintenance free. They do not require stays to hold them open.

Casement windows

In construction, a traditional casement window resembles a door in its frame. The side jambs are mortised and tenoned into the head at the top and the sill at the bottom. The frame may be divided by a vertical mullion and a horizontal transom. Side-hung sashes may be fitted with butt hinges or "easy clean" extension hinges, which allow better access for cleaning the outside surface from the inside. The window is secured with a fastener attached to the stile on the opening side. A casement stay set on the bottom rail holds the window open.

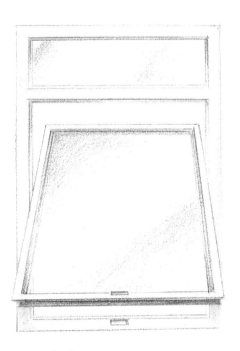

Below *Extruded aluminum window in wooden frame, common in modern homes.*

Pivot windows

This type of window is similar to a casement window, but instead of being side hung, the sash rotates on a pair of pivot hinges to allow cleaning from the inside. If required, the window can be fitted with a safety roller arm to limit its opening to about 4½in (11.5cm). Specialized pivot windows are commonly used in attic refurbishments, where they are set into the pitch of the roof.

Glazing and security

Abroken window needs to be repaired promptly both as a security measure and to keep the weather outside, where it belongs. Carefully clear up and safely dispose of all broken glass. Wear leather gloves and clear away any shards from the window sash, working down from the top of the frame.

Security locks

Windows are weak areas in home security, but they can be made less vulnerable. Ground-floor windows should be fitted with key-operated locks, as should upstairs windows. Make sure the key is accessible to occupants, in case of emergencies, but it should not be visible to anybody looking in from the outside.

The window mortise rack bolt, installed in the edge of the frame with the bolt sliding into the sash, is a good choice for wooden casement windows. Large side-hung casements will need two bolts. Top-hung sashes can be fitted with these locks, but they can also be fitted with window stay locks. These can be used to lock the window in a closed position or slightly open. The casement window lock, which is screwed to the opening sash and to the window frame, locks automatically when the window is closed.

Sash windows can be secured by bolts inserted through their meeting bars to lock them shut, or sash stops to prevent windows from being opened more than is required for ventilation.

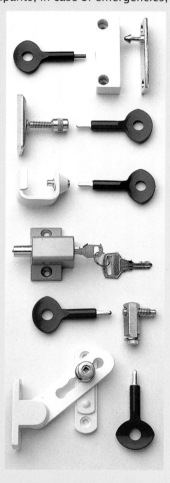

Casement locks, from top *Catch-type lock Stay bolt Screw-down stay lock Push-bolt lock Stay lock Child safety stay lock*

Replacing a pane of glass

The first thing to do with a broken window is to clear up and carefully dispose of all loose and broken glass. As a safety precaution, it is best to wear thick leather gloves when handling this material and clear away any shards from the window sash, working down from the top of the frame. If there are any stubborn or large pieces of glass still firmly attached to the window frame, these can be removed by running a glass cutter around the perimeter of the pane and gently tapping out the glass with a hammer. It is also advisable to wear some form of eye protection in case splinters of glass fly up.

With all the glass removed and safely disposed of, you can now turn your attention to the window frame itself. As a first step, you will need to chop out all the old putty with a hacking knife or an old chisel. Look out for the original glazing sprigs. If these are still in good condition, they can be carefully removed and reused to hold the new pane of glass in position. Alternatively, buy ⅝in (1.5cm) long replacements. Metal window frames use clips instead of glazing sprigs; mark their positions around the rabbet as you remove them.

Where lengths of wood beading hold the glass in place and form the decorative finish for the pane, remove these carefully for re-use, as well as the tacks that held them in place.

Now you should be able to see the unobstructed window rabbet into which the glass fits. The rabbet should be brushed clean of all dust so that the new putty will adhere.

Measuring and fitting

The replacement glass must be cut exactly, allowing a 3mm (⅛in) gap all around for expansion and using the shortest distance between opposite sides of the frame. Measure each way in three places and take the shortest distance. If the frame is crooked or awkwardly shaped, make a cardboard template as a cutting guide.

Buy the right putty for the frame: linseed oil putty for timber; metal casement putty for metal frames. If the putty is hard, roll small pieces of it in your hands until it softens. You can add a little linseed oil to linseed oil putty and wetting your hands will prevent the putty from sticking as you work.

To install a new pane, run a continuous bead of soft putty, about ⅛in (3mm) thick, into the rabbet and press it in with your thumb. Next, press the pane onto the putty, with the ⅛in (3mm) expansion gap all around, applying pressure to the edges only. Now drive the sprigs in flush with the glass, about 6in (15cm) apart, to hold the glass securely. Replace clips in their original positions.

Finishing

Run another strip of putty around the outside of the glass and smooth it at an angle with a wet putty knife to match the surrounding windows; trim surplus putty off with the knife on both sides of the glass. Running a brush dipped in water all over the bevelled putty will make it stick to the glass, thus creating a tight seal. The putty should be allowed to dry out thoroughly for one or two weeks before being painted.

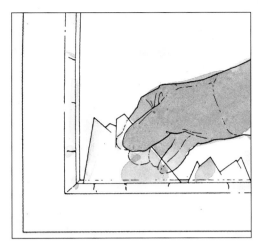

1 Clear the frame of any remaining broken glass; wear leather gloves and eye goggles for protection.

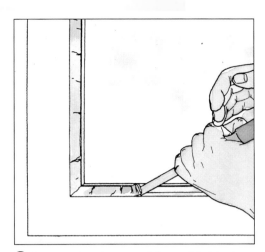

2 Remove hard putty with an old chisel and take out any glazing sprigs. These can be reused if they are in good condition.

3 Brush the window recesses, or rabbets, clean of any dust and debris to allow the new putty to adhere properly.

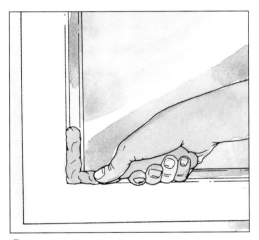

4 Run a bead of softened putty, about ⅛in (3mm) thick, right around the window frame rabbet.

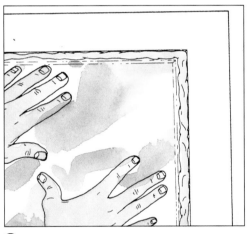

5 Offer the new pane of glass into the rabbet, pressing it around the edges only.

6 Tap the glazing sprigs in with a small hammer or the side of a square-edge chisel to secure the glass in place.

7 Press another bead of softened putty around the outside edges of the glass and bevel it neatly with a wet putty knife.

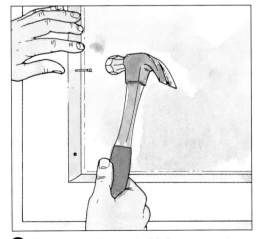

8 If using beading to hold the pane, miter the corners and tack it in place. Punch the heads below the surface for a neat finish.

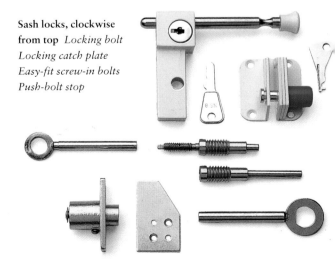

Sash locks, clockwise from top *Locking bolt Locking catch plate Easy-fit screw-in bolts Push-bolt stop*

Curtain hardware

Windows are functional parts of a room's structure, but if they are left unadorned they can look stark and uninviting. Curtains and drapes can greatly influence the visual impact of a room. A wall interrupted by just two small windows, for example, can be dramatically transformed at night if the entire wall is covered with floor-to-ceiling curtains; while a large window provides endless opportunities for either extravagant or subtle draping.

Below *This simple country-style wooden pole is hung with double curtains. The soft, natural fabrics are suspended from loops in the same fabric.*

Track and pole types

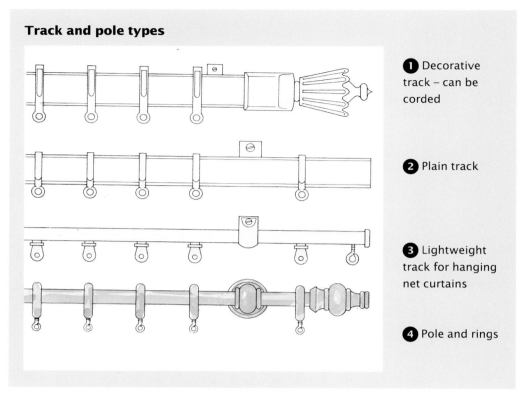

❶ Decorative track – can be corded

❷ Plain track

❸ Lightweight track for hanging net curtains

❹ Pole and rings

Tracks and poles

Curtains and drapes are hung from rods, tracks, or poles, and there are literally dozens of different styles from which to choose. The type of heading curtains have will determine how the top of the curtain will pleat and fold and whether it will hang below a track or hide it when drawn. If the track or pole will be seen, then consider a more ornamental type.

Tracks are usually available in plastic or aluminum, both of which are flexible enough to be bent into curves or awkward shapes. The simplest type of track has visible sliders that clip over the rail. Others have the sliders inserted in grooves along the back or in a recess below it. Whatever the type, treat tracks regularly with a grease-free lubricant to keep curtains and drapes running smoothly.

More expensive tracks have cord sets that mean the curtains can be opened and closed by pulling a cord.

Poles are usually made of wood, brass or wrought iron. The curtains hang from rings that simply slide along the pole.

Wherever possible, screw the holding brackets for tracks and poles directly to the wall. Battens are useful in some situations to help the curtains clear the window frame, but they can look clumsy. To allow a full-length curtain drop, some tracks can be screwed to the ceiling. If you want this effect, make sure you can attach the brackets to the joists, or mount wood between the joists for a secure anchor.

Valances

A well-fitted valance has a threefold effect – it forms part of the window dressing, hides the curtain track or pole, and protects the head of the curtains and the track from dust and dirt.

Valances, such as the one shown opposite, are simple to make. The front edge can be given an ornate shape before assembly. Make a pattern half the width of the front board, trace it on to the wood, turn the pattern over and trace the other side to match exactly, and then cut out the shape with a jigsaw. The valance can be painted or covered with fabric.

Fabric valances can be made from stiffened material or from ruffled or pleated curtain material mounted on a valance rail that clips onto a matching curtain track. The valance may be curved to fit around a bay window.

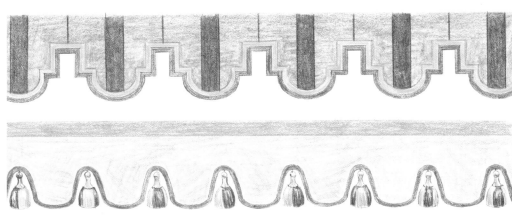

Left *The shape-defining pink border at the top and bottom of this elaborate, fabric-covered valance makes a strong statement in the otherwise soft muted tones of the room. The pelmet is further ornamented with braiding and multicolored tassels. All the colors blend well with that of the main pattern and the braiding on the valance is repeated down the edges of the curtains as an effective decorating accent.*

Above *A mock-heraldic mood is represented by these two examples of fringed valances. The stripes represented by the top valance, if repeated in the associated curtains, would tend to emphasize the vertical nature of the window area. The stripes are colorful and bold and so would perhaps be most suitable in a generously proportioned room. The predominantly single-colored valance, with its discreet tassels along the lower edge, is more neutral in nature and so would be easier to accommodate in most room settings.*

Making a valance

To install the holding batten, drill holes, insert anchors, and screw the batten to the wall; it should represent the top of the valance, less the thickness of piece **1**. If drilling into concrete, use a hammer-action drill and a sharp masonry bit.

Cut all the lengths to size, smooth them with sandpaper, and then glue and tack them together. Allow the glue to dry thoroughly.

Partly insert two screws into the top of the wall batten and cut off their heads

with a hacksaw. Try out the valance on the batten and tap it with a hammer to make indentations where the tacks are located. Drill holes into the valance top at these marks so the valance can slip over the tacks.

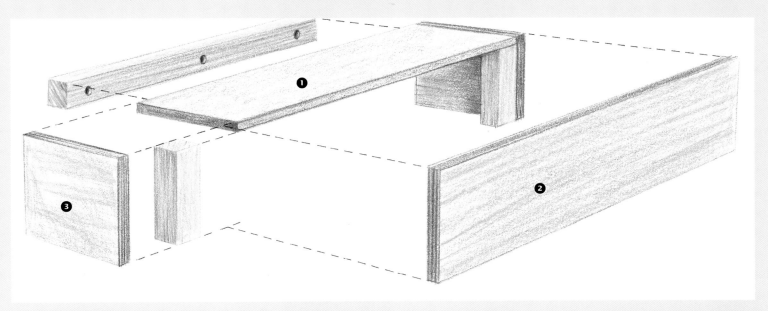

The front 2 should overlap the ends 3 for a stronger construction and better appearance.

Stairs

Intricate though their construction often is, staircases are rarely the cause of any serious concern to the householder, although they may require some routine decorative maintenance from time to time. The most common problems are to do with squeaking treads. Because the staircase is one of the most perilous areas in a home, it is important to repair any problems that do arise as soon as they are noticed to avoid the possibility of an accident. Fortunately, most defects can be rectified fairly easily.

1 *Cap* 2 *Newel post* 3 *Landing*
4 *Handrail* 5 *Balusters* 6 *Nosing*
7 *Riser* 8 *Tread* 9 *Closed stringer*
10 *Well trimmer* 11 *Apron lining*
12 *Nosing* 13 *Drop* 14 *Outer stringer*
15 *Newel post* 16 *Going* 17 *Riser*
18 *Baseboard* 19 *Half landing* 20 *Line of spandrel panels* 21 *Landing joists*
22 *Landing trimmer* 23 *Floor joists*

Replacing a nosing

Worn nosings are potentially dangerous and should be repaired or replaced. Cut off the damaged section using a padsaw or jigsaw. Fit a strip of wood the same depth as the tread and the same width as the other nosings, and glue and screw it in place. The screws must be deeply countersunk to allow you to shape the nosing with a small plane or spokeshave. Finish off with sandpaper.

Stabilizing a newel post

Tightening a moving newel post involves lifting a floorboard to reach where it is screwed to the floor joist. Try tightening the screws or make a new, firm base by installing two bolts through the base of the post into the joist. Also check the joint between the newel post and the outer stringer; if it has moved, the treads and risers might pull away. Brace the post with wood blocks glued and screwed to the inner face of the stringer and the post.

Repairing handrails and balusters

Wobbly handrails can be made firm by tapping small glued wedges into the loose joints or driving in screws at the appropriate points, countersinking and anchoring them to hide the repair. Broken balusters can often be repaired by gluing and clamping. If not, a new baluster will have to be installed. First, place the lower end into the mortise in the stringer and then screw the upper end in place beneath the rail. Sections of damaged handrail can be replaced with pieces of matching profile anchored with special bolts. Alternatively replace the whole handrail.

Fixing a wall string

Where treads and risers pull away from the closed stringer, a gap up to ¾in (2cm) can be filled. Tap narrow wedges between the stringer and the wall to force it against the treads. Cut the tops of the wedges flush with the stringer and screw through the stringer into the wedges. Fill the gap between the wedges with wood putty.

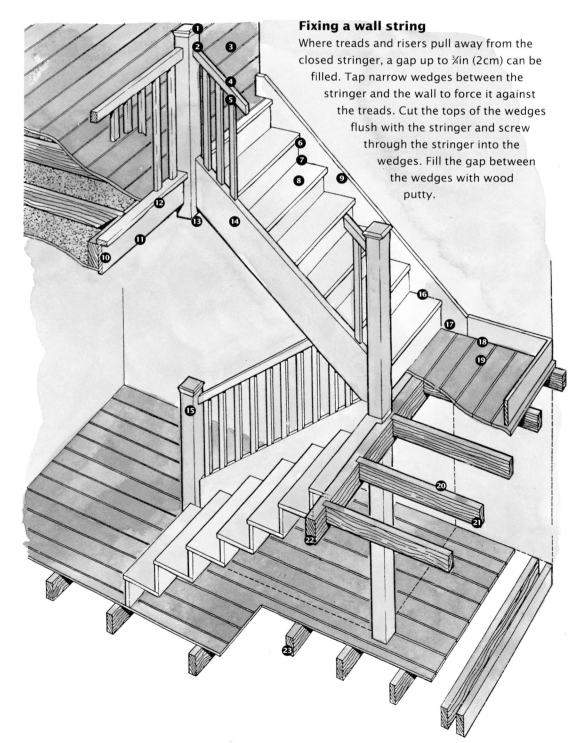

Curing a squeaky tread

Noisy stairs occur when pressure is applied to a tread that has moved in relation to its riser. If the underside of the staircase is exposed, glue and screw wooden blocks into the angles between the tread and the riser, or you can set metal shelf brackets into the angle to hold the pieces firmly together.

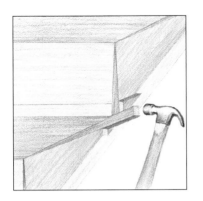

Where the underside of the staircase is covered, attempt the repair from above. Work a chisel into the crack between the nosing of the tread and the riser and squirt woodworking adhesive along the gap. Spread it evenly with a knife blade and then screw the tread firmly down onto the risers.

The rear joint cannot be opened up so easily, but try to squirt adhesive in and don't use the stairs until it has dried. As a last resort, install small angle brackets to draw tread and riser together.

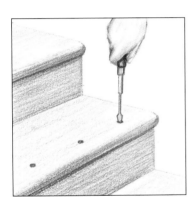

Below and bottom One of the most space-efficient methods of introducing a new stairway into your home is by installing a set of spiral stairs. Self-supporting types can also be installed adjacent to walls that are not necessarily load-bearing.

Right *Bright colors can transform an ordinary stairway.*

Fireplaces

Fireplaces give rooms a focus, and a fire in the grate adds warmth and comfort, creating an inviting atmosphere. An unsightly fireplace can be removed, or a missing one installed, with one from a vast range of second-hand and reproduction fire surrounds – but any that belong to the period and style of a house should not be unnecessarily removed.

Removing a fireplace

1 A tiled surround is held against the wall by lugs on each side. Saw off the heads of the securing screws, then lever the surround forward and lower it to the floor. Then prize up the hearthstone. If the surround rests directly on the floor, then remove the hearth first.

2 A cast-iron fireplace has resale value, so remove it carefully so that you can install it in another room or sell it. Again, the surround will be held with metal lugs. Cast-iron fireplaces can be very heavy and may need two people to move them. The cast iron may also be brittle and can crack.

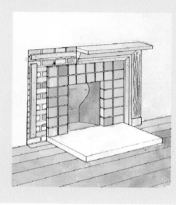

3 Wooden fireplace surrounds are usually anchored to battens screwed to the wall. The screw heads holding the surround will be covered with putty, making them hard to locate. The tiled section will probably be held by lugs fitted to the top and sides and screwed into the brickwork.

Above left and right *Whether elaborate with built-in shelves or starkly plain and unadorned, whether made of wood, cast iron, brick, or tiles, a fireplace helps to bring a room alive. Even when it is not in use, a fireplace immediately becomes a central focus. Once alight, an open fire represents an invitation to sit and relax, and just watch the flames.*

Restoring a fireplace

With the advent of alternative forms of heating, many fireplaces were removed and their chimneys sealed. Fortunately, chimneys can be re-opened and fire surrounds reinstated. This will involve some work to adjust the opening to hold the new fireplace.

Anyone without a chimney need not be denied the pleasure of a handsome fireplace in their living room fitted around an imitation fire. And those who hanker after the companionable flickering of a living flame can install a sealed balanced flue gas fire, which does not require a chimney. If only a real fire will do, a sectional fireplace opening can be built and connected to a lightweight preformed flue or chimney, which rises above the roof running either outside or through the house. This will require a concrete slab foundation to take the weight of the chimney and fireplace and to provide a non-combustible area reaching into the room. The slab should be a minimum of 5in (12.5cm) thick and extend at least 20in (50cm) into the room and 6in (15cm) each side of the opening. It should be topped with a decorative hearth at least 1⅞in (4.7cm) thick and extend at least 12in (30cm) in front of the fire.

Removing an unwanted fire surround is straightforward, but may require some muscle and, if it is to be re-used elsewhere, some care. Fire surrounds are usually attached to the chimney breast by a lug on each side near the top; large surrounds may have more lugs. Wooden fire surrounds are usually anchored to battens.

If the hearth and fireback are in good condition, all that is required is to repair any damage and make a smooth surface for the new surround. The opening may have to be modified, however, to take the new fire surround and a new fireback cast from reinforced concrete. If this is too large a job for you to tackle, employ an expert instead. If you discover there is a lot of debris at the bottom of the chimney, it is a good idea to have a specialist inspect the chimney to make sure it is safe before continuing.

1 It may be necessary to cast a new concrete fireback reinforced with ¼in (6mm) diameter steel rods.

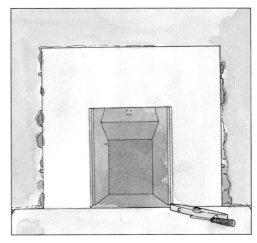

2 Place the replacement fireback over the opening and screw it to the wall using mirror plates.

3 Screw a 2 x 2in (5 x 5cm) batten to the underside of the mantel shelf to act as a support.

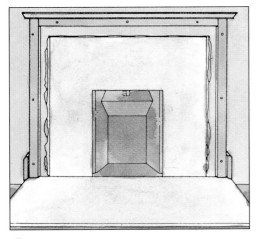

4 Anchor the side and mantel shelf battens to the wall to frame the opening. Mark the holes and check the shelf is level.

5 Cover the front face of the fireback with tiles of your choice.

6 Screw the fire surround boards to the corner blocks, working from the rear.

7 Try out the assembled fire surround on the wall battens and screw in place.

8 Attach any additional moldings to the front and sides of the boards, following the manufacturer's instructions.

9 Stain and varnish the fire surround and allow it to dry before lighting your first fire in the grate.

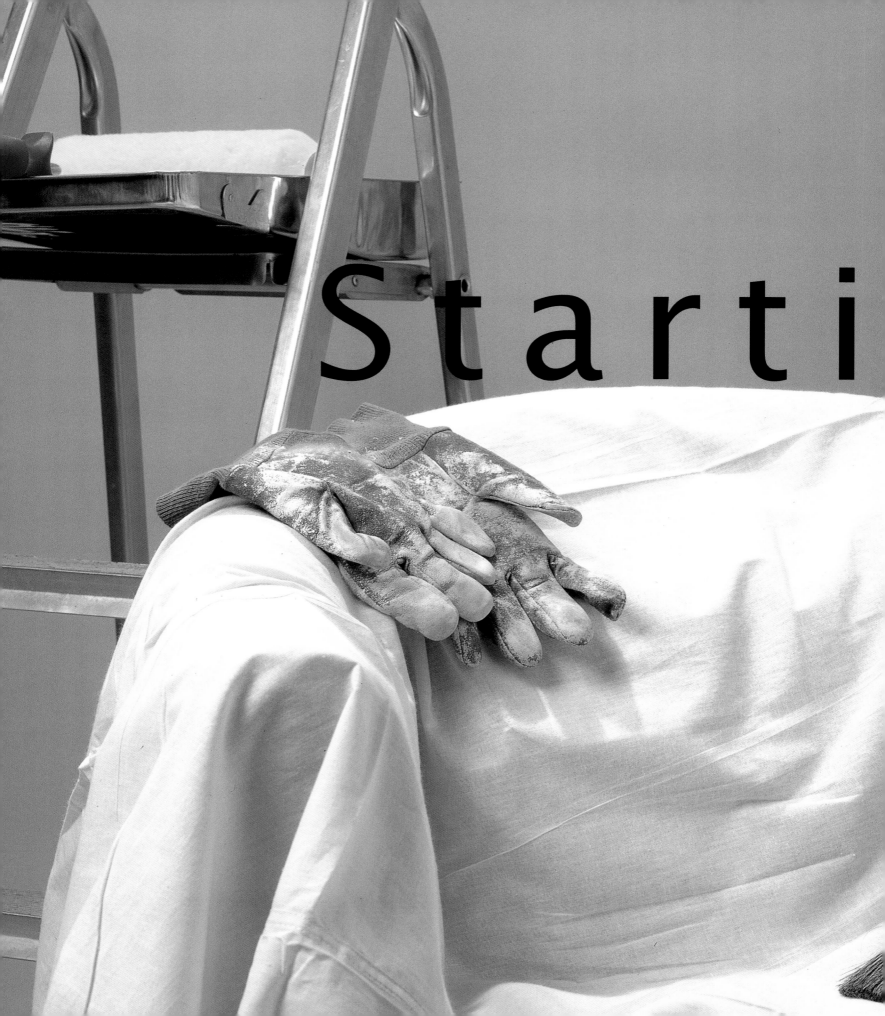

Starti

5

ng work

Choosing paint

Although there are different types and many brands of paint available, most of the ones you are likely to use around your home fall into one of two main types: oil-based and latex. Paints come in a bewilderingly wide range of colors, and you can purchased them either as pre-mixed colors or have them mixed to order. Color cards and sample cans will help you make your choice.

Which paint?

Oil-based and latex paints are available in matte, eggshell or silk, and gloss. Some primers and undercoats may be either oil-based or latex. Latex paints have some obvious advantages: they dry quickly, have little odor, and brushes and rollers are easy to clean.

Oil-based paint

- They have a typical paint smell that may linger for some time.
- They are generally thinned with mineral spirits.
- They take several hours to dry.
- They may be liquid or "non-drip" varieties.

Latex

- They have little or no odor, and what there is soon disappears.
- They dry quickly – usually in about an hour, allowing two or more coats to be applied in the same day.
- They are thinned with water.
- They are usually non-drip.

Types of paint

Traditionally, painting involves a three-step application of primer, undercoat, and top coat. An overview of which paint to choose for which job is outlined below, although not every type of paint available has been illustrated.

Primer This type of paint seals the pores of a surface to prevent subsequent layers of paint sinking in. Primers are available for wood, metal, and plaster, but universal primers will suit all three types of surface. There are also aluminum primers for surfaces that need a high level of protection and quick-primers for rapid drying. It is usually best to work with the same brand of primer, undercoat, and top coat, since they will have been formulated to work well together.

Undercoat A paint formulated to obliterate the previous color and give body to the next coating. Some gloss paints are self-undercoating.

Top coat This is a purely protective coating that is often quite thin. Top coats are available in gloss, silk, and matte finishes and some have additives, such as polyurethane or polyester, to make the paint more scratch and knock resistant. The gloss type of top coat may be liquid, in which case watch out for runs, or non-drip with a jelly-like consistency. Top coat will hide an undercolor only if it is a self-undercoating gloss; otherwise use a separate undercoat.

Latex paint Designed to cover large areas, such as walls and ceilings. Because it is water-based, latex is not suitable for bare wood, since it may cause the grain to rise. Liquid latex comes in a can, while semi-solid latex comes in a tray designed for a roller. The act of rolling softens the paint enough to spread it. Main finishes are vinyl matte and vinyl silk.

Eggshell paint This oil-based paint provides a more durable

Below from left to right 1 *Undercoat primer*
2 *Universal undercoat* 3 *Liquid gloss top coat*
4 *Non-drip gloss top coat* 5 *Vinyl matte latex*
6 *Textured latex* 7 *Red masonry paint*
8 *Rust-resistant paint*

Using aerosol paints

Paint in aerosol cans is ideal for small areas, touching-up or repair jobs, stencilling, and painting awkward objects such as the many different surfaces and twists and turns of wrought iron railings or gates. The choice of colors is not as extensive as you will find for traditional paints, since the more subtle tones are not available.

Aerosol paints are not intended to be used for painting large areas. Shake the can well before use and hold it at the recommended distance from the surface. Apply the paint in parallel bands, never in an arc. Apply only a very thin coat, allow it to dry, and build up further coats.

Because aerosol paint is released as a fine spray, objects are best taken outside for painting. Choose a still day to avoid too much paint drift. Protect the area around the object being painted with old sheets or newspapers. If you do have to work indoors, over a period of time, it is best to wear a protective mask.

surface than latex, and it is suitable for use on bare woodwork as well as walls. It has a slightly shinier finish than latex, but is much less shiny than gloss. Eggshell paint is particularly useful in rooms such as kitchens and bathrooms, since it is resistant to steam and condensation and can be wiped down.

Rust-resistant paint An enamel-formulated paint that inhibits the penetration of rust. No primer or undercoat is needed. Available in a smooth or indented "hammered" finish.

Enamel and lacquer paint A very finely ground paint with a very high-gloss finish. No primer or undercoat is needed on wood or metal and it is safe to use in a child's room.

Red masonry paint This type of paint is very useful for brightening up old brickwork or for giving a decorative finish to tiled sills. Masonry paint can be used inside or outside.

Radiator enamel Specially formulated to hold a pure-white tone and not yellow even under high temperatures.

Heat-resisting paint This type of metallic paint is available in a limited range of colors and it will resist heat up to 480ºF (250ºC) without discoloring. No primer is needed.

Textured paint This special paint or compound is spread in a thick layer on walls or ceilings and provides an easy way to hide seams in sheet rock and any visible nails. Lay the paint on thickly with a textured roller. Alternatively, apply it with an ordinary roller and, before the paint starts to dry, use a rubber-bristled stippling brush or a special toothed brush or comb to produce a variety of different effects. Note that textured paint is a permanent form of decoration and is difficult to remove. Textured paper, which can be stripped off more easily, may be a better solution.

Quantities and application

Before you start work, you will need to think about the surface you are painting and how many coats of paint it requires. This will be affected by the porosity of the surface to be painted as well as its texture. To help you plan and estimate the paint you need, the following general guidelines may be helpful:

Painting new or bare wood – allow 3 coats: primer + 2 coats primer, undercoat, finish.

Repaint – 2 or even 1 coat.

Bare walls or ceiling – primer not necessary. Use 1 or 2 coats of latex.

Household paints are sold in various sizes, from half gallons to 5 gallons. Smaller quantities are available in some brands.

Calculating quantities

To cover a smooth, sealed surface, be guided by the coverage indicated on the can.

As a general guide, ½ gallon of paint covers as follows:

General-purpose primer	11–13 sq. yd.	(10–12 sq. m.)
Gloss paint	17 sq. yd.	(15 sq. m.)
One-coat gloss	11 sq. yd.	(10 sq. m.)
Latex paint	11–15 sq. yd.	(10–14 sq. m.)

To figure out paint quantities for a given room, make a simple sketch and divide the walls into easily calculated areas – above the door, below the window, and so on. Multiply the width by the height of each area and then add them all together. For standard windows with several panes, simply multiply the width of the overall frame by the depth, and treat it as a solid area. For large picture windows, make the same calculation but deduct 50 per cent.

For metal windows, deduct 25 per cent. For flush doors, multiply the height of the doors by the width and add a further 10 per cent for the edges. For a panelled door, add 25 per cent. A little extra paint stored in a marked jar is useful for touch ups.

Applying paint

Once you have completed the necessary preparation of the surfaces, give a final wipe with a damp, lint-free cloth to remove any fine dust. The number of coats you apply depends on the under-color (if any), the type of surface you are working on, and the quality of the paint you are using. It is always better to apply two, or even three, thin coats than a single thick one of topcoat. Always bear in mind that you can not rush the job, and you must repaint over an absolutely dry layer of paint.

❶ Strain the paint into the bucket. Load the brush by dipping it in to about half the depth of the bristles.

❷ Squeeze out the excess paint by pressing the bristles gently against the inside of the paint bucket.

❸ Apply the paint in two parallel strips a short distance apart, working along in the direction of the wood grain.

❹ Without reloading the brush, draw the bristles across the grain to spread the paint over the uncoated area.

❺ Finish off by brushing the paint film lightly along in the direction of the grain. Pull the brush out toward the edge of a surface to avoid affecting the color with a build-up of paint.

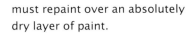

Preparing paint

Make sure the can is clear of loose dust and dirt before opening the lid. Check the can to see whether the paint needs stirring. If it does, use a length of wood. If you are using liquid paint, decant some into a bucket. This is a much less cumbersome way to carry paint around as you work. Paint buckets are also useful because if the paint becomes contaminated in any way, then only the paint in the bucket is affected.

Painting ceilings safely

Although you can paint a ceiling from a stepladder, it involves a lot of tiring leg work since you have to climb up and down to move the ladder. It is much simpler to make a platform (*see p. 00*). Erect the platform so your head is about 3in (7.5cm) beneath the ceiling.

Brushes, rollers, and paint pads

Choose your decorating tools according to the finish you require (*see right*). For a smooth surface, use a brush, a foam or mohair roller, or a paint pad; for a deeper texture, or to cover a rough surface, use a brush or a shaggy pile roller. If you prefer to work with a brush, choose the widest you can comfortably handle and work it in all directions, using a dabbing motion to fill in any crevices. If you use a roller, again work in all directions to achieve an even coverage of paint.

Don't roll too quickly or the paint will fly off. Allow the roller to shed all its paint before reloading it. Don't paint too thick a coating; instead, work two (or more) thin coats. For the second coat, work the roller across the direction of the first coat to fill in any gaps. With a paint pad work in all directions and also apply two thin coats.

Latex paint dries quickly so you will not have to wait too long between coats. If you use a roller or a paint pad, you will need a small paintbrush to finish the corners and edges.

Painting interior walls

If you choose to work with a brush, choose the widest you can comfortably hold. Begin at the top of a wall and run bands of paint downward in vertical strips, leaving a slight

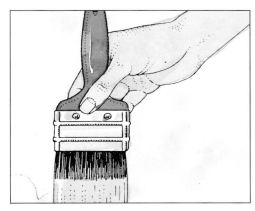

When using a brush to paint walls, choose the widest brush you feel comfortable with. Start at the top of the wall and work downward. When using a matte latex, finish off with crisscross strokes; with silk latex, use light, upward strokes.

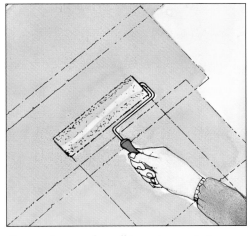

Run a roller over the wall in a crisscross pattern, being careful to merge the seams and fill in any gaps. Finish off using a small brush around the wall edges.

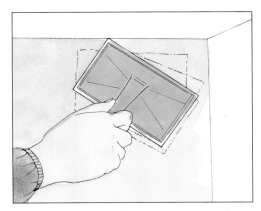

Use a paint pad in much the same way as a roller, applying paint in a crisscross pattern. Paint pads are especially useful for running along wall edges.

gap between the bands. Then brush across the wall to blend the bands of paint, finishing with light, vertical strokes of the brush.

You always produce a better finish if you apply two thin coats rather than one thicker one. If you decide to use a roller, choose one to suit the texture of the wall. For example, to cover a smooth surface and give an even finish, use a foam or mohair roller; while for deeply textured or rough surfaces, a shaggy pile roller is best.

Begin by working the roller in all directions and finish off with light strokes in a single direction. It is best to work over a small area at a time.

To use a paint pad, work the paint in all directions. Note that a pad applies only a very thin coat of latex so you will have to repeat this process to give two or even three coats – especially if you have a base color to hide. Whatever painting tool you use for the main area of walls, you will need a small paintbrush for the edges.

Painting woodwork

First, seal bare wood surfaces with a wood primer. When it is dry, rub this layer down lightly with fine-grade sandpaper, dust off with a lint-free rag, and apply a layer of undercoat (to give body to the final coat). The top coat is really a protective layer, but you can choose a paint that combines undercoat and top coat. To cover a sound, painted surface, you can dispense with the primer. Apply as many coats of undercoat as necessary until you lose sight of the base color. If you are repainting with the same color, just apply a top coat.

Paint woodwork with an oil-based paint, preferably a gloss for the highest level of protection. Apply the paint following the grain, working in strips. Next, work the brush across the grain and then, with light strokes, follow the grain as you did on the first application to ensure even coverage and a smooth finish. Note, that you should always brush out toward an edge – for example, of a door frame – to prevent the paint from forming an unsightly ridge.

When painting window frames or around glass panes in a door, mask off the panes where they meet the frame to prevent a clean-up job after the paint has dried.

Masking paintwork

A little time spent masking around glass window or door panes will save you a lot of time and effort afterwards. Run strips of masking tape around the edges of the glass where they meet the woodwork. Leave a narrow margin of paint on the glass to form a seal. Use a small brush, holding it like a pencil, and apply paint in the direction of the grain. Peel the tape off as soon as the paint is dry – otherwise it is difficult to remove.

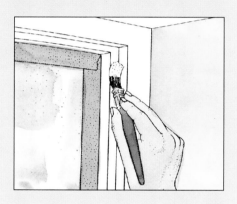

Brush care

You need a selection of different sizes and shapes of brush for many home decorating jobs, but good-quality brushes are expensive to buy. However, if you take the time to look after them properly, they become better and better tools the more they are used, and they will give you good service for many years.

Hardware stores and many large department stores stock a variety of brush-cleaning appliances. These are designed to hold brushes just clear of the bottom of the container so that the bristles don't become bent and damaged. But if you have many brushes to clean, these can work out to be expensive.

As a less-expensive alternative, you can make an effective brush-cleaning device using an old jar of a size appropriate to the brush you want to clean. Suspend the brush in the jar using a piece of string and a long nail, making sure the bristles are held clear of the bottom. Remember to change the cleaning solution regularly.

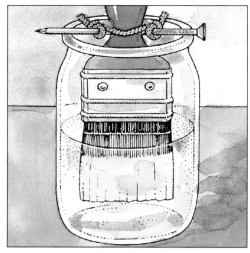

Storing paint brushes

When you have finished cleaning a brush and while it is still damp, slip a rubber band over the brush tip to hold the bristles firmly, but not tightly, together. Provided the rubber band is not too tight, it will ensure that the bristles keep a good shape, with no stray "whiskers". When all the brushes are completely dry, place them in a sealed plastic bag to keep them free from dust, and store them so that their bristles stay flat.

Paint care

Rather than discard leftover paint once you have finished a decorating job, you can store any excess by transferring what is left in the can into small, screw-top jars. Choose jars of the right size so that the paint fills them right to the top. If all air is excluded, the paint will keep almost

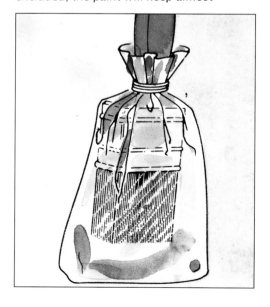

indefinitely like this and can be used later for touching up any damaged areas. If you leave leftover paint in the bottom of its original container, it will soon evaporate.

Paint that has been stored for some time can be affected in two ways. First, if there is a brown liquid floating on top, just stir it thoroughly back into the rest of the paint. It should recombine quite easily. Second, if a skin has formed on the surface, cut around this with a knife and scrape away any paint on the underside and return it to the can. Strain the paint before reuse, either with a paint strainer or by pouring it through a clean nylon stocking. Anchor the stocking loosely over the can with a rubber band and push the nylon down into the paint, then dip the brush into the nylon and the paint will seep through it.

If a can of latex has become rusty on the inside, carefully transfer all the unaffected paint into a clean container and throw away any contaminated paint and the original container.

Painting in progress

Ideally you should paint during daylight hours to take advantage of the natural light. If you paint under artificial lighting, you may overlook gaps in the coverage. For best results, paint an interior in a strict order, from the highest to the lowest point. For doors and windows, the sequence of painting is described on the following page.

Order of painting

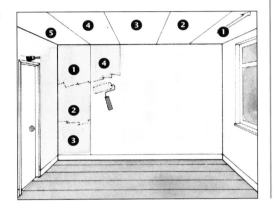

1 Start painting at the window end of a ceiling (1-5).
2 Prime and undercoat any frames and doors.
3 Paint walls, large ones first (1-4).
4 Top coat frames.
5 Top coat doors.
6 Paint floor.

To paint any room always start with the ceiling, since paint will inevitably drip or be splattered onto the walls. In an average room with a window and a door, begin painting the ceiling at the window end and work across the ceiling covering the surface in parallel bands approximately a yard wide until you reach the door end (*see numbers 1–5 on the diagram above*). Work an area that is comfortable to reach from your standing point, whether you are on a makeshift platform or a stepladder. If there is a ceiling rose or a light fixture in the middle of the ceiling, you should paint neatly around this with a small paintbrush and then continue painting in parallel bands.

The next step is to prime and undercoat the frames of the door and window and allow to them to dry (*see p. 104*).

Next paint the walls or any other large surfaces in the room. Start in the top left-hand corner of one wall and work with a brush, roller, or paint pad covering an area of about a square yard at a time. Work your way down the wall from the ceiling to the floor in vertical bands (*see numbers 1–4 on the diagram above*). Continue to paint the rest of the first wall and then the remaining walls in this order. Complete one wall in full before you begin the next. To paint around a window, first paint around the frame with a small brush and then fill in the surrounding wall space with a larger brush, roller, or pad. Once this is done, give the frames of first the door and then the window a top coat. Then paint the door of the room and add any covering to the floor last. Paint the coving and baseboards after the ceiling and walls are completed.

The decorative top coat of paint for a door should be applied as the last stage of painting a room, unless you intend to paint the floor as well.

5

STARTING WORK

HANDY HINTS

- Before you use a new brush, or one that has been stored for any length of time, manipulate the bristles by rubbing them briskly in the palm of your hand to loosen and remove any dust and broken bristles.

- If you plan to use a number of different colors of paint, line your paint bucket or roller tray with layers of foil, pressing it well down so that it takes the shape of the container. By doing this, when you need to change paint colors, you can simply remove the top layers of foil and the container is clean and ready to accept the next color.

- If you are painting a room with more than one color, use a different brush for each color. This will save you a lot of time cleaning brushes.

Painting interior doors

Whatever type of door you wish to paint, you should first remove as much hardware as possible, since handles, escutcheon plates, and hooks are all difficult to paint around. The ideal way to paint a door is to unhinge it and lay it flat on a pair of trestles. In order not the damage its surface, pad the trestle tops with old rags or newspapers. Follow the instructions for preparing and painting wood (*see p. 101*).

Select your tools for the job carefully according to the surface of the door. Use a wide brush for a flush door and a small brush for the decorative molding of a panelled door. With all types of door, paint the edge opposite the hinges last in the sequence so that you always have something to hold on to until the final stage.

To paint a flush door, divide the surface area up into small sections (*see diagram below*). Try to work quickly to avoid tide marks or visible seams. Use a 3in (7.5cm) wide brush and begin at the top left-hand corner, covering to about half the width of

the door (1). First, work using vertical brush strokes and then brush across these with light upward strokes. Complete the other sections (2–6) in the same way. It is important to work the brush strokes consistently so that the finish of the door will be even. To complete the edges of the

door (7), use a small brush. Paint the frame of the door last with a small brush (8).

For a panelled door, the sequence is a little more complicated (*see below*). First, paint the moldings around the panels (1) and then the panels themselves (2). Start with the upper panels and work from top to bottom. Begin each panel at the top and work downward, painting vertical brush strokes followed by light upward ones. Next, paint the section that runs down the

middle of the door dividing the panels (3). Continue by coating the horizontal rails, starting at the top and working down (4). Complete the outer vertical strips and then do all the door edges (5). Last, paint the whole door frame (6).

Painting interior windows

To protect the panes, mask off the glass just inside the frames with tape, leaving a ⅛in (3mm) margin to allow a thin line of paint to overlap the glass and form a seal.

To paint a sash window (*see diagrams above right*), push the rear sash down and the front one up so that at least 8in (20cm) of the lower rear sash is exposed. Paint the bottom rail of the rear sash and as much of the exposed upright sections as possible (1). Pull the rear sash up so that it is almost shut and paint the rest (2). With the front sash slightly open, paint the frame (3).

When both sashes are dry, paint the surround, shut the window and paint the exposed part of the runners. Do not paint the cords. Paint the sill last (4).

With a casement window (*see below*), anchor the window slightly ajar. First, paint the rebbets (1) and then the horizontal and vertical crossrails (2). Paint the horizontal top and bottom sides and edges (3), then the vertical sides and edges (4). When the window is dry, paint the frame (5) including the edges. Leave the sill (6) till last, to avoid smudging; do the stay last, if it needs painting, so that you can use it.

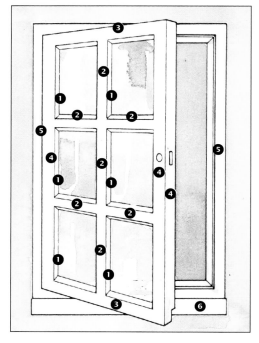

The creative effects you can achieve with paint are virtually limitless.

Problem areas

There are some areas in your home that may present some difficulty when it comes to painting – these include high-up awkward corners, stairways, covings, and picture moldings.

A stairway is one of the most difficult areas to decorate, and for some people it is enough to deter them from even attempting to do it themselves. However, with a just bit of planning and taking extra care while you work – because you will have to stand on an elevated platform – it is quite possible to paint this part of the home yourself, even if you are inexperienced.

The first thing you need is some form of scaffolding. The most reliable solution is to rent a staircase platform, which is designed to fit neatly onto stairs by means of adjustable legs. However, if you are not worried by heights, then you can construct your own platform. Make frequent checks that the scaffold board is centrally placed and has not slipped out of position, particularly as you climb on and off it.

By using a roller or a paint pad with an extension pole, you can greatly increase your reach and apply paint overhead on the ceiling and high up on the stairway walls.

Before painting picture moldings, make sure that they are free from dust, dirt, and grease. It is usual to work in a similar type of paint as for the walls, which is likely to be latex, although you may choose a contrasting color to pick out the detail of the molding. Using a small brush, paint along the entire length. Use the same method for shielding the wall as described for painting baseboards.

With covings, as with picture moldings, it is usual to use the same type of paint as for the walls. The paint can either match the walls or the ceiling or be in a contrasting color, which will emphasize any detailing. However, it is usual for coving to match the ceiling color. Use a paint shield or masking tape for a neat finish, as already described.

Painting baseboards

When the rest of the room is freshly painted, a discolored baseboard will mar the overall effect. Painting the baseboard is a quick job that is best left until after the walls are completed. Because baseboards are low down and narrow, you should work with a small brush and use a hard-wearing gloss paint that will withstand knocks. Wipe the baseboard with a damp cloth to remove any dust and vacuum along its bottom edge to remove any dirt or fluff in the carpet that may stick to the wet paint. Lay down newspaper to protect the floor. To protect the wall, use a piece of stiff cardboard or a length of thin wood and hold it to shield the wall while you brush. If the wall has been dry for some time, then you can use masking tape – but remember to peel away the tape before the gloss paint hardens or the paint may tear. Work the brush following the direction of the baseboards, making horizontal strokes and working your way in one direction around the room. When you come to painting close to the floor, make sure that your brush does not pick up dirt from below the baseboard by moving the cardboard or wood along the floor as a shield as you paint.

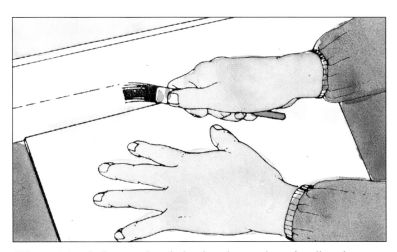

When painting the bottom edge of a baseboard, use a sheet of cardboard or a length of wood to protect the surface of the floor from paint and to prevent the paintbrush from picking up dirt or fluff and transferring it to your fresh paintwork. Slide the cardboard or wood along the floor as you proceed.

Painting faults

Good-quality modern paints rarely give any trouble, and flaws with the finished results are usually caused by problems with the surface on which the paints are applied. All too often, mistakes occur due to poor surface preparation. Here are some common faults and ways of remedying them.

Blistering occurs when air or water is trapped under the paint and the paintwork begins to bubble up. It occurs on wood if damp or resin is drawn out of the wood by heat. The only remedy is to strip back the paint, ensure that the surface has thoroughly dried out, and begin the whole decorating process once again from scratch.

Flaking happens when the paint has no grip on the undersurface and does not key on properly. The top coat of paint lifts and flakes off in dry fragments. Perhaps the surface was too smooth, as with old gloss paint, or maybe it was too chalky. Badly flaking areas are best stripped back, a key provided, and then redecorated.

Wrinkling is a fault caused by a second coat of paint being applied before the solvent has evaporated out of the first layer. It can also result if a top coat is applied too thickly. A wrinkled surface shows patches of shrivelled or puckering paint, which is rough to touch. The best remedy is to strip back the surface and redecorate, making sure you allow each coat to harden and dry thoroughly before applying the next; also avoid applying paint too thickly.

Matte patches can occur where a priming coat has been omitted. Subsequent coats then soak into the wood, which results in a loss of the gloss finish in these areas.

Unfortunately, applying further coats of paint rarely solves the problem, and the only effective solution is to strip the paint back and prime first.

Staining is often encountered when latex paint is applied over a stained area and the stain begins to bleed through. To remedy, allow the latex to dry completely and then spray the affected area with a stain-sealer, which will dry in a few minutes. You can then paint over the area again.

Crazing forms a pattern of tiny cracks. It occurs either when incompatible paints are used together or when a layer of paint is applied over a previous coat that was not completely dry. The solution is to rub the cracked surface until it is quite smooth, either by hand with a sandpaper block, or using a sanding attachment on a power drill. Repaint when it is really smooth.

Bleeding is a fault that occurs on wood containing knots that have not been properly sealed. The warmth of sunlight encourages the resin to bleed out, which damages the paint film. To correct this, strip back the damaged area, treat the knot with a suitable sealant, and then repaint.

Poor drying is usually caused when paint is applied over a dirty or greasy surface. You should strip back the paint and thoroughly clean the underlying surface. Remove any traces of grease and particles of dirt or dust before repainting.

Runs are the result of too much paint being applied with an overloaded brush, roller, or paint pad. It occurs on vertical surfaces and the descending drips are also known as sagging or curtaining. Use a wide-bladed scraper to scrape off the runs when they are dry. Then sand the surface by hand or with a sanding attachment on a power drill until the runs are eliminated and the surface feels really smooth when you run your hand over it. Unfortunately, runs can be very obstinate, so a lot of sanding may be required before you can repaint.

Color showing through is most often the result of a lack of undercoat. Bear in mind that a top coat is really just a protective layer and is not designed to obliterate what lies beneath. To remedy this problem, sand the surface well and apply enough undercoat to hide the color completely, then top coat again.

Grittiness happens when dirt that has been picked up on a paintbrush is transferred onto the surface during painting. It is particularly common when painting outside close to masonry. If the paint is still wet, you can simply wipe away the grittiness with a lint-free rag and repaint the area with a clean brush. If the paint has dried, however, you should sand it back with fine sandpaper and then repaint. If the paint in the can is contaminated with bits of dirt, you must strain it through a nylon stocking or paint strainer (*see p. 102*).

Insects can find their way into paint all too easily, particularly on a warm, sultry day in summer. Insects can also be a problem if there are any plants growing nearby. If the paint is still wet, lift off the insects with the point of a penknife, or a similar implement, and smooth out the paint to erase the imprint. If the paint is drying, leave it well alone until the paint is hard, and then rub the insect gently free with your finger.

Decorative paint materials

The following tools and materials are used in a wide range of applications, and you may find that you have some of them already around the house. Some of the specialist brushes mentioned are expensive, so look for synthetic substitutes, which can be of excellent quality. Ideally, it is best to use brushes either for paintwork or for varnishing, and not to mix them. It is a good idea to have a range of different grades of sandpaper and some steel wool on hand. One golden rule is to clean brushes scrupulously, taking special care not to leave any paint or varnish near the handle end of the brush. This takes time and effort, but it pays dividends in the long run.

Materials and equipment

Ground chalk Finely powdered chalk is applied to some wood surfaces to fill the grain and provide a smooth background for subsequent painting.

Transparent oil glaze This is sometimes called "scumble" glaze. Thin this liquid glaze with mineral spirits and brush it over the surface. It can be tinted with a stainer or oil-based paint.

Mineral spirits It is also called turpentine substitute. Use it to dilute oil-based paints and varnish and to distress oil-based paints and glazes when they are still wet.

Polyurethane varnish This is an oil-based varnish available in different finishes. It is easy to apply and provides good surface protection.

Universal stainer This is a chemical dye that dissolves in mineral spirits. Use it to tint latex and oil-based paints and glazes.

Acrylic paint Available in tubes in an extensive range of colors. It is water soluble and is useful for tinting latex paint. It becomes waterproof when dry and is very fast drying.

Mottler A brush made from hair, available in a range of different sizes. It is used primarily to drag water- or oil-based glazes to simulate wood grain.

Softening brush Use just the tip of the brush to blend oil-based glazes gently while they are still wet.

Flogger A horsehair brush made with long, coarse bristles. It is used to tap, or "flog", a wet glaze to give a finely flecked finish.

Flat fitch A hog's hair brush useful for applying glazes in small or difficult areas.

Jamb duster This is usually used to remove dust before painting a surface. It is also useful as a softening and blending brush instead of a dusting brush.

Artist's brushes Available in various sizes with round or flat bristles. They are used for detailed or delicate work.

Stippling brush A brush with a flat, square head, and with flat-edged bristles on the underside. It is commonly used for stencilling work.

Stencilling brush The stiff bristles hold only a small amount of paint. Designed to produce neat, sharp-edged stencils.

Sponge For covering large areas of stencil cutouts, a small piece of sponge is quicker to use.

From top **1** *Mottler*
2 *Softening brush* **3** *Stencilling brush* **4** *Stippling brush*
5 *Natural sponge* **6** *Flogger*
7 *Small artist's brush* **8** *Flat fitch* **9** *Graining tool*
10 *Ground chalk*
11 *Transparent oil glaze*
12 *Acrylic paint*

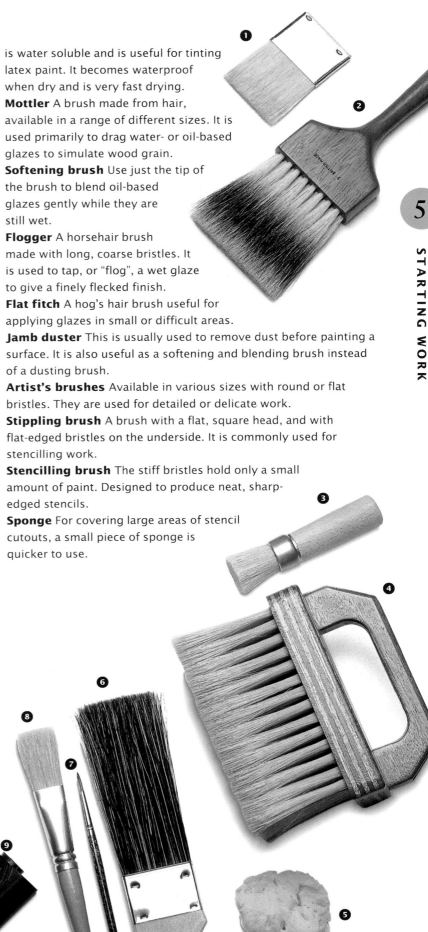

Paint effects

There are various ways of creating color effects that lend interest to a bland expanse of wall. You can either work with traditional paints commercially prepared, or you can create your own effects with readily available latex or eggshell paints, tints and pigments. Traditional techniques include sponging, colorwash, rag-rolling, ragging on, dry-brushing and liming. These methods involve the use of a base coat to cover the wall or ceiling followed by a glaze or tint applied in various different ways.

Whichever paint finish you choose, the wall or ceiling must always be properly prepared. None of these fine paint finishes will disguise bad workmanship, like unfilled cracks or dirty walls, so be prepared to spend at least the usual amount of time on surface preparation. The secret of successful paint decoration is to test all the different techniques on odd sheets of lining paper, pieces of wood or masonite. Then you can see beforehand how the impression looks and whether it is the finish you want. You may need to reduce the amount of pressure on the tool you are using, maybe thin the paint down, or just use one side of it. With practice you will soon build the skills required to achieve the results you want.

Right Rough colorwash on walls blends with the mellow wooden beams. The room is enhanced by the use of other natural materials - iron fixtures, hand-painted curtains, and a terracotta urn.

Colorwashes

You can buy ready made colorwash paint, but you can also create your own finish with latex or water-based eggshell paint and a tint or pigment.

To prepare the surface of the wall, paint a base coat of matte or silk latex and allow to dry. Either choose the same color paint or a color close in tone and mix a wash of latex and water, in equal parts. Gradually increase the water to make a thin color that will not run down the wall in heavy droplets, but will allow the base color to show through when it is applied. Once you have tested the wash on a sample area, continue to apply the remaining color with a wide brush using sweeping strokes. Further coats can be applied in a harmonizing color. For a more durable finish, you can use a thinned glaze as a wash over the whole surface. If you want a hard, protective finish, use a clear, matte polyurethane varnish, or a water based acrylic varnish.

Left Colorwash effect on wall creates a friendly atmoshpere in this country-style dining room. The walls blend in with the woodwork and provide an ideal setting for paintings and antiques.

Freehand tile

The technique of colorwashing walls lends itself to the addition of hand painting. It has an individual, crafted look and finish which, particularly in a country setting, gives an individual flourish to any wall, corner or recess.

Before you start your design, it is a good idea to carry out a small trial on a piece of paper. This helps you to establish the color combination you are going to use, the depth and tone of your paint, and the relationship between the scale of the design and the rest of the room.

Materials

- sponges, paint brushes of different sizes

- cardboard, craft knife, pencils

- latex paint for walls

- acrylic (water-based) paint, pigment or commercial paint tints

1 Select the background color for your wall and apply the paint with a sponge. Leave a generous space around the area where you are planning to paint your tile.

2 Place the cutout shape of the tile, or motif you are going to use, and sponge carefully all around the edges with the background color of the wall. Take care not to let any paint creep underneath the

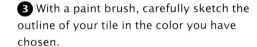
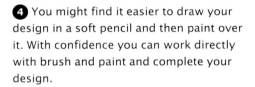

cutout. When the paint is dry, remove the template and you will find a clean area on which to start work.

3 With a paint brush, carefully sketch the outline of your tile in the color you have chosen.

4 You might find it easier to draw your design in a soft pencil and then paint over it. With confidence you can work directly with brush and paint and complete your design.

5 Working freehand gives any motif of design that you choose a highly individual look. The variations in paint add to the originality of your work, so do not try to create the same uniform finished effect of a machine-painted tile. This hand-painted tile is both pleasing and eye-catching.

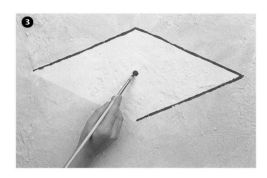

HANDY HINT

Before taking any fresh-loaded applicator to the wall, first test the imprint on a spare piece of paper to make sure it is the right size, depth, and thickness. Keep a piece of clean rag or paper beside the paint as you work and dab the applicator onto this first to ensure that any excess paint is removed. This will help to prevent unwanted drips.

Sponging

Sponging is one of the easiest decorative paint finishes to achieve. Use closely related colors give a subtle effect or contrasting colors to acheive a striking mottled finish.

Apply the base coat with matte or silk-finish latex and allow to dry. Choose your first top coat color and thin with a little water. Dip the flat side of the sponge into the paint, taking care to wipe off any drips, and apply to a test surface. Sponge the wall using a dabbing, twisting movement. Cover the whole wall; and then, if required start at the beginning again and continue to apply more coats of either color until the wall is evenly covered.

You can experiment with combining the sponging technique when working with an oil-based finish or a glaze.

1 A cool fresh mood can be achieved by using a crisp green as one of the sponged colors. The base color is applied and then sponged once with a slightly greener first coat, followed by a top coat.

2 A warmer feel can be achieved by changing the sponged color to a deep, earthy red. The base color is applied and then sponged with a warm, reddish first coat; the same top coat as in (1) is applied.

HANDY HINTS

- Practice each paint finish on paper before applying it to the wall.

- Keep a clean cloth to hand to remove any drips that may form.

- Wait for the paint to dry thoroughly before correcting errors or making improvements or additions.

- Dilute ragged-on or sponged-on paint with about 50 per cent water for a paler shade of color.

- If possible, complete a whole wall before finishing a painting session.

Right *The delicate, subtle effect on the walls is achieved by sponging. The bed linen echoes the soft creamy colors, and the furniture picks up the darker sponged color of the walls.*

Rag-rolling

This soft, mottled paint effect is an excellent technique for disguising bumps or surface irregularities. You can work with water-based or oil-based paints. When applying paint, where possible work in pairs - one person painting on the glaze with a brush, followed by another person working with the rag.

Color Recipe

Rag-rolling lends itself to working with a wide range of colors. Either match the tone of the top color with the background, or introduce a slightly darker tone of top color for a bolder, stronger impact.

Using oil-based paints, mix 3 parts of top color with 7 parts of transparent oil glaze.Thin the mixture with mineral spirits. The glaze slows the paint drying time, giving you more time to work; it also gives a soft shining finish.

❶ Here, a latex or eggshell paint is applied as the background color. While the top coat is still wet, the crumpled rag is rolled both down and across the paint to achieve an even effect.

❷ To create the stripes, use masking tape to blank out the areas you want left plain. Rag-roll the color in between the strips of masking tape. Allow to dry before removing tape.

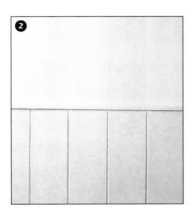

Right *A soft magnolia latex is painted on walls and ceiling, then rag-rolled with an antique grey gloss color to finish.*

Bag graining

Bag graining gives a traditional broken-paint finish using only the simplest of tools – a plastic bag filled with rags. The result can be beautifully subtle, producing an effect similar to the look of crushed velvet.

❶ Start from a right- or left-hand corner. Working in small sections, use a wide brush to paint on the background graining paint in vertical strokes.

❷ Half fill a plastic bag with small pieces of rag and secure the top firmly. When each section is completed with the brush, use the plastic bag to press down on the paint, immediately lifting off and pressing down on the next spot. Take care not to smudge the graining as you lift the plastic bag. This will produce a crinkled effect, which should be left to dry out. Glaze to finish.

HANDY HINTS

● Overlap each bag-graining slightly as you work along the wall to avoid bands where one section finishes and another starts.

● You can do bag graining either in a pale color over a white base coat or vice versa.

Broken-color effects

Dry-brushing is another color effect with a finish similar to Sponging and Rag-rolling. You can apply dry-brush technique to walls covered with lining paper as well as bare plaster. Working with a good-quality paint brush, load the paint, a little at a time, at the end of the brush and work with it dry, using a small brushing movement. The paint is spread out over the wall giving a mottled, milky effect. As with other techniques, you are building up color, layer upon layer, until you have the result you want. If you are working with latex paint, add water to thin the paint. Remember, too, that latex paints dry more quickly than oil-based paints, so you need to allow for this.

Materials

- latex (water-based) paint, darker color for background, lighter color for dry-brushing

- paint brush, paint container

- top coat of eggshell paint, slightly thinned with mineral spirits

- clean white paper and clean lint-free rags for removing excess paint

❶ Select the paint color for the background and paint the walls. Next, choose the color for your top coat. If you are working with an oil-based eggshell paint you will need to thin it (3 parts top color to 1 part mineral spirits). Choose a top coat color that is either close in tone or contrasts with your wall color. With dry-brushing, you can cover the background color completely, so your top coat is the color you will see on your finished walls.

❷ Pick up the paint on the bristles of the brush and wipe off any excess on a piece of

Ragging on

Materials

- Latex base coat

- Latex for ragging on

- Cotton, lint-free rag or sheeting

- A bowl and an old spoon for mixing paint

Apply the base colour to the wall and allow to dry thoroughly. Scrunch up the rag into a ball, and dip into the bowl of contrasting shade of paint. Remove excess paint. Dab painty rag straight onto the wall and keep dipping the same side of the rag into the paint and dabbing at the same angle with even pressure to achieve uniform pattern. For a more random effect frequently rearrange the painty rag, dabbing with even pressure.

❸

clean paper, until the brush is almost dry. With free movements, paint in all directions over the wall. Repeat dry-brush technique with layers of paint until you have built up the finished effect you want.

❸ When you have finished working with the larger paint brush, and the color is the strength and intensity you want, use a smaller paint brush to soften the edges and spread out the glaze.

Left *A dry-brushed color on the walls harmonizes with furniture painted the same color.*

Right *A country-style kitchen is enhanced by using the broken-color effect of dry-brushing to draw attention to the rustic quality of the room.*

Painting stripes

A simple way of giving a plain painted surface an interesting pattern is by using masking tape to create a simple stripe on a piece of wooden furniture. Decide how wide the stripe is to be and, if possible, turn the piece over so the surface you will be working on is horizontal. Smooth a length of masking tape along one edge of the proposed stripe and a second length along the other edge. Place the tape down firmly in place with the back of a teaspoon in order to prevent paint from running underneath. Using acrylic paint, which adheres to most surfaces straight from the tube, apply the color with a brush or cloth between the tape. When the paint is dry, peel off the tape carefully and slowly.

To create a stripe on a wall, decide whether you want a narrow or broad stripe. Then smooth the two pieces of masking tape down the wall, pressing firmly. Apply latex paint as before, with either a brush or a sponge, and leave to dry before carefully removing the tape.

Left *A striped effect created by using masking tape, gives the corner of this bedroom a fresh, attractive finish.*

Above *A colourful use of paint on wood! This child's room is enlivened with painted wooden furniture and floor boards.*

Special effects on wood

There are a number of techniques that are effective on wood. These include graining, dragging, marbling, and tortoiseshelling, Graining is probably the least complicated of these but, with time and patience, the other finishes can look quite stunning. All these finishes are achieved by the careful use of a background paint colour followed by a painted top coat, or an oil-based glaze which is tinted and then thinned. Always remember to prime raw wood before painting on it.

Dragging is a soft, striped effect which is often used on wood, although it can also be used on walls. Applied to wood it gives a woodgrain finished effect by using natural tones of paint and working with the brush to create marks which are characteristic of natural woodgrain. Use a stiff brush, the width of grain require

Marbling is best used on heavy materials such as skirtings, floors, and fire surrounds. If you like the idea of marbling then have a look at the patterns and grains in real pieces of marble until you find the one you would like to copy. Draw out some designs and ideas to work from before you start. Feathers can be used to apply the veins and fine artist's brushes will help to soften the effect.

Tortoiseshelling creates a warm look, particularly when applied to wooden picture frames or small boxes. A soft artist's brush will help to give a mottled finish. Walnut can also be imitated by using a paint finish combined with a glaze.

An interesting effect can be obtained by taking a piece of torn cardboard and dragging it through the top coat that you have applied. Sponging and stippling can also be combined with other techniques. Experiment for yourself and find your own unique technique and effect!

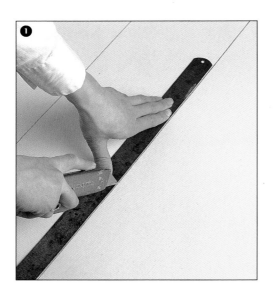

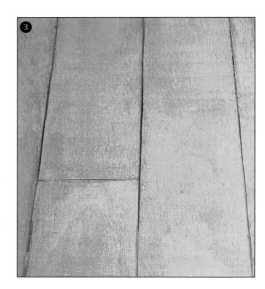

Wood graining effect

The graining technique demonstrated here is used to give painted woodwork the appearance of high-quality woods. The technique offers an affordable means of creating the beautiful golden tones of oak in your own home.

Before you make a start, it is a good idea to study the colours and grain patterns in the sample of the piece of wood that you wish to imitate. For successful results, always work with good reference sources alongside you.

Materials

- Metal rule, Stanley knife, pencil

- Paint or stain, paint brush, felt pen

- Clear polyurethane varnish, matte or satin

❶ Work on either hardboard or vinyl that has been glued to the floor. Mark out the width of floor board you want with a pencil. Using a long metal rule, run down the lines with a Stanley knife to score and mark the boards.

❷ Paint the boards with your chosen paint colour or stain.

❸ You can highlight with a felt pen, or use a small artists' brush, to imitate floor boards. Finish with clear or matte varnish.

Wall frieze

This paint effect can be fun to do and has the quality of originality that comes with free-hand painting. Choose a design that you really like, since you will be working closely with it until the frieze is completed!

Materials

- Latex paint

- Artist's acrylic paints

- Pencils, colors, paper

- Artists' brushes of various sizes

- Acrylic glaze to finish and protect

- For a harder finish and protection, clear polyurethane varnish, matte or satin

❶ Prepare your wall and paint frieze background with your chosen color.

❷ Working from your design, mark the lines using a ruler and cardboard. For accuracy you can lay masking tape down either side of the line. Paint the line freely, with a firm brush and a steady hand!

❸ To make a carbon copy, draw your design onto tracing paper, turn over, and densely scribble over the back of the design. Place wrong side of design against the wall and trace over again. Remove tracing paper and check the lines. Paint your design with the size of paint brush that suits you. If you prefer to work completely freehand, take a soft (B) pencil, draw in the running stalks and leaves. Now you are ready to paint. Wall friezes can run both horizontally and vertically on walls, in recesses, and on wooden doors.

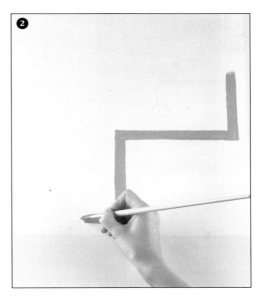

Left *A delightful effect is created in this part of the room by the wall frieze. Its carefully hand-crafted look adds warmth and liveliness to the area.*

Stencilling

Painting is one of the least expensive ways to decorate the home, but on large expanses of wall it can appear fairly bland. The decorative paint finishes described so far offer a variety of attractive effects to make surfaces more interesting to look at and exciting to live with. Of all the paint effects, stencilling has by far the most decorative potential; and the basic technique can be applied to create an array of two-dimensional patterns that can be used to embellish walls, ceilings, floors, doors, wooden panels, furniture, and window frames.

The following pages give step-by-step descriptions of how to use pre-cut stencils and also how to make your own designs. You can create your own designs or copy patterns and transfer them on to stencil paper. There are many places you can turn to for ideas such as a motif on a rug, piece of fabric or wallpaper. You can also look for inspiration in magazines, children's stories, art books, or on postcards in museums or art galleries.

Top *A country feel created using this lacy stencil motif which is repeated throughout the walls, corners and sloping ceiling of this delightful attic bedroom. The design is picked up in the deep ruffle of the sheer curtains at the window. A luxurious quilt in a traditional geometrical design contrasts effectively with a country-check bedspread to completes the look.*

Above and left *An example of stencilling used on walls and a stove to create an oriental look. A large, bold motif runs along the wall below the dado and runs along the top of the wall. The muted yellow, blue and red tones of the stencil contrast and harmonize with the bold, geometric fabrics and ornate furnishings in the room.*

Using a stencil

There are a number of ways you can apply color to pre-cut stencils, and many different effects can be achieved. Shades of color can be built up in layers or colors can be blended into one another. You might like to experiment, and find the method of applying paint which best suits the work you are doing or which you prefer.

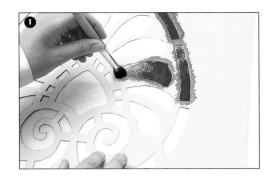

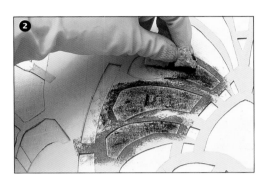

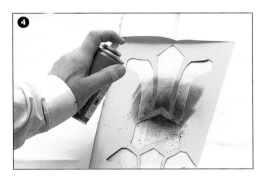

1 Using a stencil brush with firm bristles, pick up a little color, remove any excess, and apply with a light, dabbing motion.

2 Using a sponge is a very economical method and give a distinctive mottled effect. Dampen the sponge slightly, pick up a small amount of color, remove any excess, and apply with a light, dabbing motion. Colors can be blended as you work, or left to dry between coats.

3 Using a small foam-sponge roller is probably the most economical method of achieving a dense, even coverage, especially on fabric. This roller was bought in a toy shop and is ideal for this technique.

4 Aerosol sprays are not ideal for use with stencils. Not only can the fumes be hazardous, but careful masking with newsprint is essential if you do not want to spray the surrounding area. Seepage of paint under the edges of the stencil can also be a problem. Sprays are wonderful, however, for working with large areas of flat color and particularly good if you are working on fabric.

STARTING WORK

5

Repeating patterns

Repeating patterns needs some planning and measuring, but it is equally important to keep the visual balance and harmony of the room in mind. When placing your stencil pattern on the wall, start from the center and work outward, until you come to a corner or a break. Step back and have a look at the effect on the whole room before you decide what to do at this point. To repeat the pattern (above), overlap to line up with the motif at the right side as you work.

Stencilling materials 1 *artist's brush to apply tints or paint free-hand* 2 *small stencil brush* 3 *large stencil brush* 4 *artist's acrylic paint to apply tints, details or highlights* 5 *oil painting brush* 6 *natural sponge to create sponging effect* 7 *pre-cut stencil* 8 *dish for mixing colors*

Making and cutting a stencil

When you are looking for patterns or stencils, work out the different elements carefully so that they are joined together by a small "tie" of stencil paper. When your design is ready, draw it on tracing paper using a soft 2B pencil; on the reverse of the tracing paper, scribble over the lines with the soft pencil. Lay the tracing paper right side up on your stencil paper or board, secure with masking tape and draw over the lines again with an HB pencil. If you are working with acetate, trace your design direct with a felt-tip pen. Standard stencil paper is good as it is specially treated to resist absorbing paint. Strong brown wrapping paper painted with shellac varnish makes a good alternative.

Cut the stencil with a sharp craft knife, taking care always to cut away from your free hand and your body. Never cut towards yourself in case the knife slips. Work on a cutting board or piece of plywood larger than the size of your work. When working with stencils, it is a good idea to mask the edges with tape so that the stencil does not slip and cause your design to smudge.

Below *Bright colors give this design a modern look. A more subtle effect can be achieved by using pale blending colors on a pale background.*

Two-color stencil

This stencil design was taken from a multi-colored 19th century wallpaper design. Bright contrasting colors were chosen for a dramatic effect. A sponge is used to apply the paler shades of yellow and green. This gives a mottled, uneven effect of light and shade to the pattern. Two coats of the dark yellow and one coat of light yellow and green are applied over the darker blue. The stencil is attached to the wall with masking tape on the upper and lower edges.

Materials and equipment

- Stencil card, craft knife, pencil

- Paint brush and sponges

- Latex paint (matte)
  Suggested colors - deep blue, bright yellow, light yellow and pale green

- Wide-topped jars or saucers for every color you intend to use

- Clean, lint-free rags

- Masking tape

- Matte-finish clear acrylic varnish or polyurethane varnish (optional)

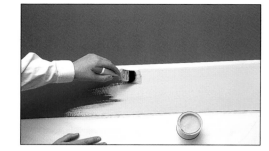

❶ Mark the dado by measuring up 33in (82.5cm) from the floor; mask with tape, paint and leave to dry. Mark the baseboard by measuring 6 ½in (16.5cm) up from the floor; mask with paint and leave to dry.

❷ Copy the pattern shown below (left) on stencil card. Cut out carefully with a craft knife. You may find it helpful to secure the stencil card with masking tape so that it does not move while you are cutting.

Adjusting the scale

It is quite likely that the stencils shown on these pages, as well as designs from other sources that you may intend to use, will not be to the correct scale for your purposes. Unless you feel confident to adjust the scale by copying the design free-hand, you should make use of a photocopier – many outlets offer fast and efficient photocopying services. All you have to do is enlarge or reduce the size of the design to a suitable size and then use the photo-copy to make a tracing of the correctly scaled image.

3 Secure the square motif stencil centrally between the dado and the baseboard. Make sure that this stencil is straight as the first stencil will set the angle for all the rest. Using a sponge, paint with bright yellow. Allow to dry. Apply a second coat.

4 Remove the square stencil and position the diamond stencil, using the two small cut-out shapes in the corners to line up with the corresponding parts of the square. Secure the stencil. Apply light yellow with a clean piece of sponge to central leaf motifs only. Allow to dry leaving the stencil in position.

5 Apply bright yellow to the straight sides of the diamond shape only. Omit the leaf shapes. Leave the stencil in position and allow to dry. With a fresh sponge apply the pale green latex over the light yellow on the leaf motifs only.

6 On a piece of stencil paper, cut a circle 3in (7.5cm) in diameter, either using a compass or a round cup. Cut out and position in the center of the square design.

7 Apply a coat of light yellow and allow to dry. Apply a coat of green. Remove stencil and reposition on center of diamond shape. Apply two coats of bright yellow.

5

STARTING WORK

HANDY HINTS

- Test your design and colors on a piece of board before you start.

- Always make sure that stencils are firmly secured at corners or edges with masking tape.

- Acetate stencils are ideal for uneven doors or walls. They mold themselves to the surface and so prevent paint seeping behind the pattern.

- When accuracy is essential, align your stencil card with a faint pencil line ruled with the aid of a level.

- Make sure the paint is completely dry before untaping the stencil card from the surface.

Below *The soft, muted tones of simple paintwork are reflected in this stencilled frieze that gently meanders around the walls. The bows break the pattern of ribbons and add interest to the overall style and decorative effect of this elegant room.*

Stencilling on fabric

This project was inspired by a Florentine design of gold fleur-de-lys, the emblem of the city, on walls painted in intense, and now faded, blue.

You may want to create a wall hanging or curtains, and to use a big, colored background with a simple, symmetrical stencil which can then be repeated. Silk and cotton are both available in a range of beautiful, commercially dyed colors. Gold stencil cream has a crumbly texture which makes it ideal for stippling through the stencil. Once you have gotten used to positioning the stencils accurately, and working around the parts that are still wet, this becomes a very simple and direct method.

Materials and equipment

- Silk or cotton fabric

- Graphite stick, pencils

- Tracing paper, masking tape

- Stencil card, craft knife

- Gold stencil cream

- Thickened textile pigments or fabric dye

- Stencilling brush

1 Place the scroll border stencil securely on the background fabric. Apply gold stencil cream using the brush upright and using short, sharp downward dabs.

2 Make sure that you complete each shape before you move on to the next one. Gold stencil cream takes up to 24 hours to dry, but it is possible to continue building up the stencils immediately.

3 Position the fleur-de-lys stencil carefully above the scroll pattern and lower it gently onto the cloth, taking care at the scroll border. Apply the gold paint as before. The bottom part of the scroll border can be used on its own as vertical and top borders and the large scrolls can be filled in with the fleur-de-lys.

Stencilling is a part of the decoration of the interior of your home. You can make your own individual mark by creating original stencils. It is important that they work in the context of the room so that they flow and become an intrinsic part of the surface they are decorating.

Left *A traditional design of acorns and oak leaves makes a perfect border pattern which can be used on a wall to highlight the rich browns of antique, polished wood furniture.*

Right *This is a perfect design for carrying a leaf-based pattern around a corner.*

Right *Create your own design for a medallion, using this one as inspiration. Make sure that you work with a really sharp craft knife or a scalpel to cut your stencil clearly.*

Right *Central border patterns need careful positioning. Walls are not always vertical, so measure the position of the repeat each time, working from some constant - either a ceiling, or a marked line, rather than from the last motif.*

Stencils come in a wide range and variety of patterns and shapes, and can be applied to many different surfaces. At its simplest, a stencil can be used by a child to make a greeting card; more elaborate stencils can be used on walls, floors, around doorways, windows, and on small pieces of furniture.

It is worth making sure that the surfaces you are going to work on are well prepared. Walls should be cleaned and filled, old paint removed from furniture and cracks filled, floors repaired and sanded, and fabric washed and ironed according to its fiber content.

Above *Leaping fishes inspire this decorative theme for a bathroom wall, and add a liveliness of their own.*

Left *Apply tonal contrast to this shell design and you can increase the depth and change the quality of the finished painting.*

Below *This bold fruit motif would look good in a kitchen or dining room. Combine it with a leafy border pattern and carry the theme around the wall. Paint it on the doors of a small kitchen cabinet to add interest.*

Left *Pick out a dominant color in a fabric, or in a piece of art, and use this simple motif to highlight it. Subtle, related tones give a delicate finish to this stencil design; bolder colors would make it more dramatic.*

Stencilling motifs

Below *Stencil designs can be used to make mobiles out of cardboard, cut with a craft knife. Use this sailor boy and combine with other simple sea shapes. Or collect small shells from the sea shore and create your own seaside mobile.*

Left *The perennial theme of Teddy Bears! You can color inside the outline with more concentrated color, working freehand with a paint brush. This will give a softer look to your bear. Highlight eyes, ears and nose with darker shading or a darker color.*

Left *Nursery rhyme themes and traditional stories offer a wide range of stencil design inspiration for a room with a child in mind.*

Above *Bird motif for a child's room or nursery.*

Left *Coloring this stencil can be done with ready-mixed flat colors or built up with overlapping tones. If you build up the color on this large motif, you will achieve a more interesting, natural finish. Like an Impressionist painter, you can create your own palette of tones which relate to the paint colors in the room, as well as the furnishings.*

Below *Repeating floor patterns can be different sizes - a larger motif for the center, surrounded by smaller ones to echo it. Work over the floor in the same color or in related tones.*

Right *Always use paint sparingly with either stencil brush or spray. This pineapple motif can be painted in graduated tones of yellow through to green, to give a delightfully realistic appearance.*

Above *A border pattern ideal for use on floor or wall. Work in one color, which highlights a dominant theme or introduce a new contrasting color.*

Below *Bold contrast of primary colors look good on the floor. When the floor has dried, varnish with several coats of polyurethane varnish.*

Right *Two motifs working well together to create a border and a corner feature. They can be repeated and carried around a wall or door frame.*

Left *A floral motif which brings out the tulip shape very clearly and focuses attention on the corner. Strong purple flowers enliven the corner.*

Right *A pretty medallion in a simple two-color combination. It can be used in a dark corner to lighten it up, or to decorate a small piece of wooden furniture.*

Above *This floor stencil is carried down the stairs and around the bottom of the banister to create a delightful design.*

Stencilling a floor

In an otherwise plainly decorated room, a bold, well-designed stencil pattern used as a border running around the floor can have real impact. Stencils look fantastic on painted or sanded floors. To prevent the paint from creeping behind the stencil card and spoiling the design's outline, the floor will have to be sanded and sealed. Once the stencilling is complete, give the design at least three coats of varnish, sanding again between each coat. Make sure that you work in a well-ventilated room and wear a face mask while you are painting.

Materials and equipment

- Steel ruler or tape measure

- Soft pencil

- Stencil card

- Masking tape

- Clean newspaper

- Aerosol paint

1 Measure and mark at regular intervals from the edge of the wall or baseboard so the stencil can be positioned exactly parallel with it. Make small, light pencil marks that will not show afterward, and then use masking tape to line up the stencil card. Use more pieces of masking tape to hold the stencil card straight and in position.

2 Use sheets of clean newspaper to mask all the areas around the

stencil, including the wall, to shield them from paint. Don't forget the strip between the stencil card and wall. Shake the aerosol thoroughly and spray a light coat of paint from about 8-10in (20-25cm). Leave the paint until it is completely dry.

3 Lift the stencil card and line it up with the pattern on the floor, overlapping the last two elements on the end of each line. Secure the stencil, it does not lie flat use a little double-sided tape on the reverse side to increase the contact with the wood.

4 Use fresh sheets of newspaper around the stencil card and continue to work as before - shake the aerosol thoroughly, and apply a light coat of paint. Leave the paint to dry before repeating this process as many times as necessary to complete the entire floor border.

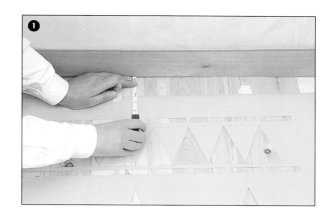

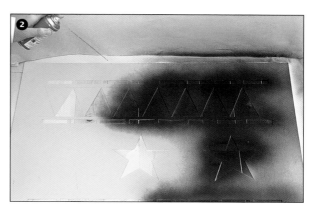

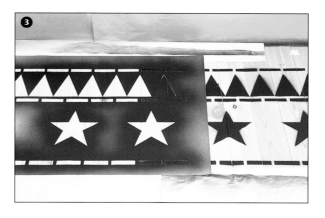

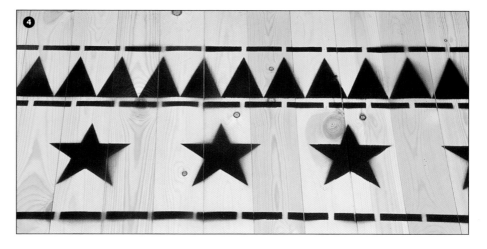

Wallcoverings
Styles and types

Although the term "wallpaper" is commonly used, "wallcovering" is more accurate since many of the patterns and textures now sold for walls and ceilings are made from plastic or fabric. The variety of wallcoverings on the market is enormous, so choosing the right one for your needs can be a daunting task unless you are familiar with what's available.

Right *Blacks and whites and tones of grey can form the perfect foil for color introduced in curtains, chair fabrics, pictures, and ornaments.*

Below *Chinese willow-pattern theme is repeated on the wall, in the furnishing fabric and on the wall frieze. Darker*

Ready-pasted wallpapers This type of product has a dry adhesive on the back. To activate the adhesive, each length of paper is soaked in a small trough of water and then applied directly to the wall or ceiling.

Relief papers Available in a range of designs from formal patterns to simulations of such textures as plaster, pebble-dash, and brick. Generally, the more heavily embossed the paper, the more expensive it is. This type of paper requires expert hanging, since once it is hung and painted it is extremely difficult to strip.

Flocks These are expensive papers. They are available mainly in traditional patterns – originally developed to mimic velvet wall-hangings. The designs are made from chopped fibers of rayon or silk stuck to a backing to give the effect of a raised pile. They require expert hanging.

Papers

Lining paper A smooth, unpatterned paper designed to cover poor wall or ceiling surfaces before a decorative covering is applied. It is always laid at right angles to the main wallcovering. Lining paper is not now often used, since textured covering can disguise poor-quality surfaces without the use of lining paper.

Pulps and Woodchip papers Pulps are an inexpensive covering made from a single thickness of printed-pattern paper.

When wet with paste, pulps are easily torn. Woodchip paper has chips of wood bonded to the front surface. It is a cheap form of covering and is often used to disguise less-than-perfect surfaces. The woodchips are available in a range of grades from fine to coarse.

Duplex papers Made in layers, they are stronger and easier to handle than pulps. There is a vast range of designs, often with matching or toning fabrics. Some duplex papers are also embossed.

Dry-strippable paper A good choice if you are thinking that you will want to redecorate, since it can be removed without soaking or scraping.

Washable papers A coating of clear plastic on the surface makes them easy to hang and clean. Use a damp sponge only for cleaning – too much water may weaken the wallpaper paste.

Vinyl wallcoverings These papers have patterns printed with vinyl inks onto a layer of vinyl fused to a paper backing. Textured vinyls are also available – solid-colored but textured to imitate other types of surface. Heavily textured vinyls mimic tiles and such materials as glasscloth and stone. Roll lengths of these may be less than standard. There are also flock vinyls, in rich or pastel colors in a variety of designs. Metallic vinyls are sophisticated (but expensive), with areas of gold, silver, bronze, or copper. Most vinyl papers are dry strippable, ready-pasted or unpasted.

Materials

Fabric wallcoverings Paper-backed fabric coverings are available, either in wallpaper-sized rolls or by the yard. Burlap is bonded to backing paper and comes in a variety of colors.

Felts and Silks Paper-backed felt is often used to deaden sound and to insulate against heat loss to some extent. Paper-backed silks are luxurious, but they are expensive and require expert hanging.

Wool cloths These offer you the choice of a range of natural colors, plus some brightly dyed effects. Textures range from coarse fibers to fine cloth in herringbones and other weaves. Crushed suede and velvet cloths are also available.

Grass cloth This material is sold by the yard. It is made in the Far East by hand and has a unique charm.

Cork Colors include a choice of browns ranging between a light pale shade to a rich, deep color. This material is often used as an alternative to cork wall tiles.

Metallic coverings This consists of thin metal foil bonded to a paper backing.

Preparation

Wait until you have finished all the painting in a room before applying your wall or ceiling covering. Give the walls and ceiling a final check for uneven putty or rough areas where any old wallcovering has been removed, and sand with medium sandpaper where necessary.

Vacuum the room to pick up fine dust. Remove any old newspapers you may have spread over the floor while sanding, and wipe baseboards, doors, and window frames with a damp rag. Then spread clean newspaper around the walls to catch any splashes of size. Size may either be a separate material, bought as a powder and mixed with cold water, or it can be paste diluted as recommended on the package. Apply it to all the surfaces to be papered and leave it to dry – usually about an hour or two – before papering. Size prevents too much wallpaper paste from being absorbed by the plaster of the walls or ceiling.

It is best to paper the ceiling before the walls. Check how you will reach the highest point of the room. A short step-stool may be adequate, otherwise, use a small stepladder. Two stepladders with a plank between them may be necessary for papering a ceiling.

Above *The use of textured wallcoverings can add an extra dimension to a decorative theme. Choose from flocks, anaglyptas, false plaster effects, woodchip (in various grades), false burlap, grass cloth, cork, and many, many others.*

Measuring

As we have seen, the term "wallpaper" refers to more than just a paper covering applied to a wall. Although wallcoverings do have paper backings, they may be faced with a great number of different materials, from silk and burlap to metal and cork (*see p. 122-3*). However, for convenience, the word "paper" is used here as a generic for all types of wall and ceiling coverings.

The chart below will help you determine the number of rolls of paper needed for a particular room, but remember to take account of any pattern repeats and roll sizes.

Right *When faced with pattern repeats, make sure you allow a generous amount of wallpaper. This pattern may appear random, but careful matching results in a lively appearance to the room.*

Calculating number of rolls for walls

Height from baseboard	27ft 9in (8.5m)	32ft (9.75mt)	36ft (11mt)	39ft 4in (12m)	44ft (13.4m)	46ft (14m)	52ft (16m)	55ft 6in (17m)	59ft 5in (18.5)	63ft 5in (19.5m)	67ft 4in (20.75m)	72ft (22m)	75ft (23m)
7ft–7ft 6in (2.13–2.29m)	4	4	5	5	6	6	7	7	8	8	9	9	9
7ft 6in–8ft (2.30–2.44m)	4	4	5	5	6	6	7	8	8	9	9	10	10
8ft–8ft 6in (2.45–2.59m)	4	5	5	6	6	7	7	8	8	9	9	10	10
8ft 6in–9ft (2.60–2.74m)	4	5	5	6	6	7	8	8	9	9	10	11	11
9ft–9ft 6in (2.75–2.90m)	4	5	6	6	7	7	8	9	9	10	10	11	12
9ft 6in–10ft (2.91–3.05m)	5	5	6	7	7	8	9	9	10	10	11	12	12
10ft–10ft 6in (3.06–3.20m)	5	5	6	7	8	8	9	10	10	11	12	12	13

Calculating number of rolls for a ceiling

Measurement around room	32ft (9.75m)	32ft 10in (10m)	36ft (11m)	37ft 9in (11.5m)	39ft 4in (12m)	42ft (12.8m)	44ft (13.4m)	46ft (14m)	47ft 6in (14.5m)	52ft (16m)
Number of rolls required	2	2	2	2	2	3	3	3	3	4
Measurement around room	54ft 2in (16.5m)	55ft 10in (17m)	57ft 5in (17.5m)	59ft (18m)	62ft 4in (19m)	64ft (19.5m)	65ft 8in (20m)	67ft 3in (20.5m)	69ft (21m)	73ft 10in (22.5m)
Number of rolls required	4	4	4	5	5	5	5	6	6	7

Measuring and calculating

Calculating the number of rolls required for any given room is not an exact science, but the charts here will help you estimate quantities. You must work in either standards or metric, but not a mixture of both. To make your own calculation for paper requirements, proceed as follows.

First, measure the distance from the baseboard to the picture molding or ceiling, depending on how far up the wall you are papering. Then measure the total distance around the room, taking into account standard (but not picture) windows. If you have picture windows, deduct their area from your calculations. Next, multiply the distance around the walls by the height to find the total area to be covered. Now multiply the width of your chosen wallcovering by the total length of a roll to find out the area of each roll. Divide the wall area by the roll area and the resulting figure is the approximate number of rolls you require. Do not forget, however, to order extra rolls if you have a large pattern repeat to account for.

For the ceiling, simply divide the area of the ceiling by the area of a roll to find the number of rolls required.

Roll sizes

A standard roll is 33ft x 21in (10m x 53cm). The paper comes trimmed and will usually be wrapped to keep it clean.

The charts for calculating wallpaper quantities (*see left*) are based on the standard roll size. However, some imported papers may be narrower, and some widely available ones are twice as wide. If selecting any of these papers, look in the sample book for guidance on coverage.

Batch numbers

Each roll of paper should be stamped with a production batch number. When selecting rolls, check that all the production numbers

Repeats

Another variable to be aware of when calculating quantities is the pattern repeat. The larger the repeat, the more likely it is that extra rolls will be required.

Free-match papers are printed with nondirectional designs that do not require pattern matching, and so involve little wastage. Set-match papers have motifs that repeat in a straight line across the paper. They, too, can be matched with little wastage, although the overall size of the pattern repeat will affect the amount of paper required.

The final repeat is known as a drop-match. These papers have patterns that repeat in diagonal lines, and so each new length of paper has to be moved either up or down to allow for this. You can minimize wastage with drop-match patterns by cutting alternate lengths from two rolls.

are the same. If they are not, this means that the rolls have been produced in different batch runs and there may be slight variations in color and shading. For this reason, it is a good idea to over-order. If you have to buy one or two more rolls at a later date, you may be supplied from a different batch. If you do order too many rolls, the supplier will usually allow you to return any that have not been used, provided that the wrappings are intact. If you have to accept rolls from a different batch, plan to use this paper in an alcove or recess, or somewhere in the room where any slight differences in color will not be immediately obvious.

Counterclockwise from top *Free-match papers have patterns or stripes that don't require matching; set-match papers have patterns that repeat in straight* *lines across the paper and involve little wastage; drop-match designs repeat diagonally across the paper and involve most wastage of all.*

Pasting and hanging

Before starting, you need to find the starting point for the first length. To do this, measure out 19in (48cm) from the window wall corner and make a pencil mark just below picture molding level. Extend a plumb line cord and let the line hang down to just above the baseboard. Have a helper make marks on the wall behind the line. Check the distance between each mark and the corner. If the wall is out of true, and the reading is more than 19in (48cm) at any point, move your plumb line nearer the wall and make a new set of marks. Adjust the measurements if using non-standard rolls to be sure to get a good turn of paper onto the window wall.

HANDY HINTS

- With coverings such as burlap, silk, cork, or foil, check if you paste the wall or ceiling or the back of the material itself.

- If bubbles or blisters appear, you may have left insufficient time for the paper to soak.

- You can often shrink bubbles back into place by wafting the surface of the paper with a hair dryer.

Papering walls

Successful paper hanging depends on preparing the walls properly beforehand, having the right tools and equipment, making sure that your pasting table is kept clean and dry throughout, and using a sharp knife or scissors to trim the paper lengths to size.

❶ Make sure the pasting table is dry and clean. Then, if you are right-handed, lay the bottom of the paper on the table pattern-side down with the surplus to your left, loosely rolled. If you are left-handed, place the spare paper to your right. Load the brush with paste and apply a strip down the middle of the paper (*see* **a**, *right*). Reload the brush and work out from the middle, herringbone fashion (**b** *and* **c**), lifting the brush off as you reach the edge of the paper. Check that the edges are well covered.

❷ Carefully fold the pasted paper back on itself, lift the paper, and ask a helper to wipe any paste from the table with a damp cloth. Lower the paper to the table and then slide it to the right, thus bringing the unpasted surplus paper onto the table. Reload the brush and apply paste as before. Fold the paper in on itself so that it almost meets the other fold. The last fold will be the top of the piece. Fold it again to make the length easy to move, and place it out of the way to soak. This is important, since the paper will continue to expand for some minutes. If it does not expand fully, you may get bubbles later. While the paper is soaking, paste one or two more lengths. Wipe the table with a damp cloth each time.

❸ Carry the first length of paper to the wall (*as shown right*).

❹ Unfold the top fold and let the paper drop. Position the left-hand edge on your pencil line, making sure you have about 2in (5cm) spare at the top for trimming. Once the left edge is positioned, wipe

Ready-pasted paper
Ready-pasted paper will not stretch so there is less chance of its bubbling through expansion. Before soaking, check the manufacturer's instructions and follow them if they are different from those below.

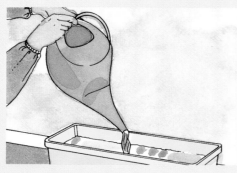

❶ Place the special wallpaper trough on some sheets of newspaper to protect the floor, and fill it two-thirds full with clean, cold water.

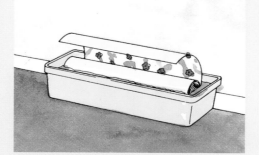

❷ Measure and cut a length of wallpaper. Loosely roll it, pattern-side in, and submerge it in the trough.

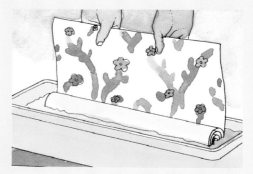

❸ Agitate so that the water makes contact with all of the paper. Lift it slowly from the trough, allowing excess water to drain off. No soaking time is necessary.

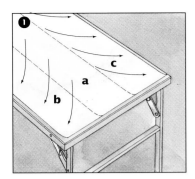

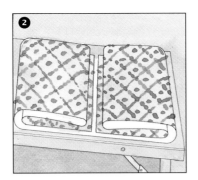

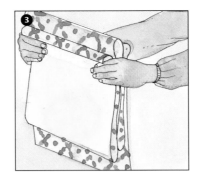

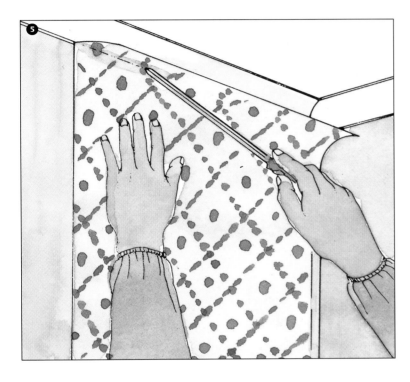

the surplus removed, carefully dab the paper back in place. Repeat this at the dado and/or baseboard end of the length of paper.

To trim heavy vinyls and heavy papers, you can use a very sharp knife and steel straightedge. Once you have creased the vinyl or paper to form a guideline, place the straightedge just above the crease and cut with the knife.

6 When you have finished the first piece, check that the edges are well stuck down – heavy wallpapers tend to curl at the edges. If so, try dabbing them down with a clean, dry rag; if the paste has dried, smear a little extra under the edge of the paper with the paste brush. Wipe away the surplus and then dab the paper down. This problem occurs most often with smooth vinyls, where the edges frequently seem to curl away from the wall. In this case, apply a special seam adhesive, not extra paste. Use it sparingly under the edge and then press the edge down in place. If you use a clear resin adhesive, take care not to get any on the surface of the vinyl – the adhesive will soften it.

7 With the second length pasted, folded, and soaked, carry it to the wall, drop out the top flat, and position the right corner on the wall (assuming that you are working right to left), lining it up with the edge of the first length. Match any pattern by sliding the paper up or down. Then smooth the top of the paper to the wall, run the smoothing brush down the length of the paper and brush outward toward the first length. Check that the seams align perfectly, and then continue adding lengths. As you progress, clean up between each length. Use a damp cloth or sponge to wipe paste from picture moldings, baseboards, and window and door frames while it is still soft. Keep any trimmed pieces for patching. Wipe the pasting table clean after each length.

your hand across to the right to secure the top of the paper to the wall. With the paper correctly positioned, take the smoothing brush and run it down the middle of the length, pressing the paper lightly to the wall. Now use the brush in light, outward strokes until the length is in place. About 1 in (2.5cm) of paper should have turned onto the window wall. Lightly press this into place, ensuring that there are no wrinkles. Don't force the paper down at the baseboard and picture molding in the corner, since you still have to trim the paper. If the turned edge seems dry, apply a little extra paste. Before trimming, smooth the paper again from the middle out, making sure that the edges are securely stuck down. Lightly dab any bubbles flat and leave the paper to dry. Bubbles usually disappear as the paper shrinks and tightens.

5 Use the edge of the closed scissors to press the paper firmly into the top edge, baseboard, and picture molding. Press very lightly to avoid tearing the damp paper. Use scissors rather than a knife for trimming, again to avoid tearing the paper. Pull the paper away from the wall just far enough to allow you to position the scissors and then cut about ⅛in (3mm) outside the score mark. With

Ceilings

When papering a ceiling, it is important to be able to reach it safely and in reasonable comfort. So, the first thing you need to do is secure a platform to stand on so that your head is about 3in (7cm) from the ceiling. Place the platform along the line of the first length of paper that you are planning to hang.

If the ceiling has been newly plastered, you will first have to "size" it to prevent too much of the wallpaper paste from being absorbed by the plaster and weakening the adhesion of the paper (*see p. 123*). An application of "size" also helps to slide your paper into place, by making the ceiling surface more slippery.

Hanging overhead lights

With a ceiling pendant, cut the paper to length and mark it on the back. Allow for trimming. Paste the paper and make a series of star-shaped cuts from the middle of the light position.

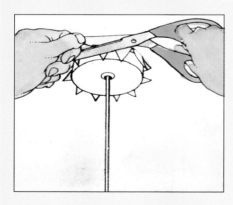

Hang the paper normally. Then, when you reach the light fixture, feed the pendant through the hole and press the paper into place around it.

Crease each flap with the blunt edge of the closed scissors and carefully cut off the surplus paper ⅛in (3mm) outside the crease marks. Press the paper into place and wipe the paste off the fixture.

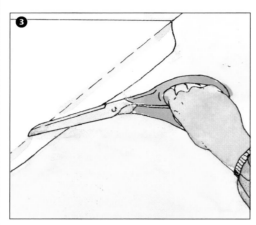

Positioning the first length

The best starting place is parallel with the window wall. This ensures that no shadows will be thrown should any paper overlap. The simplest way to indicate the position for the first length is to mark the ceiling at each end, the width of the paper away from the wall.

Rub a length of string with chalk. Secure it to the ceiling at one end, just over the mark you have made. Ask a helper to hold the other end tightly to the other mark while you pluck the string, leaving a line on the ceiling.

1 Measure the ceiling for the first length of paper and add 4in (10cm) for trimming. Cut and lay the length on the table with the surplus on the floor to your left (if you are right-handed). Using thick paste, pull the paper onto the table and fold over about 20in (50cm). Fold again until fresh paper is in place, and continue to paste and fold until you reach the end of the length.

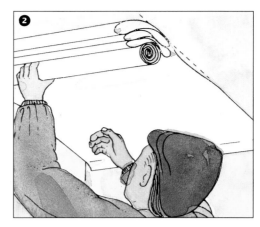

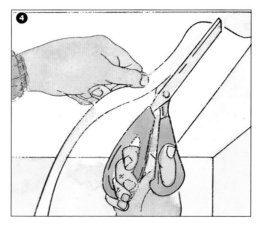

2 Allow the paper to soak and then lay it over a spare roll of paper, with the edge to be stuck first uppermost. Hold the roll in your left hand (if you are right-handed), grip the top edge with your right hand, turn it paste-side up, and apply it to the corner where you plan to start. Slide it to the chalk line and smooth it onto the ceiling.

3 Move along the platform, releasing the fold as you go. Smooth the paper to the ceiling and get a helper to hold the paper in place with a broom as you move along.

4 Continue until the length is in position. Run over it with your smoothing brush, making sure the edges are well stuck down.

5 Press the paper into the end walls and crease it with your closed scissors.

6 Trim ⅛in (3mm) outside the crease so that the paper just turns onto the wall. Dab the paper back into place. Hang the second length, matching it to the edge of the first.

Problem areas

Papering flat areas of walls is straightforward. However, many rooms present problem areas, especially if you are inexperienced! These may include features such as alcoves, radiators, light switches, and fireplaces.

Radiators

If you have a central heating system with radiators, it may be possible to swing them away from the walls to allow you to paper behind. Try lifting the radiator. If it rises enough to clear the holding brackets, slightly loosen the pipe nuts on each side and lean the radiator forward. If the radiator will not move, you will have to tuck the paper down behind it. Cut two slits corresponding to the holding brackets. Then use a radiator roller – or improvise with a length of wood wrapped in clean rag – to smooth the paper down into place.

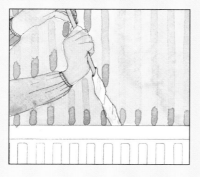

Recesses

Position the unpasted length that will turn into the recess on the wall and mark the area of surplus paper. You need enough for the depth of the recess plus about 1 in (2.5cm) for trimming. Continue a strip above the recess, plus about 1 in (2.5cm) to turn onto the ceiling of the recess. Cut away surplus paper. If the paper will not reach the full depth of the recess, cut it so that 1 in (2.5cm) turns the corner and add a further panel of paper later.

1 Make a horizontal cut at the window ledge and then at the top edge, leaving about a 1 in (2.5cm) overhang of paper. Turn the side panel into the recess wall and gently smooth it down flat. Be careful not to stretch or tear the wet paper. Crease and trim the surplus paper with your scissors.

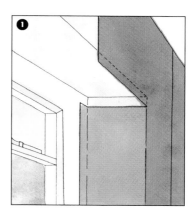

2 Paste your next length of paper as normal and hang it, allowing enough paper to reach the full depth of the ceiling recess, plus about an extra 1 in (2.5cm) for trimming. Carefully crease and then trim the surplus paper with your scissors.

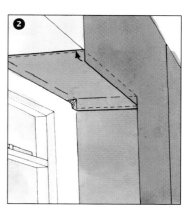

3 Now cut a panel to finish the ceiling recess. Test it for size before pasting, remembering to add about an extra 1 in (2.5cm) for trimming at both the window and recess walls. Paste the length as normal, and bring the front edge of the ceiling panel to meet the front edge of the recess. Smooth the paper onto the ceiling and trim the surplus at the window and recess walls. Cut into the corner of the overhanging paper and fold it back onto the ceiling panel for a neat edge.

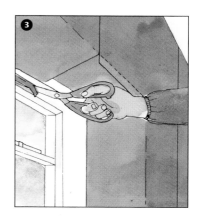

Left *Coping with the pattern matching, window recesses, and an angled ceiling in the attic bedroom is not recommended for a novice wallpaper hanger.*

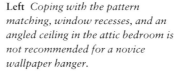

Fireplaces

If the fireplace is a feature of the room – and if it is on a chimney breast – it is best to hang a length of paper centrally on the breast, and then paper out in each direction. Then, any slight discrepancy in pattern can be lost around the internal corners of the chimney breast.

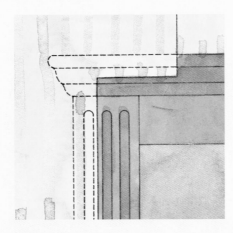

1 At the sides of the surround, cut the paper as if you were tackling a door frame (*see right*). You will also have to make cuts in the paper to let the mantelpiece come through. When measuring, allow extra paper to push into the moldings.

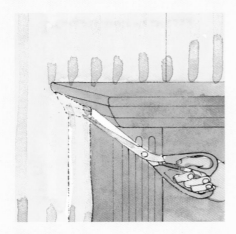

2 Trim along the crease marks with scissors. With odd shapes, such as those made by a stone fireplace, make small cuts in the paper edge, mold it to the contours, and crease it. Trim ⅛in (3mm) outside the creases so that the paper just turns onto the stone.

Wall-mounted light switches

If you need to paper around a light switch that can't be unscrewed from the wall, first drape the pasted length of paper over it. Feel for the middle and press to mark the paper. Now make star cuts in the paper out from the middle of the switch to the edges and then finish hanging the length. Press the cut paper lightly around the switch and mark it with the scissors. Pull each flap away and trim it to overlap about 1⁄16in (2mm). Dab the pieces back and wipe the paste from the switch.

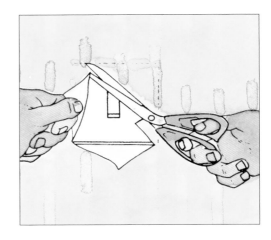

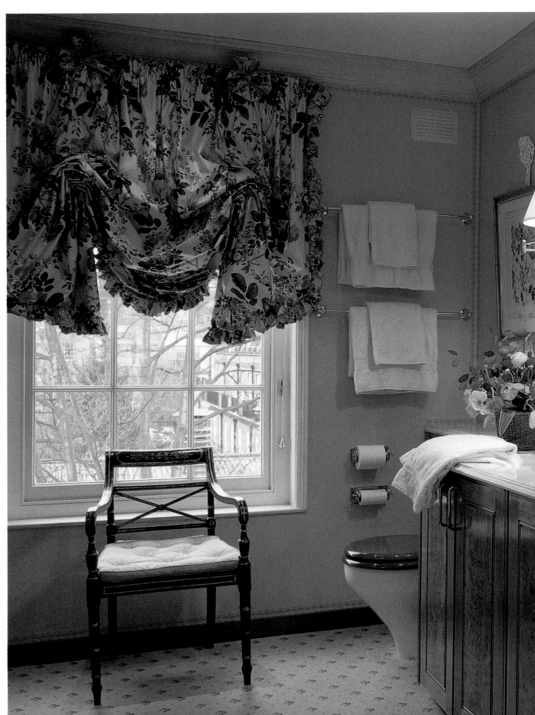

Below Bathrooms, which usually have a high percentage of built-in features, often represent a real problem when a professional finish to the wallpaper is required. Wherever possible, unscrew fixtures from the walls before papering. In the bathroom illustrated here, the towel rods, paper holders, wall light covers, wall vent, and the hooks supporting the mirrors were all removed prior to papering.

Flush-mounted switch

First of all, cut off the power supply to the circuit. If you are papering around a switch that has a removable faceplate, loosen the screws and ease the plate away from the wall. Drape the paper over the switch, find the middle, and make two diagonal cuts out to the plate corners. Trim the paper ¼in (6mm) inside the switch area and tuck the excess behind the plate. Retighten the screws and wipe away the paste.

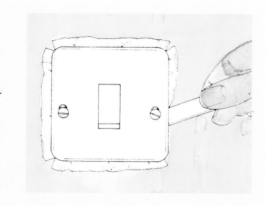

Wallpapering around doors

❶ Cut the length of paper to fit around the door, marking a spare 2in (5cm) on the back for trimming top and bottom. Measure the distance from the last hung length to the door frame and add 1in (2.5cm). Do this near both the top and bottom of the door and mark these distances on the prepared length of paper. Draw a line between them. Measure the height from the baseboard to the top of the door frame and deduct 1in (2.5cm). Mark this point on your drawn line and draw a horizontal line from it to the doorway side of the paper. Cut out the surplus.

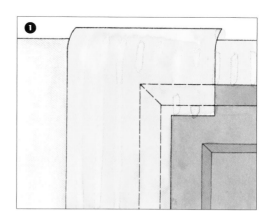

❷ Hang the length as normal, running it over the door and pressing it into the frame. Make a diagonal cut at the frame corner to allow the surplus paper to be pressed down.

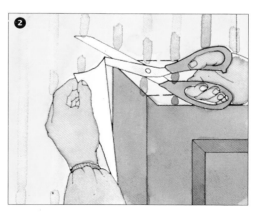

❸ With the paper smoothed down, use closed scissors or a stiff brush edge to score a crease around the door frame to make a cutting guideline.
   Pull the paper away from the wall and trim. Now work from the other side of the door, and cut your length in the same way if the two pieces will meet above the frame. Even so, it is wise to drop a plumb line to the right-hand edge of this length so that you hang the piece vertically. If the two pieces will not meet, cut an infill piece. If there is a pattern to match, cut and hang the infill before the next length is cut. But if pattern matching is no problem, hang the next full length and then the infill piece

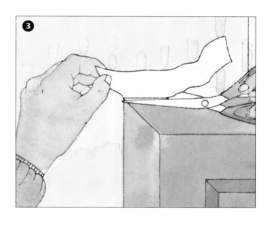

Wallpaper borders

Materials and equipment

- Wooden batten and spirit level
- Soft-grade pencil
- Pasting table and brush
- Tape measure
- Wallpaper paste
- Seam roller
- Craft knife and metal rule

A selection of borders

Wallpaper borders are available in a wide choice of designs and colors.

Anaglypta – embossed paper designs

Mock-stencil border design

Modern self-adhesive border paper

Traditional geometric Greek-key design

Mock painted plaster moulding

Mock-braid trimming

Design suitable for child's room

Most borders are meant to complement a wallpaper design, and to this end many wallpaper manufacturers produce decorative friezes to coordinate with their own products. Pattern books, for example, often contain samples of wallpapers with two or three suggested border papers for each included, perhaps in different shadings or designs. Bear in mind that these are only suggestions, however – what looks best in the context of your own home, with your belongings and decorations in place, is an entirely personal decision.

There are two basic types of border paper to choose from: ready-pasted and ordinary. Some people prefer the ease of use and lack of mess of the ready-pasted types, while other decorators feel that they can achieve a better finish with ordinary papers. Ready-pasted types are more expensive to buy. But no matter which type you use, the base surface must be completely dry, clean, and sound.

Above A border frieze placed low on the wall above the decorative dado, draws the focus of the eye to this part of the room. The patterns and colors in the chair covers and cushions pick up particular elements in the wall frieze and wallpaper.

Marking and pasting a border

Before cutting or pasting your border paper, first determine the height at which you want it to run and then draw a pencil guideline with the help of a straightedge and level. If pasting a border over freshly hung wallpaper, leave at least 48 hours for the base paper to dry out thoroughly. If pasting a border over new paint, wait at least a week. Vinyl border papers require heavy-duty paste to make them secure.

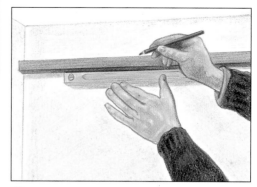

1 To make sure that your border is completely straight and level, use a wooden batten and a level to draw a guideline for the bottom edge of the border.

2 Measure and then cut a length of border paper and paste it carefully, paying particular attention to the edges. Use the appropriate paste for the type of border paper you are working with. Check the manufacturer's recommendations if you are unsure. Vinyl papers require a stronger adhesive than non-vinyl papers, for example. Align the edge of the paper with the edge of the pasting table to help keep adhesive off the decorative surface. Check that no loose hairs from the pasting brush end up on the back of the paper.

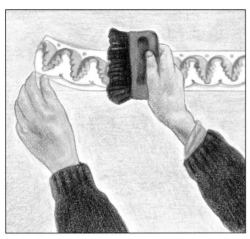

3 Align the edge of the border with your ruled pencil guideline. When you are satisfied that the border paper is straight, brush it onto the wall. Until the paste dries, you can make minor adjustments to the position of the paper, if necessary. Just carefully lift a corner, peel back as much paper as you wish to reposition, and then brush it down in place once more. Don't overstretch the border paper at this stage. By tugging it, you may get a perfectly flush fit, only to find that it shrinks back slightly as it dries out. This will leave unsightly gaps that cannot then be rectified.

4 If a seam in the middle of a wall is unavoidable, abut the ends of the papers very carefully, matching the pattern if necessary. Use a seam roller to press the seam neatly into place. Don't use a seam roller on embossed papers, however, because it will flatten the texture and simply draw attention to the seam. Carry on measuring, cutting, and pasting until you have a continuous border.

Turning corners

Depending on the effect you want to create, there are two different ways of taking a paper border around a corner. The simpler of the two involves overlapping the paper from one wall to the next and then pasting over the overlap with your next strip of paper. Where you want to emphasize the shape of a room feature, however, mitered corners are very effective.

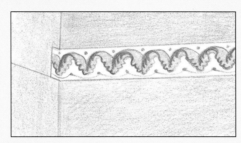

1 When turning a corner, take about ½in (12mm) of border paper around onto the next wall as an overlap. Never cut the paper flush with the corner. Then, cut and paste your next length of border and lay it over the overlap you have created.

Creating optical effects

Wallpaper borders can be purely decorative features or they can serve a more practical purpose, such as disguising a crack in a wall. Wallpaper borders are also useful for altering the apparent proportions of a room. By running the border at, say, the height of a traditional dado, you can visually break up the dimensions of a room – useful when you want to create an intimate, cozy atmosphere in a large or imposingly proportioned area. You can also use wallpaper borders to enhance the visual impact of a room's architectural features – stairways can look very stylish, for example, if they are outlined with a suitable border paper, or you can emphasize the slope of a ceiling or window recess in an attic room by following its line with a strip of border paper.

2 If creating a 90° bend, overlap the two pieces to cut diagonally through both layers.

3 Trim off the waste border and ease the edges together to make neat mitered seams. Use this technique to make a frame on a wall, mimicking the decorative plaster frames found on some walls. Press each seam lightly with a seam roller.

Above *An intricate border around a molding and door links with a simple star pattern on the walls and creates an optical effect.*

Ceramic wall tiles

In use for many centuries, ceramic tiles are highly decorative, hard wearing, hygienic, and easily maintained. Manufacturers produce a variety of patterns and colors that can be used for imaginative designs to blend with your existing fixtures and furnishings in bathrooms and kitchens.

Ceramic tiles are the perfect protection against water penetration and, therefore, are extensively used to decorate any room where water is in frequent use. But ceramic tiles should not be used only in specific parts of rooms, such as protection behind baths and sinks, they should also link these areas decoratively with the rest of the room – for example, by using them as surfaces for bathtub panels or kitchen counters to give a coordinated finish.

Ceramic tiles for floors are more robust than those used for walls. Floor tiles are more like those tiles used for kitchen counters and other surfaces that need to be hard-wearing.

Right *The decorative theme established on the walls can be taken through to the floor.*

Below *Non-patterned tiles can be used on their own or teamed with border or other tiles featuring all kinds of repeating decorative patterns.*

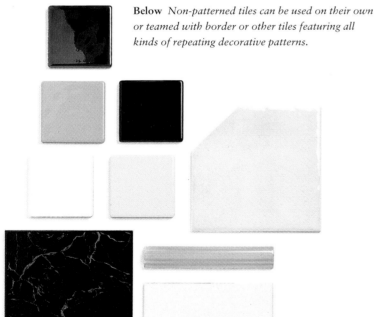

Tile sizes

The best size of tile to use depends on the area to be covered. The 6in (15.2cm) square size, for example, may be best for large expanses of wall, since you can cover a given area in less time using large tiles than you can with smaller ones. Tiles measuring 4¼in (10.8cm) square work particularly well in small rooms – such as bathrooms – where the tiles have to coordinate with fixtures and may form a major part of the decor. These tiles make for easier cutting and shaping around typical built-in bathroom fixtures – cabinets and sanitary ware – and other awkward areas, such as recesses and window rabbets.

Bear in mind that some imported tiles are available only in metric sizes, including 4in (10cm), 6in (15cm), and 8in (20cm). Always check carefully that you know the precise size that you are intending to use before figuring out the quantity you need.

Smaller than the standard sizes already mentioned are tiny mosaic tiles. These obviously take much longer to mount in position, but they can look extremely attractive as low splashbacks around, say, kitchen counters. Find out the colors available and then find a pattern that uses them to best advantage. You could create a geometric pattern, for example, or simply use graduated shades of the same color across the area to be covered.

Rectangular tiles are available, too, for creating interesting herringbone and other traditional brickwork patterns, and there are other shapes that interlock for special decorative effects.

You can also choose from lines of extra-large ceramic tiles. These tend to look best covering very large areas of wall – and perhaps the ceiling, too – and they can produce dramatic, eye-catching effects.

Plain and patterns

It can be difficult to know how to intersperse decorative feature tiles among plain ones to create the best effect. In order to get a feel for the right design balance, first cut out tile-sized squares of paper and tape them to the walls, then move them around until you are happy with the effect. In general, it is best to keep feature tiles at least one tile out from the corners of a room. If you don't, the eye will tend to be drawn to the wall edges and away from the central areas of pattern.

Tile spacing

For a professional-looking finish, it is vital to get the spacing even between the individual tiles, otherwise the grouting will accentuate these irregularities, especially a colored grouting. To get the spacing correct between tiles, plastic spacers are available. These are left in place and grouted over. Other tiles have sloping edges and are laid so that they abut. The grooves thus formed are then grouted and even tile spacing is assured.

Estimating quantities

When planning a tiling job, draw an accurate room plan on graph paper, using each square to represent one tile. As a general rule, to figure out the quantity needed, measure the width and height of the area, expressing the dimensions as so many whole tiles, and rounding up as necessary. Multiply the two figures together, and add 10 per cent extra to allow for cutting and some inevitable breakages. Try to order all the tiles you need for the job at the same time. Variations in the firing process can mean that batches of tiles differ slightly in appearance.

Tiles commonly come in boxes of 25 or 50, or in packs to cover, say, one square yard. Included will be tiles for both main body tiling (unglazed edges) and for external corners (finished edges). Before ordering, figure out how many edging tiles are needed, and check there are enough in the pack or box.

Tools and materials

You will need a tile cutter, a level with a vertical vial, a steel ruler, a few long, straight wooden battens, a serrated adhesive spreader (usually supplied with the adhesive), tile clippers or pincers, a sponge, and a soft cloth.

Basic tiling materials are spacers, if needed (or matches will do), plus adhesive and grout. For condensation-prone areas, or those areas that will get regular soakings – as in a shower stall or behind the lavatory – use water-resistant adhesive and a good-quality waterproof grout.

Above Tiles are often used in the kitchen, not only because they offer hardwearing floors, but because of their decorative qualities. This is a good example of mixing plain and decorated tiles on the walls.

Above Patterned tiles can be used to create an overall design or interspersed among plain background tiles to become random feature tiles.

Cutting and installing

The principal fact to remember about ceramic tiles is that they are brittle. This means that once you have introduced a line of weakness, by scoring a straight line in the tile, for example, it can be relatively easily snapped. More problematic, however, is shaping a tile to fit around a pipe or the edge of a sink. Here, it is best to nibble away at the tile until you have the shape you need.

When marking tiles for cutting, never use a felt pen on the tile's reverse side. The ink may soak through the tile and appear as a stain under the glaze where you cannot reach it.

Marking

❶ To help you position your tiles, mark a long, straight batten with tile widths along its length to act as a gauge stick, allowing gaps for grouting. Next, tape tile-sized paper squares to the walls to remind you where any patterned tiles will be set. As well, mark the positions of special tiles – those carrying a soap dish or towel ring.

Mark out a rough tile grid on the wall, starting on the window wall. Use your gauge stick to get the right balance horizontally, then use the stick vertically to ensure you will get a whole tile at the window sill. Avoid having cut tiles where they will show. If you need to do any tile cutting at floor level, make a pencil mark to indicate the base of the first full tile above floor level.

If you are tiling a large area and have several boxes, always take a number of

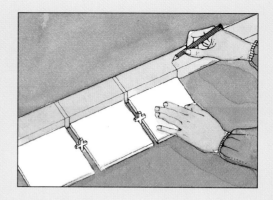

tiles from each one and mix them up to minimize the effect of any variation in color between boxes. Lay out a row on the floor, positioning them to the marks you have made on the walls. Check for balance on each side of the window. Look at any pattern on the tiles. Is it really random, or is there a motif that suggests that the tiles should go a certain way up?

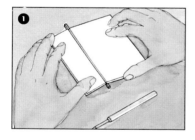

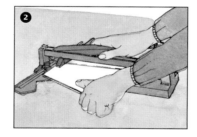

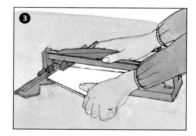

Cutting

❶ Mark the tile on the glazed side with a china marker and, once only, run a tungsten-tipped stylus cutter along it, guided by a steel ruler. Press hard enough just to penetrate the glaze. Place matchsticks under the score line and press each side to snap the tile.

❷ If shaping tiles with pincers or pliers, mark and score the line with a pencil and stylus first. Support the tile on a flat surface with the area to be shaped overhanging. Hold the tile firmly and start nibbling away from the tile edge, slowly working to the score line.

❸ Use a platform cutter for extra-hard tiles. Set the gauge to the width of tile to be cut; position the tile on the platform and, gripping the cutter arm, use it to push the cutting wheel across the tile. Exert just enough pressure to leave a score mark.

Then snap the tile between the jaws at the end of the arm, or by applying downward pressure on the arm.

❹ A tile saw simplifies the task of cutting irregular tile shapes. The saw has a circular cutting blade, tipped with tungsten carbide, held in a metal frame. The blade cuts in any

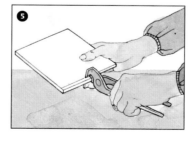

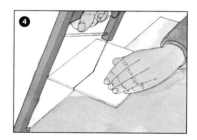

direction, and the size of the frame enables you to turn the saw around a tile without obstruction.

❺ If a pipe has to pass through a tile, mark the hole position, then cut the tile in two through the center. Nibble away the waste from each half until you have the right shape.

❻ A template former, or profile gauge, is a helpful tool for drawing awkward shapes. It consists of a number of needles or strips of plastic held in a frame. When pressed against a shaped surface, the tool takes up its exact shape, which you can then transfer to a tile by following the outline with a china marker.

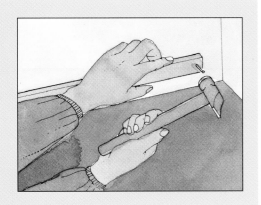

2 Starting on the window wall, look for the pencil mark representing the first full tile above floor level, and position a batten there. Check the batten is horizontal with a level, then secure it to the wall with masonry nails. Position a vertical batten at the outer edge of the first row of full tiles from the corner. Check the batten is vertical and secure it.

Materials and equipment

- China marker and steel ruler
- Wood for batten, hammer, and nails
- Carpenter's level
- Tile adhesive and notched spreader
- Tungsten-tipped cutting stylus
- Platform cutter
- Tile saw
- Pincers or pliers
- Profile gauge
- Tile grout and spacers
- Polishing cloth

Grouting

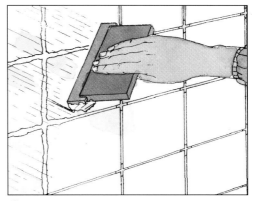

1 If the grout is in powder form, mix it to a thick paste according to its instructions. Grout from a tub is ready-mixed. Force the grout into the gaps between the tiles, making sure no holes are left.

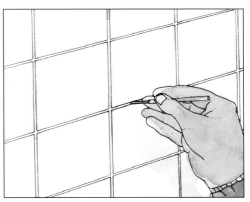

2 Wipe away surplus from the tile surface, then smooth the grout with the special grouting tool supplied with tiling kits. Alternatively, make use of an item such as the top of a ballpoint pen.

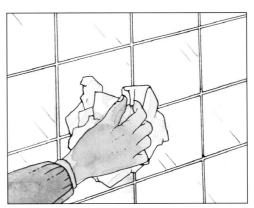

3 Allow the grout to dry, then rub the surface of the tile with a cloth. This removes surplus grout and polishes the tiles at the same time.

Installing

1 Starting at the batten, apply tile adhesive to the wall with the notched spreader, covering about 1 sq yard (1 sq m) at a time. The spreader should leave a layer about ⅛in (3mm) thick. Lift away any surplus adhesive.

If you find it easier, you can apply the adhesive to the wall with a small trowel, and then use the notched spreader to get the correct thickness.

2 Place your first tile against the wall on the inside corner of the batten, pressing it firmly in place. Try not to slide the tiles into position, since this forces adhesive up onto the tile edge.

With the first tile in place, insert a cross-shaped spacer at the top corner and position your next tile alongside so that it sits tightly against the spacer.

Continue tiling until the horizontal run is complete. You can leave cut tiles until later, completing all full tiling in an area of wall first.

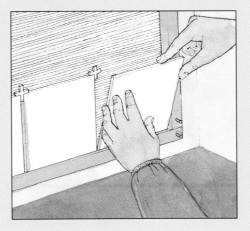

Awkward spots and fittings

Equipped with good-quality tile cutters and a degree of patience, tiling around tricky shapes and into recesses should be a reasonably straightforward task – provided that you plan for it carefully in advance. As for fixtures, remember that many of these, particularly for bathrooms, can be bought integrated with a tile. If you do have to drill to make a fixing, there is a simple technique for avoiding the risk of cracking the tile.

If you are planning a room from scratch, or building partition walls, ledges, or recesses in an existing room, take the size of tiles to be used into consideration from the outset to avoid too much tile cutting and shaping later on.

Below *Bathroom accessories finish off a room and are important decorative items. All of these can be drilled and installed easily on tiled walls and other surfaces using the technique shown opposite.*

Tiling around corners, doors, windows, and fixtures

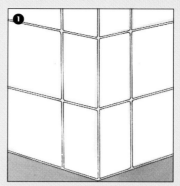

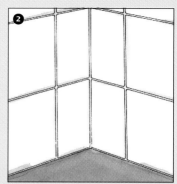

1 Finish external corners with edging tiles, equally cut. With patterned tiles, it is better to use whole glazed-edged tiles and work away to where a cut tile and a pattern break are less obvious.

2 Internal corners should, wherever possible, be completed with tiles cut to equal size. With patterned tiles, use the pieces left from tiling one wall to begin the next. This maintains the continuity of the pattern.

3 The door into a room is very much a focal point, so try to maintain a visual balance by tiling around it evenly, using whole tiles. The

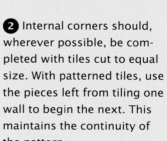

door frame may not be vertical, so don't use it as a guide for your tiling rows unless it is completely true.

4 A window is an important focal point in a wall. For symmetry, position the tiles within the recess on each side of the exact center line, and

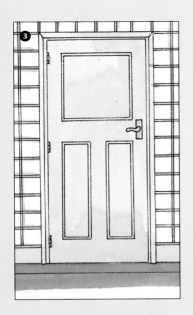

make the tiling of the wall as a whole correspond.

5 Try to tile around sinks and other fixtures in a symmetrical fashion. Ideally, plan to use a row of whole tiles above fixtures, since cut tiles can look messy. Where this is impossible, be sure to fill any gaps with good-quality waterproof sealer.

6 In bathrooms, light fixtures can be fitted with a cord pull. To produce a neat

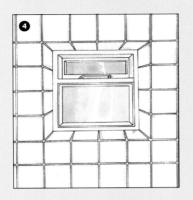

finish around a razor outlet, turn off the power, undo the screws in the face plate, and ease the front of the switch clear of the wall. Tile up to the edge of the mounting box so that the faceplate will cover the cut edges of the tiles when you screw it back in place.

Drilling

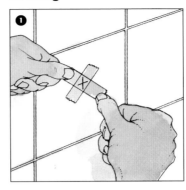

The problem with drilling into ceramic tiles is penetrating the glaze without the drill tip skating over the surface. Use a pointed tile bit or a sharp masonry bit. Don't, however, drill right through the tile into stone or brick with a tile bit. If you have a variable-speed power drill, run it at its slowest setting to maximize your control. Never use a power drill set to hammer action – the vibration will shatter the tile.

1 Mark the spot to be drilled with a china marker, then apply two strips of clear tape in a cross over the spot. This helps hold the bit in place until the glaze is pierced.

2 Insert a drill bit wide enough to let the shaft of the

screw pass through. Hold the bit firmly against the spot for good contact. Apply gentle pressure while drilling.

3 Push the anchor gently into the drilled hole and use a screw that matches the anchor for size. Don't attempt to force the screw. If it does not pass through freely, widen the hole with a larger bit.

Tiling a recess

Planning the work carefully in advance is one of the secrets of doing a good job of tiling a room, taking into account such architectural features as recesses. For a professional appearance, make sure that the tiles are "balanced" across a window recess – in other words, that the cut tiles on each side of the recess are in symmetry. Tiles on external corners must have glazed edges.

1 To produce the neatest effect, tiles lining a window recess should project to overlap those on the wall. The tiles in the recess should therefore have glazed edges.

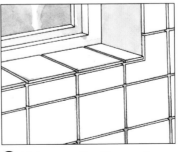

2 Make sure the tile spacings in the recess are precisely in line with those on the wall. Use cut tiles with glazed edges at each end of the ledge to finish it off neatly.

3 Start the sides of the recess with a cut, glazed-edge tile so that the spacings remain exactly consistent with those between the horizontal rows on the wall.

Splashbacks, showers, and counters

Some tiling projects call for attention to particular details, and for the use of specialized materials. This is especially true of showers, when it is vital to seal every gap to prevent water penetration. Also, should you wish to replace the tiles behind, say, an existing bathtub, or anywhere else, it may be possible to leave them *in situ* and simply tile over them.

Right *This fully tiled shower stall looks dramatic – but it takes a lot of work.*

Below *When tiling around fixtures, always use water-resistant adhesive and grout.*

Splashbacks

If you have never tried tiling before, then tackling a small area such as a "splashback" is a good introduction. Check that the back of the lavatory is horizontal – if it is, the tiles can follow this line.

With a freestanding lavatory, extend the tiling by one tile on each side. Place a ruler across the back of the lavatory and mark a pencil line on the wall where the extended tiles will sit. Pin a piece of masonite to this line to give the tiles something to rest on while the adhesive sets.

Use water-resistant adhesive to set the tiles and waterproof grout to finish. If the wall is papered, apply adhesive to the back of the tiles that overlap the paper, within ⅛in (3mm) of the edges, rather than risk getting adhesive on the paper. If this does happen, wipe off the adhesive immediately.

Shower stalls

In most situations a shower stall will involve two walls of the room, but should a third wall need to be constructed, use marine plywood on a framework of pre-treated lumber. The plywood will be unaffected by damp. Make sure you use both waterproof adhesive and grout.

The most vital factor with a shower stall is to ensure that all gaps are carefully sealed, particularly where tiles meet the shower tray. The tray must be firm, not flexible, and meeting edges must be dry before you apply sealant.

Use silicone rubber sealant, either clear or in a color to match the tray as closely as possible. Leave the sealant to set before you use the shower. Always follow the manufacturer's instructions.

Preventing water penetration

Sealing gaps is also important behind sinks and bathtubs. Use silicone rubber sealant or a plastic sealing strip, stuck in place with the adhesive supplied or with a clear silicone rubber sealant. Ceramic quadrants, or edging tiles, may be available in matching colors. Stick these to the wall with waterproof adhesive and seal them to the fixture with silicone rubber sealant.

Kitchen counters

Tiles for counters must be tougher than those used on walls. Flooring-grade tiles can also be used.

Applying sealant

Applying sealant so that gaps are completely filled can be a difficult job. Some dispensers have winged applicators that help to shape the sealant as it leaves the cartridge, but when using a straight nozzle the simplest way of getting a neat result is to run a strip of masking tape on each side of the area to be sealed. Apply the sealant between the tape, and then, while it is still soft, wet your finger and run it quickly along the sealant, pressing it in and shaping it precisely. Next, carefully pull the masking tape away from the wall straight away, leaving behind a neat line of sealant. If any sealant does stray and starts to set, let it cure and then cut it with a sharp blade and peel it away to leave a clean finish.

Since these tiles are tougher than normal, you may find that your existing tile cutter cannot cope. In this case borrow or rent a heavy-duty cutter that can handle tiles of about ⅓in (10mm) or more thick.

Try to plan your counter so that you can use multiples of tiles without the need for cutting. This will also look neater. Shaping can be a problem, however, for while a tile saw will cut hard tiles, its blade will blunt quite quickly.

Some counter tiles have matching edging strips to give a neat, rounded look to tiling. For many tiles, however, you will need to produce an edging, and this can be formed with plastic trim strips designed to lay under the row of edge tiles as they are laid.

Always use waterproof adhesive, and space the tiles with the larger spacers used for floor tiles. Finish with waterproof grout, and seal seams between counters and walls with a silicone rubber sealant or with a plastic edging strip. Some of the latter may need sticking in place with the adhesive supplied, while others are self-adhesive.

Right *Counters need to be covered with hard-wearing tiles, such as those made for flooring.*

Tiling over old tiles

If you have a room where old tiles are firmly attached to the wall and removing them could be a problem, you can tile over them, provided that the surface is firm, flat and clean.

Start one tile up from the floor, working to a horizontal batten. To save drilling into the old tiles, hold the batten in place using a number of double-sided adhesive pads.

If the walls were previously half-tiled, you will end up with a thick ledge where the tiling ends. Finish this with edging tiles or make a feature of the step by bonding a hardwood strip along the top.

When attaching towel rods and other hardware, use anchors and screws that are long enough to reach into the wall behind – the old tiles alone will not support the weight of these fixtures.

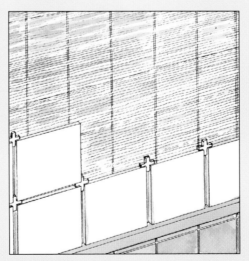

1 If removing the existing tiling is likely to cause damage to the supporting wall, you can tile over the top if they are firmly attached. Lay out new tiles so that the joints of the old and new tiles don't align. Simply use conventional tile adhesive.

2 Where the existing tiling finished part of the way up the wall, you will be left with a wide ledge of double-thickness tiles. Either finish off this edge with hardwood strips or use tile edging tiles.

Textured tiles

As well as providing a decorative surface in a vast range of colors and patterns, tiling, especially non-ceramic types, also has the dimension of texture. How this aspect of wall or ceiling tiles affects the appearance of a room depends, to a large degree, on the type of lighting employed. Frontal lighting tends to suppress the appearance of texture because the peaks and hollows that make up the surface are equally lit. To emphasize texture, use oblique lighting, which throws the hollows into shadow and highlights the peaks.

Below *Cork tiles make a warm, decorative wallcovering for bathrooms and other rooms, and they do much to camouflage poor wall surfaces.*

Cork wall tiles

Most people think of wall tiles as being of the glazed ceramic variety, but for a textured finish to a room there are other types, such as cork.

Cork tiles, as well as a being a popular choice as a floorcovering, also make a decorative surface in bathrooms, where they contribute to insulation and warmth; in offices and children's rooms, where they can double as bulletin boards; and in other rooms where they are used simply as a decorative device.

Cork tiles are most commonly 12in (30cm) square and about ⅛in (3mm) thick. The type suitable as a wallcovering are usually untreated, whereas flooring-quality types are sealed.

Always use the adhesive recommended by the tile manufacturer. Contact adhesives are applied both to the wall and to the back of the tile, while cork adhesive is spread only on the wall. It is important that the wall should be clean and free of grease.

HINTS AND TIPS

- Natural cork is difficult to clean, so consider treating the tiles with a clear (or, if you wish, colored) polyurethane sealer in a room where frequent cleaning may be necessary.

- When tiling into corners, cut the last tile by holding a tile over the last whole set one. Then take another tile and place it over the two, but reaching right into the corner. Mark a line along the edge of the top tile onto the surface of the middle one and cut along it with a craft knife to give a perfect fit.

- Battens for installing fibrous tiles on a ceiling need to be screwed into each joist to support the combined weight of the tiles.

Above *Mirror tiles are perfect in a bathroom, but the supporting wall must be perfectly flat.*

Don't worry if the surface is uneven as long as it is reasonably firm – cork tiles are very forgiving and do an excellent job of camouflaging rough surfaces,

With the aid of a plumb line and level, mark vertical and horizontal starting lines for the tiling work. Even though cork tiles abut closely and do not show obvious seams, it is still worth applying the same principles of good procedure as you would when installing ceramic tiles, so cut tiles at each end of a wall are in symmetry.

Mirror tiles

Convenient for bathroom use, mirror tiles are usually supplied with self-adhesive pads or strips attached to their reverse side. If you intend to install more than one, bear in mind that any unevenness of the supporting surface behind may cause the faces of the tiles to produce some very distorted reflections. Unless walls are perfect, it may be preferable to install a sheet of plywood backing to the wall first, and then stick the mirror tiles to it for a completely distortion-free finish.

Quarry tiles and mosaics

Although equally hardwearing as ceramic tiles and requiring similar installation techniques, quarry tiles are unglazed and have more of a casual, country appearance – a look that is emphasized by their predominantly earthy coloration. Quarry tiles contain a high proportion of quartz and are not particularly porous, which makes them a suitable choice for kitchens. There may be slight natural color variations in quarry tiles, even in those from the same batch – a fact you can exploit when planning a color scheme. Small quarry tiles in a variety of shapes are also available, and these are suitable for creating mosaic patterns.

If left untreated, quarry tiles have a matte appearance. If you want to produce a more shiny finish, then you need to treat them with linseed oil and turpentine.

Right Quarry tiles are a natural accompaniment for wood in a country-style kitchen. **Below** *A mosaic "splashback" made from water-worn pebbles.*

Ceiling tiles

Made from a variety of synthetic materials, ceiling tiles can add interesting textural qualities to a ceiling. These tiles are also a useful means of disguising a ceiling that is in poor condition.

Styrofoam acoustic tiles are the most common, and are usually 12in (30cm) or 24in (60cm) square with chamfered edges. They should be attached with special tile adhesive, which must be spread over the whole ceiling. Don't use the "five-blob" method of installing – in a fire, tiles melt away from the glue and drop from the ceiling. Modern tiles are self-extinguishing grade (SX), so they are not a great fire risk.

To calculate how many tiles you need, divide the squared area of one tile into the squared ceiling area.

It is best to find the center of a room, as with floor tiling, and tile out from a center point. However, if there is a true, straight wall at the entrance to the room, you could start there and work away.

Fibrous tiles and gypsum plaster tiles are also available for ceiling work, but since they are much heavier, they must be tacked to battens screwed to the ceiling. Find out which way the ceiling joists run and anchor the battens at right angles, spaced so that the ceiling tiles meet at their centers.

Battens of ½ x 1in (1.5 x 2.5cm) are enough for most tiles. If they are tongued and grooved, no cross-pieces are necessary, but with some square-edge tiles, it may be best to install cross-pieces between the battens to give support on all edges. Tack the tiles through the edges, or use special clips hidden by the adjoining tiles.

Painting ceiling tiles

If you wish to paint your tiles, the ideal time to do this is before you put them up. Bear in mind that the surface of non-ceramic tiles is not necessarily robust, and so you need to take a degree of care to avoid damaging them. Use either latex or special fire-retardant paint. Never use gloss paint, since it can contribute to the spread of flames should there be a fire.

Wood stains and varnishes

All articles made of wood need treating with a preservative or finish, not only to preserve and protect the surface but also to bring out the inherent beauty of the grain and the texture of the wood itself.

The finish of the wood is an extremely important factor. Although painting would hide any slight surface defects, any blemish in wood is immediately accentuated when a clear finish, or a stain followed by clear finish, is applied. It is important, therefore, that all woodwork is clean and smooth before decorating work begins.

When a clear finish is to be applied, it is essential that you give the surface a final sanding by hand, following the grain of the wood. If an orbital electric sander has been used at any stage, small circular scratches, resembling fish scales, will be seen in the final coat.

Non-pigmented finishes

All finishes alter the color of wood to some extent, and some woods – mahogany and walnut, for example – turn much darker even when a completely clear finish is applied.

An approximate idea of the color wood will take on when treated with a clear finish can be seen by dampening a small area with ordinary water. If this color is too light for your needs, then the wood can be stained before finishing. It is only possible to stain wood to a darker color; for a lighter shade it must be bleached.

When staining wood, it is advisable to test the stain on a scrap of wood, or on an area that would normally be out of sight. It is notoriously difficult to remove stain, even immediately after it has been applied.

If the wood has an open grain and a smooth finish is required, then you will need to use a grain-filler to fill the pores. The alternative is to apply extra coats of the finish, sanding with an abrasive paper between coats. Fill any cracks or holes in the wood with a wood-stopping material before applying the stain.

The final finish may be of a type that gives a surface film, such as French polish, varnish, or polyurethane. The latter two are available in gloss, satin, and matte finishes. Varnish stains are also available. These are convenient, since they will color and finish the wood in a single operation.

Do bear in mind that each extra coat of varnish stain will darken the color of the wood and, unless brushed out very evenly, the color will vary with the thickness of the film. When wood is stained with a penetrating dye, the color will not vary – no matter how many coats of clear finish you later apply.

Don't neglect to treat areas of woodwork that are normally out of sight. For example, when varnishing an external door, it is important that at least one coat is applied to the top and bottom edges; otherwise, water may penetrate at these points and eventually cause the varnish to fail.

Oil finishes

Oiled finishes, such as teak oil and Danish oil, are a useful alternative to finishes mentioned above. They are also easier to apply than polyurethane and varnish. On new wood, you will need to apply two coats, either with a brush or a mildly abrasive pad, cleaning off excess oil with a cloth. Teak oil and Danish oil leave the wood with a soft, lustrous finish that is truly resistant to liquids.

When a high-gloss finish is required on exterior woodwork, consider using yacht varnish. This usually contains tung oil, which has outstanding exterior durability.

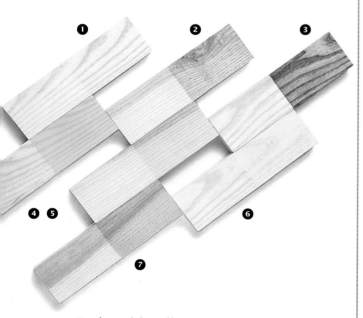

Finishes and their effects on sycamore:
1 Matte polyurethane varnish 2 Tung oil
3 Patinating wax-black 4 Yellow acrylic stain
5 Gloss polyurethane varnish 6 Liming paste
7 Staining varnish

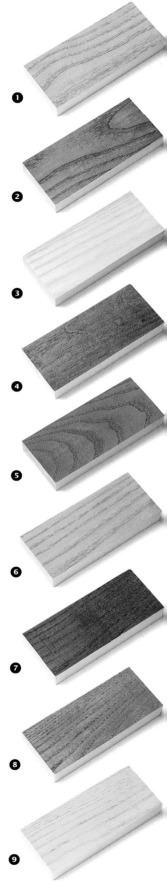

Selection of dyes on sycamore.
1 Ash grey 2 Medium oak 3 Light oak 4 Walnut
5 Bright green 6 Apricot 7 Deep mahogany
8 Mulberry blue 9 Antique pine

Waxing

This is popular for treating newly stripped pine. Some waxes color the wood a little – improving the bleached-out look of pine that has been immersed in a caustic solution, and giving the surface an "antiqued" appearance. If you don't wish to alter the look of the pine, make sure the wax you buy is colorless.

Always sand the wood down first with a fine-grade of steel wool. If the wax is applied with a soft cloth, it will produce a natural satin finish. If you want a higher gloss, however, allow the new wax to dry completely and then buff it vigorously with a soft dustcloth or clean, soft shoe brush.

Right *When stained to produce the right color and then treated with a protective top coat of varnish, the true beauty of natural wood is unsurpassed.*

French polishing

This traditional form of wood treatment produces a rich, deep, lustrous finish, and is often applied to fine furniture. However, applying French polish is a skilled task for which you will need energy, patience, and a willingness to follow the instructions supplied. As a basic guide, use this sequence of steps.

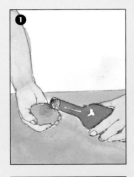

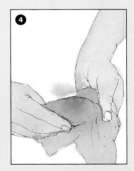

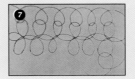

1 To charge the fad, remove the cloth and saturate the batting with polish. Replace the cloth and squeeze until the polish oozes through.

2 Rub the fad along the grain with a minimum of pressure, overlapping each stroke. Too much pressure will force out too much polish and leave the surface sticky.

3 Leave the polish to dry for 10 minutes and smooth the surface with abrasive paper.

4 Dust the surface to remove any grit and then fill the fad with polish again.

5 Now work the fad along the grain of all the surface, overlapping each stroke.

6 Next, work the fad in a series of figure eights.

7 After that, work the fad in a flowing, circular movement.

8 Finally, work along the grain of the wood once more, overlapping each stroke.

9 If the wood is panelled, use the fad's nose to work the polish into the corners.

10 Use the fad's nose in the same fashion when polishing a carved wooden surface or when dealing with any awkward crevices.

145

Home fu

6

nishings

Fabrics

Decorating your home involves far more than selecting the most pleasing combination of wall and floor coverings. By incorporating fabrics – curtains, shades, furniture covers, and cushions – you can change the decor from plain, drab and lifeless to one that has softness, warmth, and vitality.

Fabrics are available in an enormous range of colors, patterns, textures, and weights. They vary from fine to coarse weave, shiny to rough surfaced, flimsy to heavyweight. Each is best suited to a particular range of uses and creates its own special effects. Heavy fabrics – primarily used for curtains and fitted upholstery – give a feeling of solidity, while sheer ones have a graceful movement that is ideal for loosely draped furnishings and curtains. Strongly patterned or textured fabrics can be used as a focal point for your decor. Ones with subtle designs and colors can complement your chosen color scheme or work as splashes of contrast.

Fabrics in the home

The range of possibilities for using fabrics in the home is enormous. By making your own home furnishings, you can select the colors, designs, and textures that best complement or contrast with your decorating scheme. If you have to make do with old furniture, you can give it new life by making slipcovers, tablecloths, or throws in your choice of fabric. Selecting the right cloth for your needs can be a daunting task, but, by following a few guidelines, you will soon be familiar with the fabrics and their relative merits.

Natural fabrics

Cotton is the most widely used natural textile. Its fibers are thin, fairly smooth, and very strong, and the material is economic to buy and easy to sew. A huge variety of cottons is available, varying in quality, thickness, weave, surface, and design. For example, some have a single-colored patterned weave; others have a printed design. Some have a glazed, shiny surface; others are plain and uncoated.

Of the self-patterned cottons, moiré is a good choice for a multicolored, lightweight-to-mediumweight, economical fabric, while damask is a single-color, mediumweight fabric that is a little more costly.

Many velvets are 100% cotton. They vary

Left The weave of a fabric – its coarseness or fineness – largely affects its textural appearance. All woven fabrics have warp and weft threads. The warp threads run the length of the material, from top to bottom, while the weft threads run across.

Slub silk has more texture than other types of silk. The silk yarn used is a little like unevenly spun cotton thread.

Plain silk often seems to shimmer in different colors, depending on how the light strikes it.

The long, strong fibers of cotton make it an easy material to sew – ideal for embroidered patterns.

The unevenly spun fibers of slub cotton give the material a random, self-patterned effect.

Machine-woven lace became popular in the 19th century. Most was used for making lace curtains.

Made from the fibers of the bark of the flax plant, linen is strong and smooth, and stiffer than cotton.

Left The use of pattern and colour dictates the mood of a room. Large, bold patterns and strong colours are more suitable for large areas. More restrained colours and patterns make an ideal background for other decorative items and themes.

enormously in quality and cost, and can be plain cut or have a looped weave – known as chenille. They have a warm, soft texture, but can be hard to sew as fluffy bits of pile tend to accumulate.

Inexpensive cottons in checks and stripes often have a mix of fibers from different origins. Check carefully because some are not colorfast or durable.

Chintz is a closely woven, lightweight, durable cotton fabric with a shiny, glazed finish. It usually comes in solid colors or a floral pattern and is generally used for furnishings in informal decor.

Linen – an ancient fiber from the stem of the flax plant – is another popular natural textile. It has a slightly uneven, coarse texture and matte appearance. Although linen is expensive, its long fibers make it very strong and durable.

Synthetic fabrics

Fabrics with synthetic mixes are also extremely popular and versatile. They are strong, hard-wearing and relatively inexpensive. Their main disadvantage is that they tend to attract dirt particles.

Synthetic dupion is a lightweight, fabric that hangs well and looks like silk. Economical and easy to sew, it is available in a range of plain colors.

Brocades are a heavier, better-quality synthetic mix of dull and shiny yarns in matching or contrasting colors. They come in a range of colors, patterns and thicknesses that make them an exciting choice for home furnishings.

Choosing fabrics

With so many fabrics to choose from, it is important to look at a selection in a large department store. Compare how they look, feel, and hang. Crush a corner of the fabric in your hand to see if it creases easily. Hold it up to the light to examine the weave – the closer the weave, the more durable the fabric. Examine the raw edge to see how readily it frays.

It helps to bring along sample swatches of any wall or floor coverings that you are trying to match. Keep in mind a balance of color, pattern, texture, and weight. If in doubt, ask for fabric samples and examine them at home before making any final decisions. The way the light interacts with the fabric is an important consideration, so don't make up your mind until you see the samples in your own home environment.

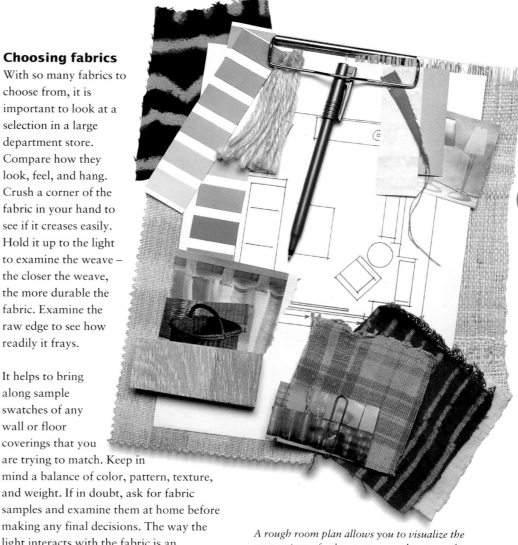

A rough room plan allows you to visualize the proportions of color, pattern, and texture of different fabrics before making any purchases.

Materials and equipment

- Hand-sewing needles – a comprehensive collection

- Upholstery needles

- Steel dressmaker's pins

- Pincushion

- Seam ripper

- Tape measure

- Tailor's chalk or pencil marker

- Polyester or cotton thread in assorted colors and weights according to fabric used

- Thread for basting

- Dressmaker's scissors

- Small embroidery scissors

- Paper scissors

- Pinking shears for finishing seams

- Sewing machine

- Steam iron and ironing board

Curtains

Everyone is aware that curtains serve a practical function – offering privacy and insulation from drafts. However, the role that they can play in a decorative scheme is frequently underrated. Varying enormously in size, style and material, curtains can have a striking influence on the mood and atmosphere of any room in your home. Floral cotton curtains, reaching to the windowsill, create a fresh, casual atmosphere, while elaborate floor-length velvet drapes give a stately formality.

The kind of curtains you choose depends on your personal preferences, your need for warmth and privacy, and the kind of atmosphere you are trying to convey visually. Your choice also reflects the physical characteristics of the room – the height of the ceiling, the dimensions of the window, and the amount of available light.

Right *Heavy floral curtains, made from an abundance of fabric, hang elegantly from a pole. Fabric of the same tones, but different pattern, is swirled and draped luxuriously. Furnishings in the room echo the colors in the curtains.*

Below *Elaborately frilled and scalloped floor-length voile curtains, combine with a very full sheer cafe curtain hung softly on a simple wire.*

This curtain heading uses pencil pleat tape and simple hooks attached to rings hanging from an iron pole.

A pleated curtain is made with triple pleat heading tape and pronged hooks hanging from a simple track.

Hand-sewn curtain headings, made from fabric loops secured with a button, suspend curtains from an iron pole.

Colors and patterns

Your choice of colors will be based largely on the atmosphere you want to create and whether the effect is to be warm or cool. Generally, colors in the red range are warm and lively; those in the blue range cool and relaxed. Colors become softer when muted with black or white.

Rich colors and strong patterns are better for large rooms, where there is space to make them a dominant feature. Smaller rooms look less overwhelmed with curtains in gentler tones and small, subtle patterns. Pale-colored curtains are a good choice for dark rooms, reflecting the maximum available light. If the decor is bland, you can make a feature of the curtains with highly contrasting colors and patterns. It is best to match the size of any pattern to the size of the windows. To unify a room, use matching or complimentary colors.

Left *A quilted-style fabric makes these bedroom curtains look warm and luxurious. The simple wooden pole allows the curtains to run freely on rings, so that they are either pushed wide open to allow light to enter, or tied back to prevent the room from filling with too much daylight or sunlight.*

Above right *Cool colors combine with fine iron work to create an elegant atmosphere to this room. An Eastern look is achieved by softly draping the window with a sheer oriental fabric and covering the chair seat with the same material.*

Right *A lively feature is created by hanging a light-colored pole with a bright yellow patterned curtain across the doorway. The colors bring freshness and sunshine to the room.*

Far right *The unusual pattern and shades of the curtains and bed cover reflect the wood in the room. Subtle pastel shades of the window curtains harmonize with the bed linens. Iron curtain hardware creates a rustic feel to the room and works together with the wooden beams, floor and furniture.*

Sheers and nets

Draping windows with sheer or net curtains has many advantages. Sheers and nets give a room daytime privacy, screen it from unpleasant views beyond the window, and at the same time let in plenty of softly diffused light. They also form a shield from the glare of the sun and lessen color fading of delicate fabrics.

Choosing a style

Nets and sheers can be hung like curtains – from tracks or poles – if they are to be opened. If they are to remain closed, hang them from spring wires. Alternatively fold or tie them in your own imaginative styles. If they have an intricate design, hang them without gathering the material.

There are natural and synthetic sheers and nets in all thicknesses, weaves and patterns. Examine as many samples as possible at home before making a choice.

Many shrink, so buy extra material and prewash it before measuring and cutting.

Sheer curtains are often made with a ready-stitched heading down one side and a finished edge down the other, and come in sizes to fit standard window lengths. All you have to do is sew the side hems.

Above *Hazy muslin drapes with a blue printed pattern that reflects the deep blue of the walls.*

Left *The texture of layers of lace is brought out by the strong sunlight pouring through the window.*

Making sheers and nets

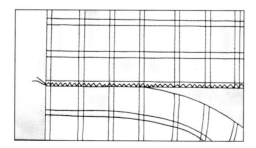

1 When cutting the fabric, carefully follow the line of the weave to ensure that the edge is even. Some weaves are prone to fraying. To prevent this, zigzag stitch along the cutting line before you cut it.

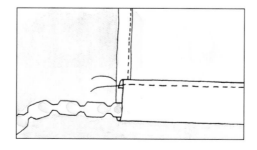

2 Sew the side and bottom hems in exactly the same way as for simple unlined curtains. Lightweight sheers and nets hang better if the bottom hem is weighted with flexible, lead-weighted tapes available from fabric stores.

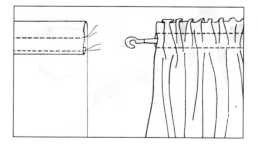

3 To make a heading for a spring wire, thin brass rod or wooden dowel, allow about 2in (5cm) of fabric. Turn under and fold again to make a 1½in (4cm) hem. Sew two rows of stitches to make a channel for the wire or rod.

fabric
delights

Below *This bathroom is enhanced with decorative fabrics which echo the wall frieze and fall softly to surround the bathtub.*

Left *This is an ornate, mediterranean style, glass-panelled door decorated with a heavy fabric which relates to all the other elements in the room - the mosaic wooden table, copperware, and floor rugs.*

Right *Detail of border fabric on bath drapes and window shade. This elaborate border brings a new atmosphere into a traditional bathroom.*

Above *A heavy satin cushion is accentuated by a tassel fringe, which picks up the color of the wall.*

Above *This upholstered chair is draped with a plain throw to soften the formal pattern of the fabric.*

Above *Rich velvets and plum browns create a warm atmosphere to a room.*

Left *A simple straight-backed chair is dressed with a cover which make a feature of large, elegant bows. This is a dramatic, yet simple way of finishing and securing the cover. The painted wood color of the chair matches the stripe in the fabric.*

Right *A beautiful finishing touch to this elegant cushion is provided by a softly knotted corner.*

Furnishing fabric can be used by the yard to drape walls, tent a ceiling or create a fantasy headboard; to make cushions, chair covers and throws; to decorate the dining table; to furnish the bedroom and bathroom with linen and to make household items such as sheets and mattress covers. Traditionally, fabrics are used for tents, and woven cloth decorates nomadic dwellings.

Light is an important factor in selecting fabrics. Not only does the climate in which you live have an impact from the outside, but the quality and amount of light inside your home is of great significance. Whether you are working with natural light or artifical light using bright or low levels of intensity, you will notice that it has different effects on the color and texture of the fabrics you intend to use.

Left *These elaborate bed curtains and quilted and fringed bed cover combine to create a luxurious effect. They are set off by the simple, fine lines of the iron work in the bed frame.*

Below *A crown of frothy white voile or gauze is a simple and effective addition to this country-style bed. The delicate, transparent material softens the hard lines of the wooden beam and traditional country images on the cushions.*

Above *A stunning arrangement of fabric, supported by a frame, gives this bed a luxurious appearance, with a hint of mystery.*

Left *Cushions and pillows match in an interesting mixture of muted tones and squares and stripes.*

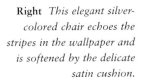

Right *This elegant silver-colored chair echoes the stripes in the wallpaper and is softened by the delicate satin cushion.*

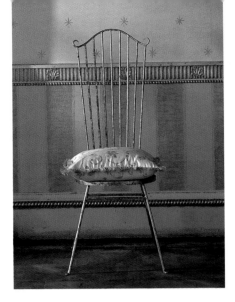

Below *Fabrics in the same family of color and tone, and patterns based on straight lines, work well together to create a lively, harmonious collection.*

Below *This bolster has an elaborate finish, including piping and silky tassels.*

Below *A strip of black and white tassels sewn onto the edges of a wicker chair transforms its image.*

Measuring

First select the style and decide the length of curtain – to either the sill or the floor. Once you have installed the curtain track or pole, select your curtain heading – always choose this before buying your fabric.

To estimate the amount of fabric needed for your curtains, measure the width of the track, and multiply by the number of widths the curtain heading dictates. Divide by the width that the fabric is sold in and round up to the nearest full measurement. The total figure is the number of widths you will need. Measure the length of the curtains, including an allowance for hems and headings. Add an allowance for any pattern repeats, and round your total figure up to the nearest half yard.

HINTS AND TIPS

- For gathered headings, allow material one and a half to twice the width of the track or pole.

- For pencil pleats, allow 5-6in (3-15cm) per pleat and about 4in (10cm) between them. Allow material about two and a half to three times the length of the track or pole.

- Allow extra for pattern matching. The larger the pattern, the more fabric you will need.

Making sheers and nets

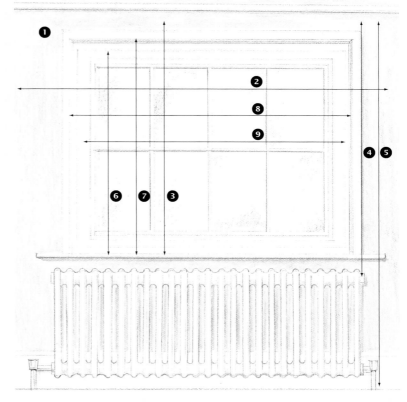

You can make curtains to hang to the floor, level with the top of a radiator, or to the sill. Remember to measure the width of the track, not the window frame itself. Take note of the measurements in the diagram above when planning curtains, shades, or blinds.

Curtains: **1** curtain track **2** measurement of track width **3** drop from track to sill **4** drop from track to top of radiator **5** drop from track to floor. Blinds: **6** height, without recess **7** height, inside recess **8** width, no recess **9** width, inside recess.

The lining

Curtains do not need to have a lining, but it's worth including one. Linings increase the life of the curtains by protecting them from sunlight, adding insulation and giving a fuller, more luxurious finish.

Once you know how much fabric you'll need for the curtains, it's a straightforward matter to figure out how much you'll need for the lining. Since the lining is slightly smaller than the curtain, simply allow 6in (15cm) less in the length and 5in (12.5cm) less in the width.

Making the calculations

Estimate the amount of fabric and take the pattern repeat into account, so that all widths match. Allow one complete repeat for every width except the first. For example, if you are joining widths, add an extra 12in (30cm) to the overall width of the the curtains to allow for turns and side seams,

For the headings, if you use a standard heading tape on short curtains, add an extra 8in (20cm) for hems and headings, and allow up to 15in (37.5cm) for deep headings on

full-length curtains. If you are using velvet, the pile of the fabric should always hang the same way.

The amount of fabric used depends on the width of the track or pole and the style of curtain heading. Use a generous amount of fabric to give fullness to the the curtains. As a rule of thumb, fabric should measure at least one and a half times the width of the window; if necessary, you can join narrow fabrics together. When buying, allow an extra half a yard for trimmings and tiebacks.

Curtains

Almost any upholstery fabric may be used for curtains, from heavy velvets to the lightest of cottons. The fabric should drape well to ensure the curtains hang in balanced, graceful folds from the gathered headings. Upholstery fabrics are normally wider than dress fabrics, so check the width of the fabric you intend to use before measuring and calculating fabric.

Lining fabrics specially designed for curtains are available in a range of colors, as well as white and off white. If you wish to use colored lining, check the effect with the fabric you intend to use, to see that the color of the lining does not affect that of the curtains when they are hung together. Curtain lining fabrics are usually slighter narrower than curtain fabrics: when calculating quantities simply use the same number of widths of fabric.

Materials

- Curtain and lining fabric

- Curtain tape and hooks or rings

- Sewing thread in predominant color of the fabric

- Needle – of length and thicknesses according to weight of fabric

- Long dressmaker's pins

- Marking pencil

- Strong thread and larger needle for making gathers

Making unlined curtains

Unless curtains are sheer, they will hang better when lined. However, there can be occasions when unlined ones are preferable, and the technique for making them is basic to any curtain.
Begin by matching patterns were necessary. Join the widths and any half widths using a flat seam. Trim off selvages or clip to prevent puckering. Press seams open.

❶ Turn in and press fabric 2in (5cm) on each side edge. Make a 1in (2.5cm) double hem, pin, and baste to within 2 1/2in (6.5cm) of the top edge and 6in (15cm) of the lower edge.

❷ Press in the miter at each corner, then turn in and press the raw edge to make the double 3in (7.5cm) hem. Use a loose slipstitch to sew the side hems for a more professional finish. Stitch the miter, then stitch the hem.

❸ Turn down and press 2½in (6.5cm) along the top of the curtain. Make a line of tacking 1½in (4cm) down from the foldline.
Cut tape to the width of curtain plus 2in (5cm). Pull out about 2in (2.5cm) of cords at each end of the tape. Knot the cords together on the wrong side at one end of the tape and knot them loosely together on the right side at the other end. Turn tape under 1in (2.5cm) at each end, pin, and baste the tape to the wrong side of the curtain with the top edge along the line of basting. Machine stitch the tape.

❹ Pull up the cord from the loosely knotted end to fit the track or rod, and space the gathers evenly. Knot the cords to hold them in position, then tie the ends and hide them behind the curtain with a stitch if necessary. Insert the hooks, and hang the curtains. Check the length and then make a 6in (15cm) hem and slipstitch.

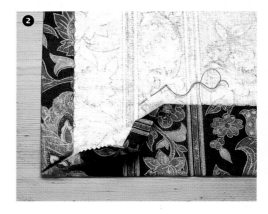

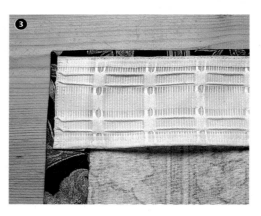

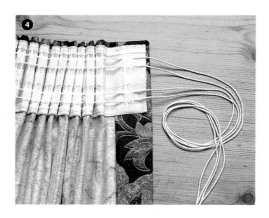

Making machine-stitched linings

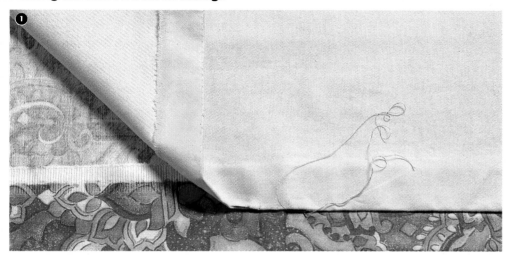

Unless curtains are specifically intended to filter light and create a semi-sheer effect, it is best to line them. This will give insulation and protect the main fabric from dirt and from being damaged by strong sunlight.

1 The lining should be cut to the size of the finished curtain. The finished curtain should be 5in (12cm) wider and 22.5cm (9in) longer than the lining. Position the lining on the curtain, right sides facing, with the top edge of the lining 3in (7.5cm) below the top of the main fabric, with side edges matching.

2 It is a good idea to secure the lining to the curtain as this helps the two layers to hang well together. With the lining facing you, work long catch stitches down the center of the lining, from top to bottom.

3 Adjust the two layers. Pin the side edges together. Machine stitch and press. Remove the selvages or clip the seam allowance. Turn a 6in (15cm) hem along the lower edge of the curtain, and a 2in (5cm) hem along the lower edge of the lining (which should be 2in (5cm) shorter than the main curtain). Press. Turn the lining and the fabric right side out. Slipstitch the remaining edges of the lining to the curtain.

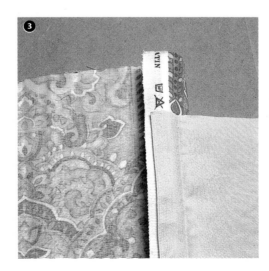

Curtain hardware– tracks and poles

Choose tracks or poles that are strong enough to support the weight of the curtains. They must also be long enough to overhang each side of the windows by 10-12in (25-30cm), depending on the fullness of the curtain (*see p. 90-91*). It is advisable to install tracks and poles before measuring curtains because the shape of the window or the style of curtains intended will govern where the hardware is placed. Curtains can also hang from ceilings, and in front of shelves.

Cotton heading tape

Gathering tape

Pencil pleat tape

Pinch pleat tape

Metal-pronged hook

Cotton lining tape

Standard hooks

Pin hook

HOME FURNISHINGS

6

155

Shades

Shades are an inexpensive alternative to curtains, and easy to make yourself. Be sure to balance the colour, pattern and style of your shades with the rest of the decor in the room.

In general, elaborate shade styles look better with plain fabrics, while simpler styles can benefit from colourful patterns. You can purchase kits to make shades and match the fabric with your own colour scheme. When not in use, shades can be rolled up out of the way to allow light and air to enter the room. Shades, made of paper with bamboo struts, are delicate and allow the light to filter through.

Below *A simple straight blind is given a more dressy finish by making a scalloped edge, with binding, and a colourful contrasting pelmet.*

Fixings and fittings

Roller blinds have a flat pin at one end for the slotted bracket and a round pin at the other end – incorporating the spring – for the drilled bracket. To fix the blind level, first screw one end bracket into position. Then slot in the appropriate end of the roller. Use a spirit level to check that the roller is horizontal, and then you can fix the other end bracket into the correct position.

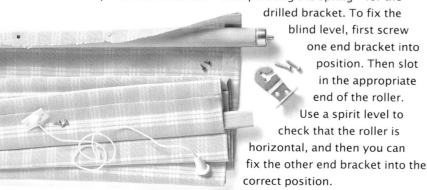

Styles of shades

The simplest and cheapest type of shade in the plain roller shade, made from stiffened fabric attached to a sprung roller. It requires a minimum of sewing and is widely available in kit form. The flat surface lends itself to almost any colour, pattern or design – whether muted background or bold focal point. You can add your own trim to complement the style of the rest of the decor or you can make a pelmet, covered with matching or complimentary fabric.

Roman shades have sewn-in vertical pull-cords that enable them to be pulled up into evenly spaced deep pleats. They can be lined or unlined, as long as you use fabric with an even weave. Roman shades look best in a solid colour or simple geometric pattern that follows the weave of the fabric. They can be trimmed with braid for extra interest.

Shades are traditionally used in kitchens and bathrooms, but with more elaborate styles you can introduce them into your bedroom or living room, and even consider combining them with curtains which close or with material that is draped over a pole.

Making Austrian shades

Austrian shades are made from fabrics, such as silk or chintz and gathered at the top like curtains, with or without a lining.

❶ Fix the blind track in position in the window recess. Measure the dimensions of the window and make up one piece of fabric to twice the width measurement and the length measurement plus 45cm (18in) for the heading and bottom hem. Hem sides of blind and fix vertical rows of looped tapes to reverse of the fabric. The outer rows should be 10cm (4in) from the hemmed edges. The inner rows should be at intervals of 30cm (12in).
For an optional frill at the bottom, cut a 16cm (6½in) wide strip of fabric to twice the width of the blind. Hem bottom edge and work two rows of gathering stitches along upper edge.

Measuring up

Decide where you want to fix the shades – either inside or outside the window recess. If the recess is deep, position the shade inside it, close to the window. Then measure across the recess and deduct 1.5cm (⅝in) on one side for the pin end and the same amount on the other side for the spring mechanism.

Next, position the shade brackets 3cm (1¼in) from the top of the recess to allow room for the full roller. The bracket must be level for the shade to roll neatly. Measure the drop of the shade from the roller to the bottom of the recess, add an allowance of 7.5cm (3in) both top and bottom.

If you're fixing your shade outside the window recess, decide on the fabric overlap on each side, and measure the total width.

For windows without recesses, the fixings will have to be mounted on supports above the window.

Right *This striking shade, set in a very white window frame , is outstanding for its bold, dark pattern which is echoed in the clear lines of stripes in the room.*

❷ Pull gathers evenly and then pin, tack and sew in position.

❸ Make headings as for curtains, fit gathering tape and curtain hooks, and hang shades in position. Fit a screw eye into window surround at top of each row of looped tapes. Cut lengths of cord – one for each row of loops. Make each cord twice the length of shade plus one width.

❹ Tie a cord end to lowest loop in each row. Pass each length of cord up through all loops in its row. Then pass all cords to the right through screw eyes along the track. All the cords will hang on the same side of the window. Knot them together and trim the ends level with the sill.

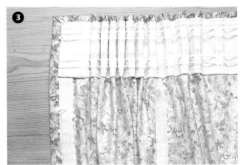

Furniture covers

When you are decorating your home, changing the entire decor can be extremely costly, and it's likely that you'll have to incorporate some existing furniture into your scheme. You may have a couch or armchair that is structurally sound but dull and threadbare in appearance. However, do not despair! Making your own furniture covers in a fabric that harmonizes with the colors and patterns of your decorating scheme is not as complicated as you may think – and it is an extremely effective and inexpensive way to bring new life and interest into a room.

Right *This beautiful cover looks elegant and is simple to achieve. Follow the method for a simple slipcover, and finish with self-color bows.*

Below *A classic style fitted slipcover with box pleats. This cover will need tucks and darts to achieve a precise fit over the arms and back.*

Selecting the fabric

There is a wide range of unhostery materials available, from which to select the one that best fits your scheme. Linen, chintz, velveteen and many synthetic fabrics are all suitable. Make sure that you choose a strong, firmly woven fabric that will hold its shape.

Solid colors are easiest to work with, since there is no pattern matching. However, fabrics with very small patterns are the most practical choice for a family home since they disguise marks – and may not need matching. Fabrics with bold floral patterns are very popular, but need extra care when cutting out because the motifs must be carefully centered and matched.

HINTS AND TIPS

● It's easy to mix up the pieces for a slipcover since they all look similar after cutting out. So, as you cut out each piece of fabric, add a small self-adhesive label to the wrong side indicating its intended position and direction, or number with white tailor's chalk.

● To join widths of fabric as inconspicuously as possible, sew them together so the seams correspond with the edges of the seat cushions.

Draped furniture covers

The easiest solution to revitalising a couch or armchair is to buy a length of attractive fabric and drape it over the furniture. How much you want it to overhang and how much you tuck it in depends of the style of the rest of the decor in the room. You can finish the cover with fringe, or a decorative trim or braid. A lovely drape can be achieved with an ethnic bedspread or a beautiful woven rug.

One way of breaking up the expanse of loosely draped material is to cover it with an array of brightly colored cushions. This is especially effective if you use scraps or remnants of expensive fabrics such as plain silk or brocade, and make small cushions in different sizes and shapes.

Right *This loosely draped cover is finished with a large knot tied in the soft fabric. An exquisite plain silk cushion is placed on the chair.*

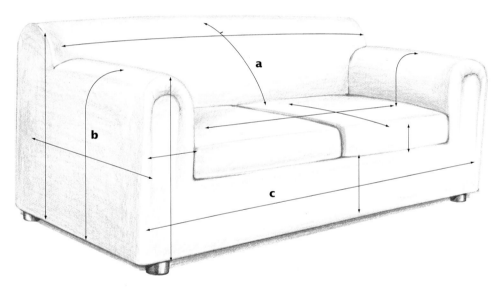

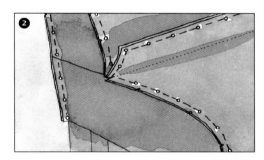

Loose furniture covers

Loose furniture covers are not hard to make, and with this method, the trick is to work directly onto the couch or chair. Working with the fabric inside out, so you can adjust the seams easily, mark the main lines with tailor's chalk and then simply cut out the main pieces as large rectangles - (a,b,c). Depending on the shape of your sofa, allow a generous amount of material, and sit on the sofa before trimming the material to the correct size and shape. Allow extra material if you have a pattern that needs matching.

1 First make a rough sketch of the sofa, and indicate the dimensions of each section as you measure it, as marked on the diagram. Always take measurements at the widest point widthwise and lengthwise, and add an allowance of 2in (5cm) for all the seams. If necessary, also include extra fabric for tucking in around the seat. Add an allowance for pattern matching.

2 Cut out all the panels on the straight grain of the fabric and position over the couch with the wrong side out. Pin to fit and then mark the seamlines. Remove the fabric, and baste with large, firm stitches, and take out the pins. Before machine stitching the seams, sit on the sofa to make sure you have allowed enough material for a generous finish.

3 You can attach piping, either in the same color or a contrasting one, to emphasize the shape of the couch. Measure the length of the seams that give definition to the edges of the furniture – the sides, top and front – and hand sew the piping over the seams. You can also use concealed piping to make a false hem. Smooth the cover into position on the sofa. Trim the lower unfinished edge all around and baste piping to right side of fabric. Remove the cover and machine sew the piping in place. Press the piping down and stitch the seam to the wrong side of the fabric.

Table linens

With a little imagination and a minimum of expense, the most worn-out of tables can be transformed into a decorative feature when draped with an eye-catching tablecloth. And you can turn any meal into a sense of occasion by displaying your own personalized tablemats and napkins as well.

It takes only the simplest sewing stitches to make a basic tablecloth, tablemat or napkin. And you can easily make them more special by adorning them in one of a variety of ways. For example, you can make the table linens from several different-colored fabrics – cut in strips, squares or other shapes and sewn in patterns much like a quilt. Alternatively, you can adorn them with embroidery or applique, or edge the border in satin ribbon, ruffles, or scallops.

Tablecloths give scope for all kinds of imaginative effects. You can superimpose layer upon layer of translucent fabric, put lace over darker contrasts, or drape and knot soft fabrics. You can knot the corners of a very large square tablecloth and if you have a round tablecloth, you could catch up the sides to make flounces.

Below A simple round table is transformed into a dining feature with a flowing circular tablecloth covered with a washable half-length gingham cloth.

Rectangular tablecloths

Rectangular tablecloths require the least effort to make – and with a large expanse of fabric, there's plenty scope for creativity. They look best with a drop of no more than 12in (30cm). When joining lengths of fabric, position the seams so they create a central panel or else fall along the overhang. Alternatively, you can take advantage of the shape of the tablecloth and make the separate sections of fabric an integral part of the design – especially if you are incorporating material in more than one color or pattern.

Some tables are suited to covering in heavier fabric such as tapestry or damask. The fabric can hang in rich folds that show off their pattern and texture.

Circular tablecloths

Small occasional tables can be covered with a floor-length cloth. However, circular dining tables, like rectangular ones, usually look best with tablecloths that have a drop of no more than 12in (30cm). The tablecloth will look better if you can make it from a single piece of fabric rather than joined panels.

Placemats

Individual placemats are often used instead of tablecloths, saving on laundering and adding to the festive mood of any occasion. They can look very attractive, especially if made in sets with matching or contrasting napkins. When planning the color and design of your placemats, think in terms of the presentation of the entire table display – including plates, flatware, napkin rings, glasses, flowers and, of course, the food you will be eating!

MAKING A RECTANGULAR TABLECLOTH

- Before measuring, decide on the length of the overhang. The width of material you'll need is the width of the tabletop plus twice the overhang. Add an allowance of ¾in (18mm) on each side if the cloth is to be edged with lace, ruffles, or other decorations, or is floor-length. Add 2in (5cm) to each side if it is plain hemmed. The length of material you'll need is the length of the tabletop plus allowances for overhangs and hems.

- If the fabric is not wide enough to make the tablecloth from a single piece, add side panels to the center (top) one, making sure to match any patterns.

- When sewing plain hems on a tablecloth, fold the corners neatly and finish by hand. The corners look neater if they are mitered, with seams like the corner of a wooden picture frame.

Making a circular tablecloth

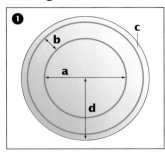

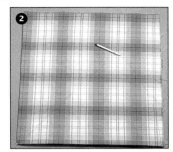

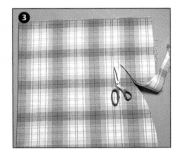

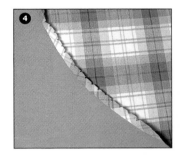

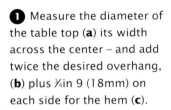

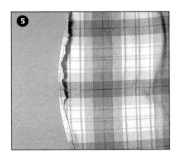

Circular tablecloths are not difficult to make and can enhance a simple, or even worn, table into an object of interest and delight.

1 Measure the diameter of the table top (**a**) its width across the center – and add twice the desired overhang, (**b**) plus ¾in 9 (18mm) on each side for the hem (**c**).

2 Now make an accurate paper pattern. To do this, take a large square of paper with sides slightly longer than the radius of the cloth (**d**) and lay it on a flat surface. Pin one end of a piece of string to the bottom left-hand corner of the paper and tie a pencil or piece of chalk to the other end, adjusting its position so that the pencil makes an arc the same length as the required radius. Draw an arc on the paper and cut the pattern on this line.

3 Fold the fabric in half and then in half again. Pin the curved pattern to the fabric and cut along the curved edge.

4 To prepare a plain hem, cut small V-shaped notches along the edge of the cloth, spacing them about 1in (2.5mm) apart and no deeper than ½in (12mm).

5 Turn in a ¾in(18mm) hem and bind the clipped edge with bias binding. If you wish, you can decorate the border with braid, tassels or a fringe.

Napkins

To finish off the table display, you can easily make your own napkins. Traditionally, cotton, gingham or seersucker are ideal fabrics for napkins. Napkins are usually square, and range in size from 12 by 12in (30 by 30cm) to 24 by 24in (60cm by 60cm). When marking up the fabric, allow at least 18mm (¾in) all around for double hems. for the neatest finish, mitre the corners. Handstitch, or disguise the machine stitching line with close zigzag stitching, or finish with a braid.

Top *A tapestry table runner, fringed on all sides, sets off the food on the old wooden table. The runner can be left on all the time, or removed when the table is used for a meal.*

Right *Fringing the edge of a napkin is easy to do and gives a hand-finished look. To start fringing, simply tease out a single thread with a needle, and gently pull it. Follow it round the edge of the fabric until the end of the thread. Depending upon the material, you may find that you need to ease the threads quite firmly in order to pull them out. Carry on pulling out threads until you have a fringe that is the depth you want.*

Cushions

Cushions mean comfort! Scattered plentifully or piled high, casually strewn or carefully placed, cushions create a welcoming atmosphere. Cushions vary from soft, small shapes and downy pillows, to foam pads and firm bolsters. With creative use of fabric, you can add a touch of surprise with cushions, by changing the covers according to your mood or the season of the year.

Quick Cover

This is an easy-to-make flapped cover.

1 Cut a strip of material 1¼in (3cm) wider and two-and-a-half times the length of the cushion. Turn both short edges under ½in (1.5cm), baste and press. Turn both edges under another ½in (1.5cm) to make double hems. Baste, press and stitch on the wrong side.

2 Centre cushion on right side of fabric, marking 4 corners of cushion with pins. Remove cushion and fold over both hemmed ends on the pins so that they overlap. When raw edges are level, baste and stitch both side seams, leaving ½in (1.5cm) seam allowances at each side. Turn cover right side out and insert cushion through overlapped opening.

Ruffles

An attractive finish to a cushion, ruffles can be a solid colour which coordinates with the main fabric. You can repeat a colour used for curtains, or reverse the main fabric and trim.

Allow three times as much fabric as the length around the edge of the cushion, and double the depth of the ruffle, plus seam allowances. Fold the fabric in half, wrong sides together and press. Gather by hand or machine, or fold into knife pleats or box pleats. Insert the ruffle into the cushion before the main seams are sewn up.

Cushion Pads Stuffing and Trimmings

You can buy ready made pads in a variety of shapes and sizes, stuffed with feathers, down or synthetic fillings.

If you want to make your own pads you will need to make your own casing. This can be made from lining material, old cotton sheeting, calico, or ticking. When you have decided upon the size and shape of your cushion, make the casing following the instructions for square or rectangular cushion covers.

Stuffing materials include foam chips, synthetic fibres, kapok (a vegetable fibre) and pieces of foam cut to size.

Cushions may be trimmed in a variety of ways. You can simply sew on bought braid or trimming (either by hand or with a sewing machine). However a more tailored finish can be achieved by using piping or a pleated frill, while the cushion is being made.

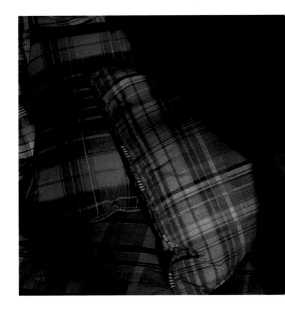

Above *Tartan check covers to cushions are given added richness with self-piping cord and trim.*

Below *The ethnic style furnishings are enhanced by the rich, burnished tones of the ceramic urns.*

Far left *Pillows are trimmed with corded piping, and the bolsters are knotted and tied with frayed corded tassels.*

Left *Beautiful, elegant pillows tied and finished with ribbons, tassels, and bows.*

Below *Extremes of color and pattern vie with each other for attention and delight the eye.*

Bottom *Floral tapestry cushions can be combined with quilting fabrics and patchwork designs to create a rich, and exciting array of pattern and texture.*

Square and Rectangular Cushion Covers

Measuring

Make the cushion cover the same size as the pad. Measure with a tape from end to end and side to side of the pad. Add 1in (3cm) seam allowance to each measurement.

Materials

- Fabric (if the fabric has a large pattern, allow extra material)

- Cushion pad

- Zipper if required - this should be 4in (10cm) shorter than the shortest edge of the cushion.

- Piping cord and braids need to go around the edge of the cushion, plus an extra 1in (3cm).

Method

Lay the fabric flat and draw cutting lines with tailor's chalk. Cut out, following the grain of the fabric as far as possible.

❶ Place the two pieces of fabric together, right sides facing and raw edges matching. Pin, and baste and stitch around 3 sides. Finish raw edges. Stitch about 2in (5cm) from each end of

the fourth side toward the center. Clip corners, press seams, and open edges.

❷ Turn the cover right side out and put the cushion pad in. Push the pad right into the corners. Finish the cover by hand sewing (slipstitch) the opening. If a zipper is required, insert before the side seams are sewn up.

163

Piping

Piping is made by covering a purchased piping cord with bias strips of fabric which is stitched into a flat seam to give a tailored finish. The cord is available in different thicknesses, so choose the size according to the scale of the item you wish to pipe. Shrink cotton cord before use or it will cause the piping to pucker during washing. To do this – boil the cord in water for five minutes and allow to dry thoroughly.

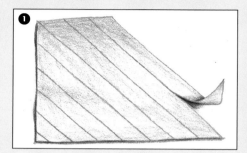

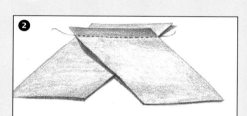

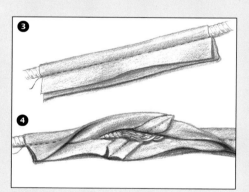

❶ To make bias bindings, mark the line of the fabric and cut out strips to the width you require. The most usual width is 1½in (3.75cm).

❷ Join the strips by placing two strips together at right angles to each other with right sides facing. This will form a triangle. Pin and machine firmly across the width, leaving ¼in (0.75cm) seam allowance. Open flat and press.

❸ Work out the length of piping required and join enough bias strips to cover the cord. Place the binding strip right side down.

❹ Position the piping cord in the middle and wrap the binding with wrong sides facing to enclose the cord. Baste close to the cord. Machine stitch. Remove the basting stitches.

❺ Place the panel of the main fabric wrong side down and lay piping on top of it so that the raw edges of the binding face outward and align with

the raw edge of the seam allowance of the main fabric. Place the second panel of main fabric right side down over the top with the raw edges aligning, and baste. Stitch the four layers together along the seamline. Remove the basting. When you turn the fabric right side out, the piping neatly edges the seam. You can finish a raw edge with bias binding by hand or machine. Ready-made bias binding has pre-folded edges and can be bought in at least two different widths and a wide range of colors.

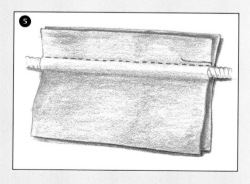

Mitering Corners

❶ With the fabric wrong side up, turn in about quarter of an inch (0.75cm) along each edge and press. Fold along hemlines.

❷ Press and unfold the hems. Fold in the corner so the diagonal fold aligns with the straight fold lines of the hem. Trim off the surplus triangle of fabric, leaving a quarter inch (0.75 cm) seam allowance.

❸ Turn in one hem along the hemline crease. Press and pin. Turn in the other hem along the hemline crease to form a neat corner. Pin and hemstitch.

❹ Slipstitch along the diagonal at the corner to secure.

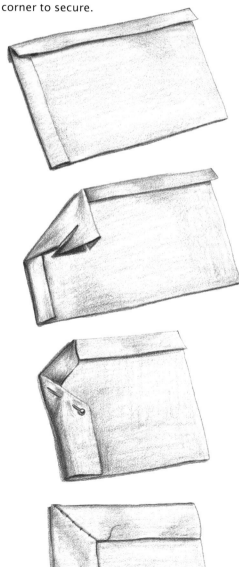

Bed linens

The bedroom is a personal haven for calm and relaxation. Whether you prefer to decorate it in a style that is romantic, exotic, elegant or flamboyant, the decor will include soft furnishings – bed linens, pillows, covers, drapes and perhaps even wall hangings or a bed canopy. There is no better way to be sure that these items are in the fabrics, colors, patterns and styles that reflect your personal taste than by making them yourself.

Bedroom furnishings can be as simple or as adventurous as you want. You can choose silk for elegance, a floral cotton for a country-style look, or white chintz for softness and diffused light. If your bedroom doubles as a study or living room during the day, you can camouflage the bed with a close-fitting, functional cover.

Top right *A bedroom with an atmosphere of rich elegance which comes from the bed drapes, the colors and patterns as well as the generous amount of upholstery fabric.*

Above *Simple lines in bold strips using primary colors and tones are extremely effective on these twin beds.*

Left *A child's bed is draped with soft voile canopy which is contrasted with bold-colored bed linen.*

Bedspreads

Bedspreads can be made in two basic styles – throw-over or fitted. Either style can be floor length and edged with pleats, fringe or braiding. Alternatively, it can be made to come halfway down the sides of the bed over a contrasting dust ruffle. You can use almost any type of fabric, as long as it is crease-resistant and has enough body to hang well.

Throw-over bedspreads are the easiest type to make, consisting simply of a plain rectangle of fabric that covers the bed from head to foot and hangs down the sides to the desired length. You can make the corners square or curved, and you can leave the hem plain or trim it with edging in contrasting fabric.

A fitted bedspread is made from five pieces: a top panel and a skirt consisting of four side panels of fabric. One of the long side panels is made in two pieces with a flap opening so the cover is easy to put on the bed.

Bed canopies

It is a straightforward project to transform an ordinary bed into one that is unusual and mysterious with the addition of a fabric-covered canopy.

You can make your own supports for the drapes with four lightweight wooden curtain poles. Simply attach them to the ceiling above the head, sides and foot of the bed, making sure they overlap at the corners.

Select lengths of soft, fine-woven material for the canopy cover. Loosely drape it around the poles, or make up the lengths into curtains with deep-cased heading through which the poles can be inserted. Add ribbons or cord to tie back the canopy if you wish.

Materials of different weights, weaves and colors produce very different effects, so experiment before settling on a particular fabric. Be generous with the amount of material you use, because a feeling of fullness adds to the effect.

Lighting

Planning lighting

When you are choosing a color scheme for any room in your home, the first thing to take into account is how that room will be used and, thus, the type of lighting you will need. Light is very important in a room, because it affects colors and makes them seem lighter or darker. Natural light from windows will change the appearance of colors at different times of the day – enlivening them in the morning sun and gradually toning them down as the day progresses. Artificial lights also affect the colors in a room, making them look lighter or darker. They can also play tricks with colors, sometimes causing dramatic changes at, literally, the flick of a switch.

Above right *The bold pattern and coloration of this pair of table lamps emphasizes the enclosed, intimate atmosphere of this living room.*

Below *The shape of this room demands a variety of lighting types to produce an even scheme overall.*

Time of day
How you incorporate lighting into your room scheme will probably depend on when and how that area is most used. A bedroom, for example, is usually the easiest room to plan, since it will be used in artificial light for the greater part of the year. A dining room is also reasonably straightforward. This room is most often used for evening meals, in which case it is the evening light that you need to consider when planning a scheme.

Living room lighting
In the majority of homes, the most difficult room of all to create a lighting scheme for will be the main living room. This is because the living room will be in use for a number of hours during the day time, as well as at night. Much will also depend on whether the room has a bright or a gloomy aspect. If it is a sunny room, you can choose cool blues and greens and rely on warm, artificial lighting in the evening. A shady living room, however, may need oranges and yellows to create a feeling of warmth.

Highlighting features
Lighting can be used to accentuate features in the room in much the same way as colors and patterns. Strategically positioned wall lights, spotlights, uplights or ceiling downlights can be arranged so that they wash a complete wall with a blanket of light. They can also be used to good effect to highlight an isolated area, such as a display shelf, or a recess filled with beautiful objects, or to light a work of art such as a sculpture or a painting.

The days are long gone when it was considered adequate to light a room with a single, central pendant light. In a specialist lighting store, you can be overwhelmed by the lighting options open to you. Light fixtures, bulb wattages, and even colored lights have been brought into the scheme of things so that, apart from practical values, there is also the esthetic appeal to consider. Lampshades, too, contribute to the interest and atmosphere of the room, coming as they do in a vast choice of shapes, sizes, materials, and colors.

Effects on colors

Light, whether artificial or natural, exaggerates the effect of colors. White and pale colors reflect light and so make rooms appear larger. Conversely, dark colors absorb light and tend to make rooms seem smaller. Under most artificial lights, blues become darker while reds and yellows become brighter. You will also find that ordinary tungsten filament lamps create a warmish red effect, whereas warm-white fluorescent tubes produce yellowish color effects.

Clockwise from top left *Natural daylight (as reference); tungsten filament lighting; "cool" fluorescent lighting.*

Energy efficiency

Approximately 20 per cent of the electricity generated is used for lighting, but about half of this amount is wasted either lighting empty rooms or as heat produced by the lamps themselves. It makes sense then to switch off lights in unused rooms.

Compact fluorescents These bulbs fit regular incandescent bulb holders. Their extended life compensates for the higher initial purchase price.

Tungsten-halogen This incandescent bulb produces a white light very close to daylight in appearance. High-voltage lamps are fine for general room lighting, while low-voltage versions make ideal accent lighting. The price of these bulbs is high, but they can last up to 4,000 hours and save about 60 per cent on the cost of energy as compared with ordinary bulbs.

Metal-halide This bulb combines energy efficiency with intensity and has about a 6,000-hour life.

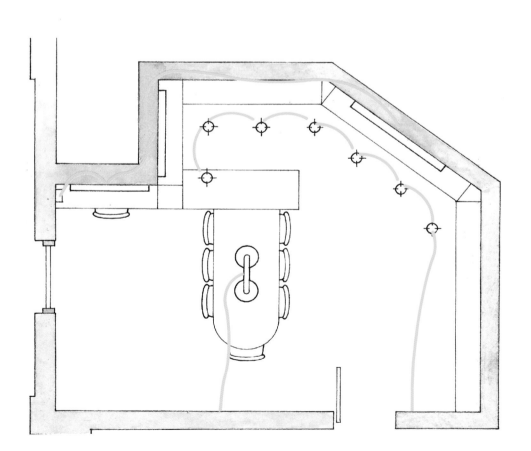

Above *In a multipurpose room, such as this spacious kitchen, you will almost certainly need a lighting diagram to make sure that all the different areas of the room are adequately illuminated – especially the dining table and countertops.*

Halls and stairs

Lighting in the entrance or hall is important because it sets the scene for the style and mood you wish to convey; it reflects the atmosphere you wish to create and ensures the entrance to your home is safe and well illuminated. Although the hall should extend a welcome to visitors, you can, if you wish, treat it in a more dramatic way than the other rooms in your home – almost like a stage set, into which you invite your guests to enter with a feeling of anticipation.

Above *If your hall or stairway is used to display paintings or other pieces of art, then the lighting needs to take this into account. Bright levels of indirect, full-spectrum lighting in this picture-festooned stairway means that glare from the glass frames is minimal and colors are accurate, without in any way compromising safety.*

Right *A good level of general illumination is useful in the hallway near the front door to your home, but this should not be dazzlingly bright. Pockets of brighter lighting to highlight specific areas can then be created with table lamps.*

Links and continuity

Halls, and indeed stairs, represent the links between different rooms and areas of your home. In order to create a continuity of style you may, therefore, wish to carry your lighting theme through from one room into the hall or stairway. Many light fixtures now available offer the choice of wall- or ceiling-mounted uplights and downlights, as well as freestanding lights, all with the same cosmetic appearance. In this way, you can take continuity of appearance into account while introducing wide-ranging lighting effects, each tailored to the requirements of each individual area.

Stairs are often very badly lit, relying entirely on the overspill of light from hallways or landing areas. From a safety point of view, stairs need to be adequately lit. The light needs to be bright enough for people to move around without fear of tripping or falling. Stairs can be made safer by installing strong directional light that draws attention to the vertical risers and horizontal stair treads. Avoid glaring landing lights and use wall fixtures to provide an additional source of light.

Varying lighting intensities

Think carefully about the lighting intensity of different parts of halls and stairs. In an entrance hallway, for example, you will probably want relatively high light levels, since this is where you congregate, at least

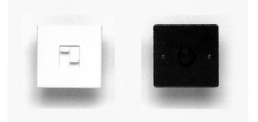

Dimmer switches

One easy way of increasing the range of lighting effects you can create is by replacing your existing on/off switches with dimmer control switches. Although designs differ a little between manufacturers, they all work in much the same way by controlling the amount of voltage reaching the bulbs, and hence varying their light output. One-gang dimmers are the most common type, but two-gang versions are also available. All are suitable for two-way switching, and installing one in place of an existing switch simply involves switching off the lighting circuit, then disconnecting the existing switch cable and reconnecting it to the dimmer. If you are not sure which type to choose, check with the retailer that it will be suitable for the combined wattage of the lights it is to control.

briefly, when people enter or leave your home. You may also not want too marked a difference in lighting intensity between, say, the living or family room, which tends to be brightly lit, and the adjacent hall, so that your eyes don't have trouble adjusting. In an upstairs hall, however, or in the area of hall in a single-story home or apartment adjacent to the bedrooms, it is a good idea to have a reduced level of illumination. This helps create a mood and also avoids an abrupt change in light level between the bedrooms, which tend to be softly lit, and the adjacent area of hall.

You may also want to differentiate areas by using lights with different color effects. For example, in an entrance hall you may want a bluer lighting effect – one that closely resembles the qualities of daylight – than that used near the bedrooms, which could be warmer orange in quality to create a more intimate atmosphere.

Candle power

Electric lights are not the only form of illumination at night. Candles are a centuries-old alternative, and the range of designs available make them a suitable option in virtually any style of dining room, especially when a romantic atmosphere is wanted. In addition to table candlesticks and candelabras, there are also large floor-standing holders and wall-mounted sconces. Many candles are scented to impart a delicate perfume to the room. To avoid too bright a flame, keep the wick well trimmed. This also means that the candle produces the minimum amount of smoke while it burns.

Candle safety

You need to exercise some basic safety precautions when using candles. For a start, never leave lit candles unattended in an empty room. It only takes a few minutes for a fire to start. Never stand a candle in a position where any material, such as curtaining, may come into contact with the flame. An open window could cause a light curtain material to billow into the room and touch a badly positioned candle. When setting a candle into any type of candle holder, make sure that it is well secured and cannot fall over.

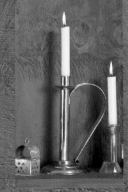

Above and right *Candle holders range from wall-mounted sconces to freestanding candlesticks made of glass, wood, china, and metal.*

Living areas

The living and dining areas of the home are often used for many different purposes. A variety of occasions take place in living areas, ranging from relaxing, talking, reading, sewing, studying, hobbies, and watching television, to daily meals, parties and entertaining. To meet these many and varied activities, you need an effective and extremely adaptable lighting plan.

Right *For a dining or breakfast room table, you often want a good level of illumination directly over the table itself. The ideal solution is an adjustable ceiling-mounted hanging light that can be moved up or down and set at the perfect height.*

Below *To show off a collection of ornaments to best advantage, concealed, unobtrusive lights are the answer.*

Ceiling pendants

Although often not producing the most attractive of lighting effects, ceiling-mounted hanging lights do provide useful general lighting in a living or dining room. The main drawback with pendants is that they rarely light a room evenly, so there will inevitably be pockets of gloomy shadow, especially in the room corners.

If mounted over a dining table, however, retractable pendant fixtures can be extremely useful, creating a bright highlight just where it is needed most. You do need to be careful, though, that the light is not low enough to dazzle the eyes of the diners. For a long dining room table, you may need more than one hanging light to light the eating area evenly.

Spotlights

Individual spots can be wall or ceiling mounted or recessed into the ceiling. This form of lighting produces highly directional illumination, ideal for reading or sewing, or as hobby light, for example. Take care to position spots correctly, however, so that

shadows are not cast over your book or work. Spotlights are also ideal for creating emphases within a room, angled to highlight an ornament, attractive architectural feature, or a plant perhaps. Spotlights can also be mounted on electrical tracks. These are available in different lengths and allow you to set the light anywhere on the track (*see p. 177*).

Uplights and downlights

These types of light can produce very dramatic lighting effects, washing walls or ceilings in bright but localized illumination. Depending on the opacity and shape of the hood used, you can create all manner of intensities and shaped areas of light, ranging from scalloped-edged highlights to relaxing curves. The decoration within the area of illumination produced by these lights is often best if left on the plain side to prevent an overcluttered appearance. An uplight on the wall adjacent to the television should provide enough general illumination to reduce any effect of glare from the screen.

Table lights

Depending on the wattage of the bulb itself, as well as the characteristics of the lampshade, table lamps can be used to create very localized pockets of illumination in a room, as well as a more general level of lighting. If a table lamp is to be used as a reading or sewing light, or for any other activity needing concentration, make sure it is positioned so that it casts an even light without any annoying shadows.

The color of the lampshade is important, too, since distinctly colored lighting can result in eyestrain. Like uplights, table lamps can help to illuminate a room sufficiently to reduce the glare from a television screen. If a central hanging light is failing to light all of the room, then consider strategically positioned table lamps to brighten the more shadowy areas.

Floor lamps

Floorstanding lamps, usually found in a living or dining room, can be interesting decorative features in their own right. And the choice of lampshades is magnificent! They may harmonize with the lighting scheme by using a material in a matching tone, or create a dramatic focus of light by using a material with a bold, contrasting pattern. Being portable, you can move them wherever you want, depending on your activity. The central column of some types can be adjusted to give a range of lighting heights, while others have multiple bulb sockets or lighting arms to increase the range of effects that can be achieved.

Top *Table lamps tend to produce isolated areas of lighting. Use them to brighten gloomy corners or, if accurately sited, as activity lights.*

Above *Use picture lights when you want to make a statement. You will be inviting close inspection of the picture, however, so make sure its quality is good.*

Left *In this area around a hearth, the lighting is pitched at the right level to produce an intimate, welcoming atmosphere.*

Kitchens and Bathrooms

In most homes, the kitchen is where people congregate and where a lot of the day-to-day work of preparing food and cooking takes place. So the main utility areas – the sink, counters, stove, and the oven – need to be not just attractive, but particularly well lit.

Below *Spotlights set into the ceiling have been positioned to give a high level of illumination directly over the main task areas in this kitchen.*

Bottom *Concealed lighting on the underside of the wall cabinets provides a higher level of illumination for the work areas.*

Kitchens

Track lighting This versatile form of lighting can work well in a kitchen, provided that the track is carefully positioned. For example, if you install a track in the middle of the ceiling with the spotlights aimed at the oven or sink, every time you stand in these areas you will be casting a forward-facing shadow. Instead, for shadow-free lighting, mount the track over the area to be illuminated with the spots directed downward.

Concealed lighting The most usual type of concealed lighting consists of light

Pendant lighting A hanging light can provide good background illumination. If it is the only light source, however, it is likely to cast shadows and leave some area of the kitchen inadequately lit. A hanging light is better used in conjunction with track and concealed cabinet or shelf lights.

Pendants can be used in a more versatile fashion, however, if they are removed from the traditional center-ceiling position and rehung so that they are directly above the main utility areas. If the surface to be lit is long, you may have to install two, three, or even four hanging lights to give even illumination.

Bathrooms

Pull-cords can be used in bathrooms to prevent you from touching electricity supply with wet hands.

Fluorescent lights Most people opt for a gentle, restful form of lighting in a bathroom, which makes fluorescent tubes an unlikely first choice. However, fluorescent tubes mounted behind translucent panels in the ceiling or, indeed, a wall can add a touch of style and panache. Bear in mind that several evenly spaced low-voltage tubes produce a more flattering light than a fewer number of high-voltage tubes. Another advantage of fluorescent tubes is that they produce virtually no heat, making them a safe form of lighting to position near water.

Downlights Strategically placed downlights can be used to accentuate different areas of a bathroom, either to illuminate task areas or simply to create interesting light and shadow contrasts.

Mirror lights A mirror is an important feature in a bathroom, either for shaving or putting on make-up. The best lighting solution is sidelighting – a row of low-voltage bulbs on each side of the mirror will give you virtually shadow-free lighting.

Shower lights A shower stall will probably require its own light. Use a specially sealed lighting unit that is waterproof against all moisture.

Top left Lights on flexible brackets attached to the shelves of this traditional hutch have been used to highlight the decorative nature of the kitchenware.

Bottom left Bulkhead lights on each side of this bathroom recess give shadow-free lighting.

Below Carefully designed lighting can help to differentiate different task areas in a bathroom.

Bottom Large areas of mirror in a room will reflect any available light and boost the overall brightness.

fixtures attached to the underside of wall cabinets or shelves suspended over the kitchen's counters. These produce light just where it is needed. But make sure that the light is low enough not to shine directly into your eyes, as this might prove to be dangerous if you are working with sharp knives or hot liquids.

Another type of concealed lighting consists of fluorescent tubes mounted behind translucent panels set into the ceiling. Fluorescent fixtures are not attractive, but this way you obtain the benefit of bright, energy-efficient lighting without the fixtures or tubes being visible.

Bedrooms

In many homes today, bedrooms have to serve more than one function. Your bedroom not only houses and stores your clothes, but may also have to double as a part-time workroom or study. It may be more like a studio or lof, or it may simply be a restful, quiet area in which to relax and retreat for a while. Whatever your own version of a bedroom is, you will take this into account when planning the most appropriate lighting plan.

General lighting

The background lighting for a bedroom can consist of a single hanging light or, in a large room, a series of pendants. Alternatively, consider track lighting or recessed spots. Position these lights so that they illuminate the areas of the room where most light is required – such as above a writing table, study desk, bookshelves, or play area. A dimmer switch is also useful. This gives you the option of soft, restful lighting or bright, full light for reading or dressing by.

Special purpose lighting

Bedside lights If you enjoy reading in bed, then some form of bedside lighting is essential. Lights can be mounted on the wall behind the bed, angled so that the light falls directly on the page. Lamps can also be placed on bedside tables, but make sure that enough light falls on the page without the lamp itself being visible when you are in your normal reading position. Switches for bedside lights should ideally be located so that you don't have to get out of bed to use them.

Mirror lights A dressing table mirror or a full-length mirror will benefit from being sidelit by a series of lights positioned on each side of the glass. If the light output on both sides is exactly matched, then this type of lighting gives a very flattering, shadow-free type of illumination.

Wardrobe/cupboard lights If the general lighting in the room is not sufficient to illuminate the inside of large closets when the doors are open, then these areas should

Above *Lights mounted on the wall behind a bed are excellent for reading by.*

Above left *A lighting scheme consisting of uplights, table lamps, wall-mounted lights, and ceiling lights produce a good range of lighting options in this bedroom.*

Below *Lighting controls situated by the side of the bed are most convenient.*

have their own internal light source. This is practical lighting and so does not need to be particularly sophisticated. A simple fluorescent tube is probably the best light to use in most circumstances. Fluorescents sit very close to the surface on which they are mounted, and so are less likely to be accidentally knocked or broken. They also produce very little heat and so they are unlikely to scorch any delicate fabrics that may accidentally touch or rest against the tube.

Recessed lights There is a wide range of light fixtures available that are designed to be recessed into the ceiling surface, instead of being mounted on it. These include downlights, spotlights, and rotating eyeball fittings, and they are often used in groups controlled from a single switch – in other words, several lights can be wired in sequence from a single power supply connection.

Low-voltage lighting As an alternative to main-voltage fixtures, you can install lights that run on a much reduced voltage via a transformer that can be concealed in the space above the ceiling. These lights are smaller and neater than main-voltage versions, and their halogen bulbs give a cool, white light that is perfect for highlighting features or providing decorative mood lighting effects in a bedroom. All you need do is choose the right transformer for the number of lights you plan to install, and provide a power supply to the transformer from a convenient connection point on the existing lighting circuit.

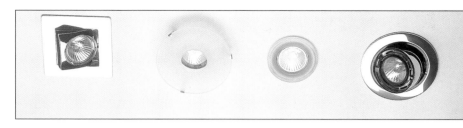

Above *Fully recessed spots make effective downlights, while "eyeball-style" lights can be swivelled to alter the lighting direction.*

Below *Lighting track systems have evolved dramatically over the last 45 years, and they are now available in as many different designs as there are types of room to accommodate them.*

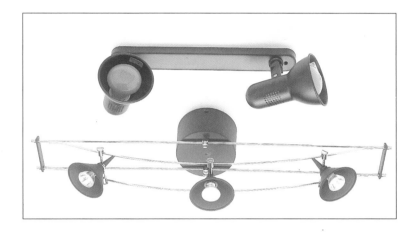

Track lighting

Track lighting was first introduced about 45 years ago, and since that time it has enjoyed a healthy popularity. This popularity is based on the unmatched versatility offered by these systems and the fact that they can be installed with little decorative disturbance.

Basically, the track itself comprises a length of metal channelling, usually about 3ft (1m) long. If a longer track is required, lengths of track can be coupled together. Running the length of the track, inside the metal casing, is the electricity supply, while a slot on the outside allows you to attach spotlights at any point you wish. The position of a spot can be altered by releasing a catch at the bottom of the light and then clipping it back in its new position. Check the instructions regarding the number of lights that can be accommodated on any length of track.

The main drawback with these systems is that the track itself is surface mounted

and, thus, always on show – so you need to regard it as a feature when planning the room's decoration. Another factor to bear in mind is that the larger types of spotlights suitable for mounting on a track can appear rather intrusive, especially in a less than generously proportioned room. Where light levels do not have to be high, you can overcome this problem by using much smaller, low-voltage lights, but first you will have to install an appropriate transformer to the main voltage supplying the track.

Many manufacturers produce their own track lighting systems and each is slightly different. This means that the spotlights from one maker will not fit into the tracks made by another. This can be particularly annoying if you already have a track installed and then discover that the lights from a different one would better suit your needs, so it is worth doing your homework before you invest in a new system.

Above *By following the shape of the walls, this ceiling-mounted lighting track has been purposely emphasized as a decorative room feature. Each spotlight has been precisely positioned, but the lights can be moved as easily as the pictures they illuminate.*

8

Flooring

Choosing floor covering

Deciding on a suitable floor covering is not just a matter of cost and taste. You will also need to consider a number of practicalities. What is the function of the room? Who will use it and for what? How much will the floor be used – whether at home or in a work space? The condition of the existing subfloor, and the maintenance involved?

Choosing the right material and color for your decorative plan will also need to be taken into account, since floor covering can be a dominant element in this regard. With so much choice available to you, you need to take care to plan carefully before you start. Indulging your personal taste can lead to unwelcome expense.

Above right Easy to lay, reasonably inexpensive, and stain resistant, fiber matting also adds interesting textures to a room.

Below Wood strip flooring makes a hardwearing, practical surface for a kitchen.

Carpet

Carpet is perhaps the most common floor covering in homes. It is comfortable to walk over and sit on, and can transform any interior instantly. Made from wool or synthetic fibers, or a mixture of the two, carpet is available in a vast range of thicknesses, patterns, colors, textures, and cost. Its durability as a floor covering depends on quality and the wear it is subjected to.

Fiber matting

Made from plant fibers, matting is easy to lay, either as a wall-to-wall covering or as loose mats. It is available in a choice of patterns and shades from cream through green to brown, it does not show stains, and it is fairly easy to clean. It can be an inexpensive flooring option, although some styles are costly.

Wood

Bare wooden floors are beautiful in their own right. Stripped, carefully stained, or colored if desired, sealed, and decorated with a rug or mat, they can look stunning. If you are not fortunate enough to have an old floor suitable for such treatment, you can buy wood strips or parquet tiles to lay over your existing one. They are not difficult to put down and can be very reasonably priced.

Vinyl

Vinyl is an excellent choice for kitchens, bathrooms, and utility areas. Available in a wide range of colors and patterns – usually textured – this durable material is waterproof, oil and fat resistant, and often cushioned for sound and heat insulation, although it will burn or scratch. It is sold as tiles, which are easy to lay, and in sheet form, which is more tricky, and ranges in flexibility from soft and rubbery to rigid and stiff. Prices vary from economical to expensive depending on the amount of PVC (polyvinyl chloride) present; the more it contains, the more expensive the vinyl. It is essential to follow the manufacturer's cleaning instructions, since the wrong type of cleaner can damage the tiles. Most advise warm, soapy water and rinsing.

Cork

Warm and practical, floor-grade cork is a reasonably priced option for kitchens and bathrooms. Usually sold as tiles, it is sometimes available in sheet form, which cuts down on laying time. Unless it is pre-sealed, cork must be cleaned and sealed with at least three coats of floor-grade polyurethane lacquer or varnish, after which it is durable and easy to clean. Cork is limited in color, but it can be stained or stencilled before sealing. A white cork tile is now available to suit pale decorative schemes.

Rubber

This is an expensive alternative to vinyl. Anti-slip and resistant to most household spills, rubber is available in primary colors, subtle two-tone effects, and with raised designs. It is sold in sheet or tile form.

Linoleum

Made from natural oils, gums, and resins, linoleum is very durable and easy to clean, although it will rot if water seeps under it. Available in an exciting range of glossy colors and patterns, it can be used to create unique designs. Linoleum is sold as tiles or in sheets, which are more difficult to lay. Price ranges from economical to expensive.

Ceramic

Ceramic tiles are available in a truly vast array of styles, finishes, colors, and textures. Good looking and easy to wipe clean (unglazed tiles need regular washing and they do absorb oil), they always remain cool no matter how hot it gets. They range from inexpensive to very costly, require a certain amount of skill to lay, and are unsuitable for all but the strongest of subfloors.

Quarry tiles

Made from unrefined silica alumina clay, these rustic tiles are usually in shades of brick red, gold, or brown. Although durable, they can become pitted – but this often adds to their charm and appeal. Like ceramic tiles, they are cold and noisy underfoot and range in price from economical to expensive. They may require a lot of cleaning, however. If permitted by the manufacturer, they can be sealed with linseed oil in 4 parts of turpentine, which should be painted on, covered with brown paper, and left for 48 hours before sweeping and washing.

Above *Usually found only in traditional style country cottages, slate floors are the ultimate in hardwearing durability. Slate can be stained darker with linseed oil before sealing.*

Below *Old floorboards can be stripped, sanded, stained, and then sealed to provide a beautiful, easy-care surface for any room in the home.*

Wood floors

If you find a wood floor beneath old floor coverings, why not refurbish it? The preparation and finishing involves a lot of physical work, but the rewards can be tremendous.

Before starting, check that the boards are in good condition and that the supporting joists and wallplates are sound. Have any serious problems rectified. Make sure, too, that there are not too many gaps between the boards. A few can easily be filled, but if the whole floor needs this treatment, results will probably be unattractive.

If you are lucky, the floor may need only a light sanding and cleaning by hand, but a floor sander is often necessary to level uneven edges and expose fresh surfaces for treatment. Where the wood is a consistent color, just seal the surface with polyurethane lacquer or varnish; but to enhance or even change the color, use a wood stain. Stains are available in natural wood colors or ones designed to harmonize with decorative schemes but still let the grain show through. Boards that are in poor condition or heavily filled can be coated with floor paint. Painting floorboards presents endless possibilities for color use and design.

Staining

You can alter the color of wooden floors using a wood stain. Since wood can only be darkened with stain and recently applied stain is difficult to remove, first test a small inconspicuous area to check that the shade is right. To lighten wood, you must apply bleach.

First, fill any cracks or holes with wood stopper or a filler that will take the color of the stain. If the wood is open grained but you want a smooth finish, apply grain filler, rubbing it across the grain.

Next, make sure the floor is absolutely dust free and remove any marks with mineral spirits. Apply the stain with a dry, lint-free rag or brush, working quickly and evenly in the direction of the grain, wiping off excess stain with a clean cloth.

An alternative to staining and then sealing is to use a varnish stain, which combines the two jobs. The varnish must be brushed on very evenly to avoid patchiness, however, and every successive coat of varnish will deepen the color.

Safety precautions

Before using stains and varnishes on a wood floor, carefully read the manufacturer's instructions on the can or the accompanying leaflet. Many of these products are highly volatile and give off unpleasant or potentially dangerous fumes. Do not smoke, drink, or eat while using them, work in a well-ventilated area, and if you are particularly sensitive wear a face mask and some form of eye protection. Keep these products away from exposed skin. It is best to apply stains and varnishes during the day so that you can keep the windows open. Daylight is also best for critical judgment of the effects you are creating.

Below left *Floors that are too old and damaged to be stripped and stained can still look appealing if the surface is sanded smooth and then painted.*

Below right *As well as natural wood shades, modern floor stains are also available in a good range of hues to complement the room's decorative color scheme.*

Left *This floor is a beautiful example of pickling, and indicates just how effective this technique can be. It is particularly striking since the color is highlighted in the fabrics, which adds an air of elegant luxury to the room.*

Pickling

Using lime to alter the color of wood is a traditional technique stretching back hundreds of years. Like staining (*see opposite*), pickling alters the color of the underlying surface without obliterating its most attractive feature, which is the grain of the wood. It can be applied to a floor which is stained with color, giving a very attractive finish over blues and greens.

The most typical woods to treat in this way, using either a pickling paste or wax, are hardwoods, since these often have the most decorative figuring. Pine is a softer wood also suitable for pickling. The most usual woods to be pickled include oak, ash and elm.

Materials and equipment

- Pickling wax or paste

- Steel wool

- Liquid floor wax

- Clean, lint-free cotton rags

- Buffing cloth, brush, or polishing machine

1 If you have stained the wooden surface to be pickled (*see opposite*), allow the stain to dry thoroughly. Open up the grain by brushing with a wire brush. This may be omitted on softwoods such as pine. Make sure that surfaces are clean and dust free before applying the wax.

2 Apply a coat of pickling wax and work it well into the grain using extra-fine steel wool. Pickling wax dries relatively quickly, so it is better to work in smaller areas in order to achieve an even finish.

3 After about 5 minutes, remove most of the excess wax using a pad made up from clean cotton rag. Change to a clean piece of the rag as it becomes clogged with wax. Depending on the area being treated, you may need to make up several fresh pads in order to remove all the wax.

4 To form a protective surface for the newly pickled wood, add a coat of liquid floor wax, making sure that it gets well into the grain. Allow a few hours for the wax to dry properly and then buff the surface to a

soft sheen. You can use soft, lint-free rags for this or a soft brush. If, however, the area is large, such as an entire floor, it is much less effort to use a floor-polisher equipped with a soft polishing pad.

Laying parquet and woodblock floors

Veneered woodblocks and panels are a convenient and economic way of laying an impressive wooden floor on an existing wood or solid subfloor. Since the subfloor needs to be sound and level, you may have to lay masonite or blockboard over a wood floor before laying a new surface.

Parquet panels

Parquet floor panels are laid like tiles on a special adhesive spread on the subfloor. The panels are tongued and grooved to fit securely and ensure that you build up the pattern correctly. Some panels are already finished, but unfinished ones will need sanding before being sealed.

You must leave a ½in (12mm) expansion gap all around the room between the panels and the baseboard to avoid lifting and buckling in damp weather. Cut a strip of wood to keep this distance while you work. Later the gap can be filled with a cork strip, although some people prefer to tack a piece of quarter-round shoe molding to the baseboard to hide the gap.

Before starting, check that the walls are square by butting a panel into each corner of the room. Any gaps between the panels and the walls indicates they are not.

If the walls are square, you can lay the panels starting from the center of the room working outward. Establish the central point by stretching two chalked strings at right angles across the middle of the room. Loose lay a line of tiles from the center to each of the baseboards. To avoid having narrow pieces of panel at the edges, adjust the starting point by as much as half a panel width either way. Move the strings and mark the floor as guidelines for laying the panels.

Left *The individual mosaic panels making up a parquet floor combine to create an attractive pattern as well as an easy-care surface.*

Right *This dramatic parquet floor works well in a large, airy country room, especially one which leads to the outdoors.*

Laying parquet panels

For square rooms, lay the tiles out from the straightest wall with a line of uncut panels parallel to the baseboard.
Note: mineral spirits will remove semi-dried adhesive.

1 Lay a panel against one wall with an edging strip placed between it and the baseboard. Stretch a string line across the room along the edge of this panel.

2 Mark a line on the floor following the string. Then push the panel into the corner. Here, the walls are not true.

3 Position the next panel to project beyond the first by the depth of the marking batten.

4 Press the batten hard against the wall and draw the outer edge of the

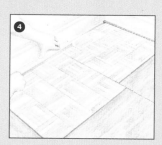
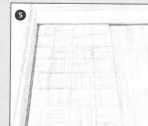
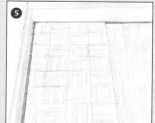

batten onto the panels to act as a guideline for cutting

5 Cut along guideline and lay edging

strip against the second baseboard.

6 Finally, apply adhesive to four panels at a time.

Woodblock floors

Provided that the subfloor has been well prepared, and is level, firm, stable, and dry, it is relatively easy to lay a woodblock floor. The wood pieces are laid in a pattern onto a self-adhesive board. Allow for an expansion gap at the baseboards.

1 Remove the self-adhesive membrane after laying the self-adhesive underlay.

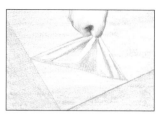

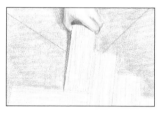

2 Lay out the blocks of wood in the desired pattern.

3 Gently bond them to the adhesive with a mallet.

4 Mark the edges, leaving an expansion gap.

5 Cut off waste wood with a knife and straightedge.

6 Fit the edging strip into place along the baseboards.

Left *A beautifully laid and polished woodstrip floor enhances this space, which is flooded with light from the tall windows.*

Carpet and matting

Whether fitted wall to wall or loose laid as a rug, carpet is hard to equal in terms of sheer comfort and warmth. But as well as being a practical floor covering, carpet is available in such a wide range of styles, colors, patterns, and textures that it can be used to complement the decorative theme in any room in the house.

Matting is becoming increasingly popular as a floor covering as the range of colors increases and modern manufacturing techniques make it easier to keep clean.

Carpet

A wall-to-wall carpet can transform an interior and, where it continues through doors, it provides a unifying feature. Carpeting a large room can be difficult and many people prefer to employ professional layers rather than risk spoiling an expensive piece of flooring. Heavily tracked areas such as halls, staircases and landings need heavy-duty carpeting.

When working out how much carpet you need, take exact room measurements. For anything other than an absolutely straight-sided room, make a plan and mark on it the precise measurements of every nook and alcove. Alcoves and bays may need extra pieces to be joined to the main carpet. Take the plan to the store and ask an estimator to calculate quantities.

To give maximum wear, a burlap-backed carpet needs to be stretched into position, using a knee-kicker, over grippers, which are nailed to the floor around the room's edges. Carpet should be laid over good-quality underlay of felt, foam, or rubber to improve comfort and durability and to minimize dust travelling up from floor-boards. Foam and rubber underlay are not suitable for stairs or heavily seamed areas. Rubberized felt and bonded underlays are also available.

Foam-backed carpets are much easier to lay, being simply unrolled in place over a paper underlay to prevent it from sticking to the subfloor. They are usually stuck down at the edges, but can be secured over special grippers. Generally cheaper than burlap-backed carpets, foam-backed ones have a shorter life. They are useful for rooms with little foot traffic as well as bathrooms – the backing prevents shrinkage.

Carpet tiles

Sealed-edge carpet squares come in a range of sizes and colors and are easy to lay. Shades can be mixed to make checkerboards or more complicated patterns. The

Above left *Carpet tiles can be cut up and joined together in a bright and cheerful mosaic pattern.*

Left *Room-sized matting is durable and hardwearing, and provides a wealth of texture.*

squares can be stuck down or laid loose, so damaged or heavily worn squares can be replaced or moved around – a boon for children's rooms, dining rooms, and even kitchens. Being removable, they also give access to underfloor services with the minimum of disruption.

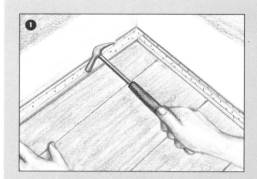

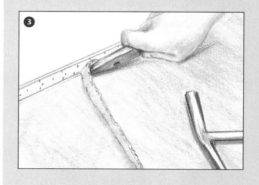

Carpet swatches
1 *Wool and synthetic mix* 2 *Synthetic fibers*
3 *Long-pile wool* 4 *Patterned weave* 5 *100%
wool* 6 *Wool patterned long pile* 7 *Wool
patterned short pile* 8 *Traditional patterned wool*
9 *Short pile wool* 10 *Modern geometric pattern*

Laying carpets
With a lot of determination, you can do a good job of laying burlap-backed carpet yourself. First-timers should start with foam-backed carpet.

Materials and equipment

- 2in (5cm) single-sided tape

- Sharp knife and carpet hammer

- Knee-kicker carpet stretcher

- Bolster

1 To lay traditional carpet, attach gripper strips ⅛in (3mm) away from walls or baseboards around the room.

2 To abut seams in rubber underlay, use single-sided 2in (5cm) tape on top of the pieces.

3 Abut underlay up to gripper and trim to fit with a sharp knife.

4 Cover gripper with carpet and stretch carpet onto gripper pins.

5 Cut carpet ¼in (6mm) oversize. Tuck it down between gripper and baseboard.

Above *Light-colored carpets may need protecting with a rug where they receive most wear.*

Threshold strips

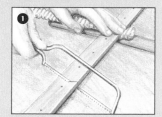

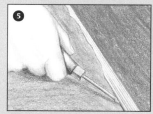

1 To protect carpet in doorways, use an edging strip. Measure and cut bar to size.
2 Nail bar down. Bars can be single or double sided.
3 On a double bar, hook carpet on both sides and trim with a knife.
4 To seal carpet edges that may fray, apply adhesive to the edges.
5 Tuck carpet under edge and hammer down.

Stair carpet

Stair carpet must be laid over underlay, which can be in the form of pads tacked to each tread and overhanging the nosing by 2in (5cm). You can tack the carpet in place, although special stair-case grippers will give a better finish.

Start at the bottom, with the pile facing down the stairs. Tack the carpet to the first tread, press the fold into the first gripper and, working upward, keep the carpet very taut. When you reach the top riser, tack it under the last nosing so that the landing carpet just overlaps it.

Angled treads (winders) need a series of folds in the carpet to take up the slack. An easier method is to cut the carpet just below the nosing and tack it in place on each winder.

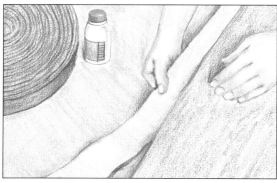

1 Make seams by placing half tape under the carpet edge when tacky.

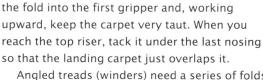
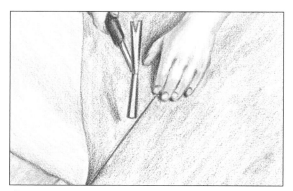

2 Abut the second piece over the tape and hammer it down to form a good bond.

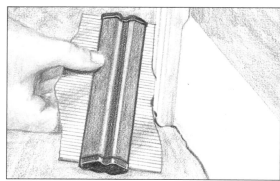

3 Use a template former to trace the contour of any difficult or awkward shapes, such as moldings.

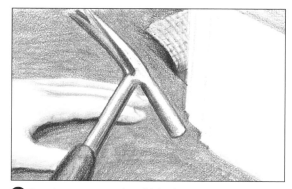

4 Fraying carpets should be hemmed 1in (2.5cm) at the edges and then tacked down into place.

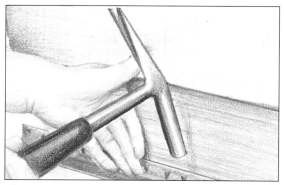

5 Nail a stair strip over the underlay pad at the back of the tread.

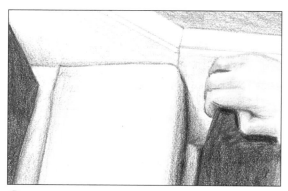

6 The landing carpet should cover the tread nosing at the top of the flight.

FLOORING

8

Matting

Matting made from sisal (agave leaves) and coir (coconut fiber) is inexpensive, practical, and hard-wearing and ranges in color from pale to dark brown. Most coir is honey gold and some sisal is now dyed in other colors. Thought to be uncomfortable and dusty, coir and sisal are now often backed with latex or vinyl, which stops dirt falling through and adds strength. Coir and sisal matting can be used in almost any area except where food is likely to be dropped.

When laying sisal or coir, it is best to cut it slightly too big and leave the matting in the room for at least 24 hours to adjust. Broadloom types are best for wall-to-wall use, although you can sew narrow lengths together or abut them over double-sided tape. It can be laid loose, but it is better to secure matting with double-sided tape.

Rush, seagrass, and maize matting is more finely textured than sisal or coir, and less robust. Available in different weaves, the squares can be sewn together with fine twine. Since they are liable to dry out and become brittle, they need to be moistened occasionally with a plant mister.

Right *Pieces of loose-laid matting can be used informally to differentiate different activity areas within a large room.*

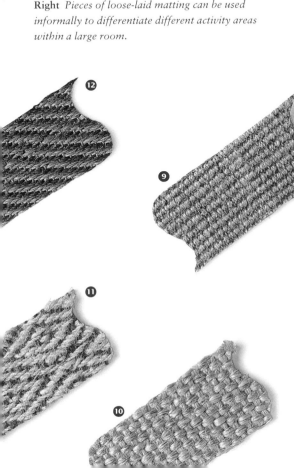

Matting swatches

1 *Coir 2-color basketweave* 2 *Sisal 2-color bouclé* 3 *Sisal 1-color bouclé*
4 *Coir 3-color herringbone* 5 *Sisal 2-color herringbone* 6 *Sisal 1-color bouclé* 7
Coir 3-color twine weft 8 *Coir 2-color bouclé* 9 *Coir 2-color bouclé*
10 *Sisal natural basketweave* 11 *Coir 1-color bouclé* 12 *Coir 2-color herringbone*

Laying vinyl tiles

Being soft, vinyl tiles are easier to handle and cut than hard tiles, and they are generally easier to lay as well. Their lightness also makes them suitable for use on suspended wooden flooring, especially in upstairs rooms, and their durability makes them particularly useful for children's rooms and bathrooms.

Since vinyl tiles require a stable, level surface, unless the sub-floor is perfect, it is best to put down masonite or blockboard before laying the tiles. Many vinyl tiles are self-adhesive; otherwise, you will have to use a special tile adhesive.

Right *Bold checkerboard patterns are easy to achieve using vinyl tiles.*

Materials and equipment

- Squared graph paper

- Colored pencils

- Metal ruler

- Marking chalk

- Tile adhesive and spreader

- Heavy-duty craft knife

Planning

 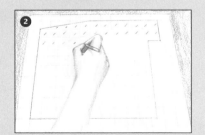 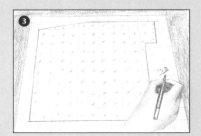

1 Make a scale drawing of the room on squared graph paper. Each square represents one tile.

2 Mark all alcoves and other irregularities. In a kitchen where much of the floor may be taken up with built-in cabinets, include them to scale as well. Mark each square as you calculate quantities.

3 Find the total of tiles needed for the room.

4 Shade in the design to figure out the pattern and quantities of each color required.

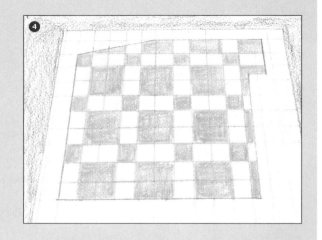

Laying vinyl tiles

Before laying, place the tiles in the room, remove the packaging, and leave them for 24 hours to acclimatize. It is usual to lay tiles from the center point and work outward, toward the edges of the room, but in bathrooms and kitchens where much of the floor space is occupied by cupboards, you will have to find the center of the area to be tiled.

1 Mark the center line with chalk and check that the edge tiles are at least a half-tile wide.

2 If not, move the line a half-tile width to one side.

3 Mark a center line in the other direction. Check as before and move the line if it is necessary.

4 Spread tile adhesive along the floor, on both sides of the center line chalk marks.

5 Lay the marked central tiles first on each side of the chalk line.

6 Continue working outward from the center tiles toward the edges until the floor area is covered.

7 Lay border tiles last. Place the border tile to be cut squarely on top of the last tile, then slide another tile over it until it touches the wall or baseboard. Mark a pencil line on the loose tile below. Cut to this line and the tile should fit exactly.

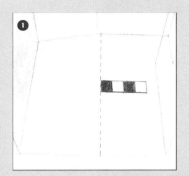
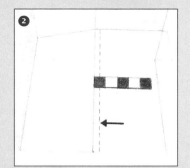
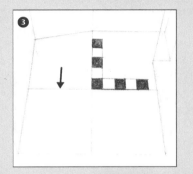
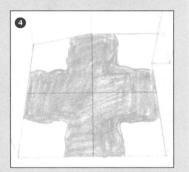
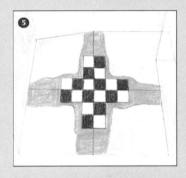
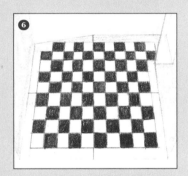
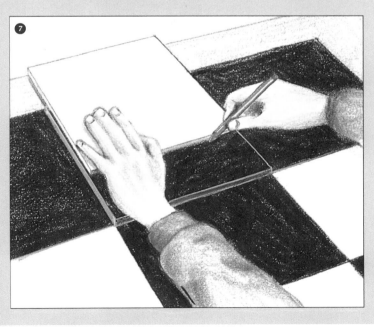

External corners

To cut around an external corner where one tile is involved, use the same technique for cutting border tiles to fit (*see left*).

1 Place two full tiles over the last full tile and slide the top one over to abut the baseboard or wall. Mark a pencil line on the tile beneath.

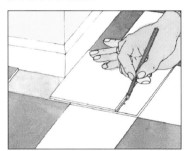

2 Move the lower tile and top tile around the corner without turning them, and place over a full tile. Mark a line as before. Cut out the rectangular shape and glue the tile into place.

Tiling around a pipe

First, cut an edge tile to fit the space, and then push the tile against the pipe and mark the center. Next, move the tile against the wall and mark the pipe center on the edge of the tile. Draw light pencil lines from both points and cut a hole where the lines bisect. Finally, make a slit in the tile to allow you to feed it around the pipe.

Sheet flooring

Vinyl sheeting is made in a huge variety of colors and designs: Spanish and Portuguese ceramic tile patterns, marble and parquet effects, and bold designs in strong colors and black and white. It always pays to buy the best you can afford. Cheap sheeting will eventually crack and does not withstand scratching, staining, or spills for long. The best type is cushioned by an inner layer of bubbles, making it soft and warm underfoot – essential for long standing in the kitchen. It is also harder wearing.

Below *The many colors and patterns available in sheet vinyl make it easy to coordinate with the decor of any room, and its easy-clean, hard-wearing, and spill-resistant surface is ideal for kitchens and bathrooms.*

Handling sheet vinyl

Although large rolls of vinyl are heavy and awkward to handle, demanding a degree of strength and skill to maneuver, vinyl sheeting does have the advantage of covering large areas quickly and with a minimum of seams through which water and other spillages might seep. For large kitchens and bathrooms use a wide sheet material.

When working out how much vinyl you need, allow an extra 2in (5cm) all around in case walls are uneven or out of square, which is likely to be the case. Decide which way you want the pattern to run and avoid seams in doorways, since this is where foot traffic is heaviest. Laying seams at right angles to windows makes them less noticeable because the light won't cast a shadow.

Cold temperatures make vinyl brittle, so if you are laying it in winter, warm it up first. Leaving it in the room overnight with the heating left on will probably be sufficient.

Laying vinyl sheeting

It is best to leave the vinyl loosely rolled in a warm room for 24 hours prior to laying to allow it to become supple.

❶ Cut the vinyl about 2in (5cm) longer at the edges to allow for trimming. Lay the vinyl up 2in (5cm) against the baseboard or wall. Sweep the vinyl with a soft broom to make sure the sheet is in close contact with the floor. Keep one long edge on a chalk guideline if you are using more than one length.

❷ Use a block of wood to press the vinyl firmly into the angle between the floor and baseboard. If necessary, make vertical release cuts into the corner flaps. Don't trim or use adhesive until the fitting is complete.

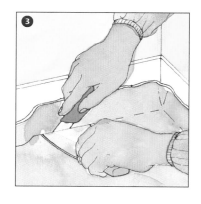

❸ If a second sheet is used, lay it overlapping the first. Cut through both sheets and re-move the waste. Use a paint scraper to hold the vinyl hard against the junction of floor and baseboard, and trim off the surplus with a craft knife.

Trimming around a door frame

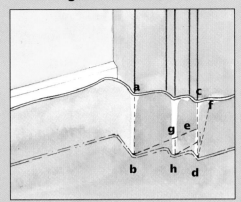

1 Make two 2in (5cm) vertical cuts in the vinyl at the projecting points of the frame (**ab** and **cd**). Next, make diagonal cuts to the same points (**eb** and **fd**). Make another vertical cut around the frame (**gh**) and cut diagonally (**ih**).

2 Press the vinyl tightly against the frame and trim off the surplus. Take the vinyl into the doorway and trim it so that it will end up halfway under the door. Finish it off later with a metal edging strip to prevent it from lifting.

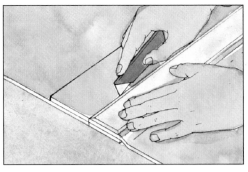

Seams

If adjoining vinyl overlaps at any point, use a straightedge and a sharp craft knife to cut through both thickness at the same time. Pull away the waste material and you will be left with a perfect fit.

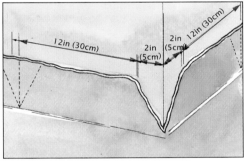

External corners

Lift the vinyl and make a vertical cut at the corner. Take the knife blade just to the floor. Make further diagonal cuts from 2in (5cm) on each side down to the base of the first cut so that the vinyl will rest against each wall. Make other cuts about every 12in (30cm) if necessary. Hold the vinyl tight against the wall with a block of wood, then position the knife with its point where the wall and floor meet. Cut into the corner holding the blade at 45° as you proceed. Repeat this process for the remaining flap of vinyl, making sure to get a neat fit on the corner. Bear in mind that it is better to trim away too little than too much: you can always pare away a little more if necessary. Finish all the fitting before sticking down the vinyl.

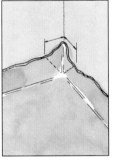

Internal corners

Leave 1in (2.5cm) of the surplus running up the wall, then cut out a triangle from the corner. This will allow you to press the vinyl against both walls for trimming.

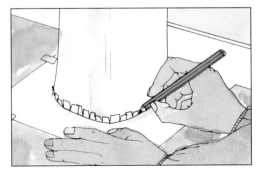

Pedestals

With awkward shapes, such as a pedestal vanity unit, it is best to make a paper template first and then transfer the shape onto the vinyl to be cut.

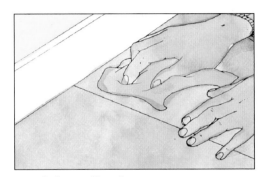

Applying adhesive

Apply adhesive with a notched spreader. Check how long the adhesive should be left before the vinyl is applied. With solvent adhesive, work in a well-ventilated area and avoid smoking or any form of naked flames.

Cutting safely

Sheet vinyl is not easy to cut and care is needed. Keep a sheet of scrap board on hand on which to make cuts: the knife may snag on floorboards. Use a sharp knife with a snap-off blade so that you always have a sharp edge. Position a steel straightedge along the line to be cut and use it so the blade cuts away from your other hand. With thick vinyl, make a number of passes, allowing the knife to follow the cut until it breaks through. If vinyl has to be cut *in situ*, push the blade through the sheet and pull it along the marked line – again make sure that your holding hand is always behind the direction of the cut.

Linoleum motifs

Linoleum – either in sheet form or tiles – will give you long and durable service if laid on a perfectly flat base. Linoleum is malleable and will readily mold itself to even quite minor inconsistencies and undulations in the underlying floor. The raised ridges then become points of weakness, which are prone to cracking or splitting. As you have already seen (see p. 78-82), the most difficult aspect of laying linoleum is cutting it to fit exactly the edges of a room, where you need to accommodate baseboards and built-in fixtures such as cabinets, toilet pedestals, central heating or water pipes, and so on.

This technique lets you transform an ordinary linoleum floor into a personal style statement. The ease with which the material can be cut means that you can make any shape of decorative motif or border, in blending or contrasting colors, and then set it into the linoleum floor covering. The example here consists of a two-color star surrounded by a border set within an overall background color of linoleum. The order of working is: lay the background linoleum to be encompassed by the border; cut and lay the border; lay the out-fill (from the outside edge of the border to the room edges); and finally, cut and inset the motif.

Although these are geometric shapes, the template from which they were created could just as easily be a fantasy figure or cartoon character for a child's bedroom or a shell-strewn beach suitable for a family bathroom.

Materials and equipment

- Plywood or latex floor covering
- ¾in (19mm) ring nails
- Hammer
- Tape measure
- Pencil
- Metal straightedge or steel ruler
- Water-based linoleum adhesive
- Adhesive spreader
- Clean rags or sponges
- Round-edged bolster
- Electric heat gun (type used for paint stripping)
- Scoring knife or pin vise
- Cutting knife
- Background color linoleum
- Linoleum for motif and border
- Paper and thin cardboard for making template
- Tape

1 Measure and draw on the plywood floor covering the area that will be encompassed by the border design. This will be the central panel. Using a metal straightedge as a guide, first deeply score the linoleum for the central panel and then cut it all the way through with a cutting blade.

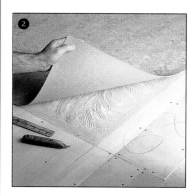

2 Spread adhesive up to the edges of the pencil lines. Align one side of the cut linoleum panel with a ruled edge and press it down into place. Remove any trapped air with the round-edged bolster. Check that the edges are well stuck. Use the heat gun to aid adhesion. Wipe off excess adhesive.

3 Cut strips of the border to fit around the outside of the central panel. Use the strips as a guide for cutting mitered corners. When all strips fit, spread adhesive over the plywood and stick the strips down. Work out any trapped air and make sure the edges are well stuck down. Remove excess adhesive.

HINTS AND TIPS

- Cover a wooden floor with ¼in (6mm) plywood as a base for the linoleum. Hammer all nail heads down flush.

- Cover a concrete floor with latex solution to give a perfectly even base on which to work.

- An electric heat gun keeps the linoleum pliable. Move the gun 6-8in (15-20cm) above the material for 3-5 seconds at a time.

- If you want small amounts of linoleum for a decorative motif, try to acquire some scraps or use linoleum tiles.

4 Measure and cut the linoleum for the outfill – this is the area outside the border and central panel stretching from the outer edges of the border to the room edges. Carry the diagonal cut line created by the border miters through the outfill linoleum. This makes fitting easier.

5 The motif shown in this example is a 2-color, 5-pointed star. As you can see, each arm of the star consists of 2 mirror-image triangles, set base-to-base. To make this design, simply cut out one triangle from the drawing and use this to make a cutting template of thin cardboard.

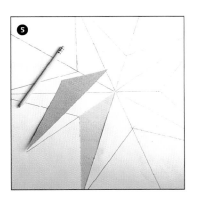

6 Use the template to cut the linoleum elements of the star. Turn the template over to create right- or left-facing triangles.

7 Stick the linoleum star motif together with tape. Place it in the middle of the central panel and trace around it. Using a metal straightedge as a guide, score around the shape. Then use a cutting blade to deepen and widen the scored line in the panels. Cut right through the linoleum.

8 Slip the blade carefully under one cut point on the central panel and then start lifting out the star. This shouldn't be a problem even if the material has been down for a few days and been walked on. Lift steadily, cutting the adhesive with a blade as it lifts away from the plywood base.

9 Clean off the old adhesive and apply fresh. Fit the star into position. Use the handle of

the bolster to tap the edges down, and the rounded blade to work out any trapped air. The heat gun will keep the linoleum pliable. When the star

is in place, peel off the tape and clean off excess adhesive. If you find there are any gaps around the star, scrape the surface off a scrap of

background linoleum, rub it into powder, mix it with adhesive, and smear it into place.

9

Storage

Choosing and planning

One of the features of modern life is clutter. The home has never been a materially more complicated place, and the need for attractive and versatile storage never greater.

In the kitchen, typically we find a range of saucepans, dishes, mixers, grinders, graters, extractors, kettles, and toasters, not to mention larger items such as stoves, refrigerators, washing machines, and dishwashers. And don't forget the table and chairs. In a mixed-activity room, such as the living room, the clutter can be far worse. How do you move for couches, coffee tables, ornaments, books, magazines, record collections and sound systems, television sets, CD players, and computers?

It would be possible to make a list such as this for every room in the home. Bear in mind, however, that the type of storage option you favor may vary from room to room, depending on the degree of clutter and the type of atmosphere you wish to create.

Awkward spaces

In a narrow galley kitchen, a combination of traditional storage – in the form of a freestanding hutch – and floor- and wall-mounted units, maximizes the amount of standing space in the center of the room.

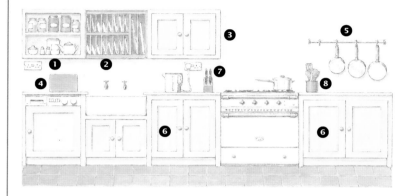

1 Open shelves for display **2** Plate rack for everyday dishes
3 Closed cabinets for storage or for things that need to be kept up high, away from small children **4** Cutting boards close at hand
5 Pot rack when shelf space is limited **6** Base cabinets are ideal for heavy objects and their tops make good work surfaces **7** Knife rack
8 Containers for utensils used daily.

Kitchens

In the kitchen, built-in base and eye-level cabinets are an effective way of keeping things out of sight until they are needed. The range of modern materials, surface finishes, and colors available is extra-ordinarily large, allowing your imagination full reign.

However, innovations from the past should not be overlooked. In a large family kitchen, or a country-style room, why not consider a traditional hutch? Hutches in traditional designs are still made today, and most offer you a combination of open shelving, on which to display your best and most attractive dishes and ornaments, as well as closed cupboards beneath for all those less-eyecatching items that you don't want on permanent show. Perhaps the answer to your kitchen storage problem may be a mixture of the old and the new – in the food-preparation area, built-in, easy-clean units may be best, while in the eating area you may favor the friendly charm of a hutch or a set of open wall shelves.

Mixed-activity rooms

Purpose-made cabinets to accommodate the typical types of home-entertainment equipment – such as televisions and video recorders – are readily available. Modular designs allow you to add on as necessary if you want your hi-fi system in the same area of the

Above *A place for everything, and everything in its place – this is the philosophy behind this immaculately planned work room.*

room. Many, too, also allow you to extend the units upward, with purpose-made units for tapes and CDs. By choosing the modular components with care, you should be able to put together just the right size and shape to fit into, say, the alcove created between the door and the corner. These units are often very simple to make, and you should have few problems in building your own if you wish.

Walls are often under-utilized for storage and display, especially hard-to-get-at areas above tables and sofas. Open shelves here may be the perfect place to display ornaments and paintings, since you will only rarely want access to them. Where books are concerned, however, make sure that you build shelving in an easily accessible part of the room, or you may wish to build or buy freestanding bookshelves instead. With these you have the added flexibility of being able to change the arrangement of the furniture at will without destroying the room's decor.

Left *If shelves and cupboards do not provide sufficient storage space, then kitchen utensils suspended above head height from the ceiling can make an attractive display.*

Above *Practical as well as attractive, this simple set of wall shelves is the perfect place to show off your dishes, or ornaments, without restricting access to them.*

Right *There are lots of ideas for storage of different kinds in this room. In particular, ways of storing in the office, using the same storage drawers repeated; and a freestanding unit to house small features, books and sound system.*

Bathrooms

The main storage requirements in a bathroom are for linen, towels, toiletries, and cosmetics. If the hot-water boiler is in the bathroom, then building a linen cupboard surrounding it, with slatted shelves to allow warm air to circulate around the towels, sheets, and so on, can be a great boon.

If you have young children, you need to take care with medicines. You could readily build or buy a medicine chest, which should then be mounted high on a wall and fitted with a secure lock.

Most modern bathrooms are not large, so there is usually relatively little scope for storage. However, in larger rooms you could include some freestanding furniture – perhaps a table with a flower display or a collection of trinkets or jars of colored sand the children have collected.

Bedrooms

The most obvious need for storage in a bedroom is for clothes and shoes. A good way of utilizing the available space is to build a closet along one wall. After the basic framework is in place, the fascia and doors can be made out of some sort of composite material or wood. A built-in closet can also incorporate a dresser and overhead cupboards.

In a child's bedroom, you will more than likely need somewhere for toys and games, as well as clothes and perhaps a study area, too, for an older child or teenager. An attractive storage solution for

Left *A period-style armoire fitted out with shelves is an elegant solution to the need for additional storage in any room of the house.*

Above *A modern freestanding column of shelves can be painted or left its natural color.*

Right *An alcove was created in this bathroom to support lightweight shelving. These, in turn, have been used to support one end of the vanity shelf.*

Above *A dazzling combination of yellow, green, and red has transformed an inexpensive chest into a spectacular hideaway for all those odds and ends that accumulate in a child's room.*

Left *Beds with spaces beneath can be utilized as storage areas, and small objects can be stored out of the way on high-level shelves.*

Below *Style has not been sacrificed in the pursuit of storage space in this basement kitchen, with a staggered series of storage cubicles moving diagonally up the wall supporting the staircase.*

toys and games, assuming you don't want to use a built-in closet, is a toy chest. This is relatively simple to make, or you can adapt an old chest or blanket box for the job, perhaps giving it a coat of paint in bright colors and making sure there are no nail heads standing above the wood. Where space is tight, modular furniture systems are available that incorporate bunk beds, an integral closet (usually quite small), and a study area.

Hallways and stairs

Since the hallways and stairways are often thought of as the connecting bits between the "real" rooms of the house, their full potential as storage areas is usually not realized. Mounted on the wall above the front door, for example, you could construct an out-of-the-way storage cupboard. Or, if the stairs are comfortably wide, you may be able to build a set of bookshelves on the wall, and be able to choose books at different heights as you ascend or descend the stairs.

The largest potential storage area in a hallway, however, is often the space under the stairs. In an existing understairs closet, you may decide to change the internal arrangement of shelves and partitions, as well as the access doors to allow better use to be made of it, for storing brooms and other cleaning equipment, for example.

Shelving

Shelves can be strictly utilitarian or attractive enough to be a positive room feature. Shelves are available in a wide range of materials and can be either fixed in one position or adjustable.

An alcove or recess, formed by the construction of the house, or put in a purpose-built niche, is an ideal place for shelves; they can be mounted flush to the walls or uprights where the fixments will be virtually invisible.

Before starting, you need to consider the composition of the supporting walls, since this will determine the size and type of hardware you choose (*see p.100-101*).

Heavy-duty goods will need strong shelves and supports. Since this usually occurs in garages and workshops, appearance is not as important as strength. The shelving is erected using the same methods as those for indoor shelves, but the hardware may be slightly different.

Left *Adjustable shelving used as a display area for a range of ornaments of different sizes and shapes.*

Above 1 *Veneered particle board* 2 *Zinc-covered medium-density fiberboard* 3 *Safety glass* 4 *Pine* 5 *Sand-blasted wood* 6 *Recycled plastic* 7 *Laminated blockboard*

Maximum spans between supports

The following table gives an indication of the distances between supports.

	thickness	span
Wood	⅝in (15mm)	1ft 8in (500mm)
	¾in (20mm)	3ft (900mm)
	1¼in (30mm)	3ft 8in (1100mm)
Blockboard	½in (12mm)	1ft 6in (450mm)
Plywood	¾in (20mm)	2ft 8in (800mm)
	1in (25mm)	3ft 4in (1000mm)
Veneered	½in (12mm)	1ft 4in (400mm)
blockboard	¾in (20mm)	2ft (600mm)
	1in (25mm)	2ft 6in (750mm)

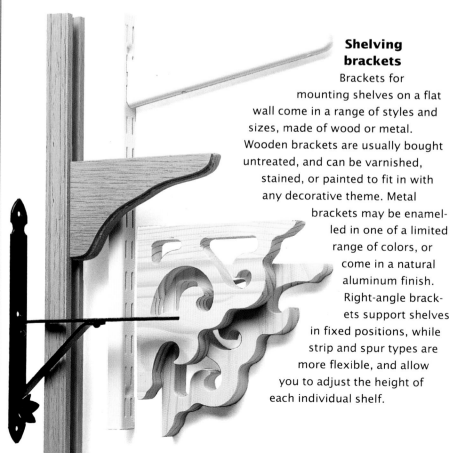

Shelving brackets

Brackets for mounting shelves on a flat wall come in a range of styles and sizes, made of wood or metal. Wooden brackets are usually bought untreated, and can be varnished, stained, or painted to fit in with any decorative theme. Metal brackets may be enamelled in one of a limited range of colors, or come in a natural aluminum finish. Right-angle brackets support shelves in fixed positions, while strip and spur types are more flexible, and allow you to adjust the height of each individual shelf.

Shelving in an alcove

There are many different ways of fitting shelves, like the one shown here:

1 Wooden or metal pegs fitted into predrilled holes in the side uprights are a neat type of recess fixing. The supports, along the width of the shelves, are almost invisible.

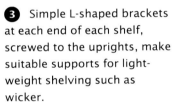

2 If you do not want the supports to be a feature for a glass shelf, then use plastic or rubber-covered dowels.

3 Simple L-shaped brackets at each end of each shelf, screwed to the uprights, make suitable supports for light-weight shelving such as wicker.

4 When shelves need to be very securely fixed in place, this type of bracket supports the entire width of the shelf.

5 Fixing strips and spur brackets allow you to vary the space between the shelves, and to accommodate different sized items. They do, however, support the entire length of the shelf and are, therefore, more visible.

6 Simple right-angle brackets are inexpensive to buy and very serviceable. Unlike strip and spur fixings, they do not allow you to vary the shelf intervals.

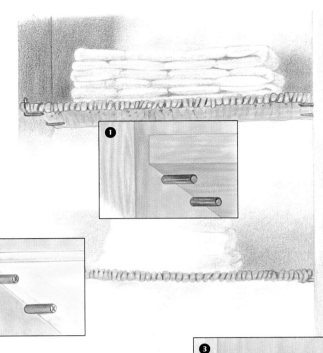

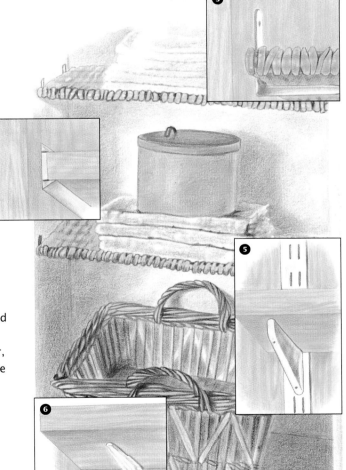

Heavy-duty shelves

1 For heavy loads a wooden upright is plugged and screwed to the wall and a stout bracket screwed to it.

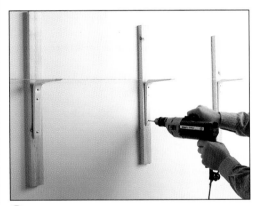

2 The outer brackets are mounted first and the center ones are positioned using a string-line. A pilot hole will avoid splitting the wood.

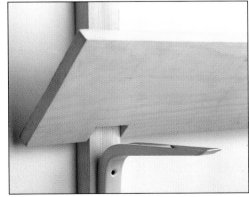

3 For a neat fit, the shelves are notched to fit around the wooden uprights before being screwed into place.

To hang a short length of shelving, you can attach the right-angle brackets to the shelf first.

Simple storage

There is an adage that states that possessions expand to fill the available space, and no sooner have you added a cupboard or set of shelves to your home than they seem full to overflowing once more. Simply building or buying more and more freestanding or built-in units all too often results in an uncoordinated, esthetically unsatisfactory look as different shapes and styles are slowly incorporated into your rooms. One solution to this dilemma is to devise some sort of modular storage system that you can add to as the need arises. By using the same materials and method of construction, you can increase the overall height or length of the storage unit whenever you choose while maintaining a design consistency within the room. For smaller objects, especially those you use frequently and need to find instantly, there will always be a need for simple, convenient, yet attractive, storage solutions.

Top *A lattice of wood makes things instantly available.*

Left *Narrow freestanding shelves accommodate kitchen overflow.*

Above *Pull-out wicker baskets arranged on drawer runners provide much welcome extra storage in this small kitchen alcove.*

Small-scale storage

It is the small-scale storage objects we collect and display that tend to give our homes charm and character and reveal, often unconsciously, much about our personalities. In any room in the house, you have the chance to make a creative statement by including some carefully chosen boxes, a basket, some spoon holders in the kitchen, or a wine rack in the dining room.

Many of these objects would be suitable as home-built projects, and yet others can be picked up for next to nothing at thrift stores and secondhand dealers. If the color is not right, they can be painted or even découpaged.

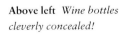

Above left *Wine bottles cleverly concealed!*

Left *Shaker-style round wooden boxes make charming storage boxes for letters, trinkets, and other small items. These boxes come in sets designed to fit inside each other.*

Top *An unusual solution to the problem of storing wood for an open fire has been provided by this columnar metal frame. Holding far more wood and kindling than a traditional wicker basket, it takes up very little floor space.*

Above left and above *Three ideas for storage systems: stacking vegetable baskets used for toys; open shelves decorated to match a collection of sea shells; and a freestanding wine rack, tucked neatly out of the way on the floor of an alcove.*

Toy box

Whereas large-sized toys can be put safely out of the way on shelves or stood in a corner when playtime is over, there is always a need to confine small toys and games somewhere safe, especially if there are component pieces that could easily become lost if left lying about on the floor. For a lightweight toy box, use ½in (12mm) plywood. However, if a large, robust box is needed, then it is best to use ¾in (18mm) blockboard instead.

Once the box is constructed, you can decide on the most appropriate form of decoration. First, choose a background color and then perhaps add a motif, such as your child's favorite cartoon character, or use a stencilled design or even cut-outs from magazines or comics pasted down and then varnished to protect them.

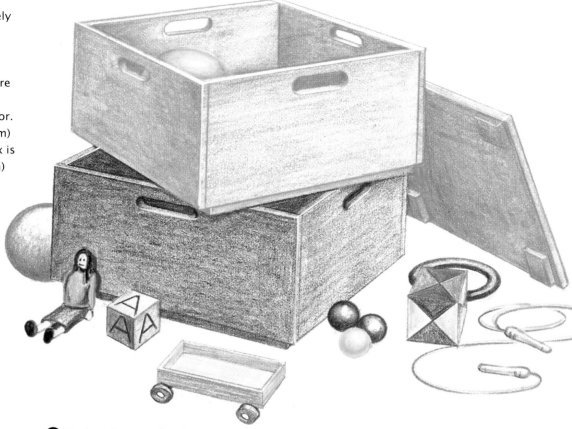

Materials and equipment

- Blockboard (or plywood) for sides, base, and lid

- Wood saw

- Try square

- Smoothing plane

- Swing brace and auger bit

- Jigsaw or padsaw

- Medium-grit sandpaper

- Nails, tacks, and hammer

- PVA woodworking glue

- Nail set

- Woodfiller and smoothing tool

1 Mark and cut out ¾in (18mm) blockboard for the sides and then smooth all edges with a smoothing plane. Bear in mind that the dimensions of all the modules must be precisely the same or they will not stack properly when completed.

2 Mark the positions of the handle holes 2in (5cm) from the edge. Drill holes at each end using a 1in (2.5cm) diameter auger bit in a swing brace and then use a jigsaw or padsaw to cut out the remainder of each hole between the guidelines. Smooth the inside of the handle with medium-grit sandpaper.

3 Drive three 2in (5cm) oval nails ⅜in (9mm) from the edges on two of the sides. The nails should just protrude through the board. Apply PVA woodworking glue to the edge of one adjoining side.

4 Position the two sides squarely together and drive home the nails. Complete the side assembly in this way by applying glue to the next side to be joined,

positioning it carefully, and driving in the nails.

5 Hold the fourth side in place, check the corners with a try square, and measure the inside open frame. Cut the base piece to fit.

6 Position the base flush with the bottom edge of the sides, then glue and tack the base between the three completed sides.

7 Apply wood glue to the edges of the two open sides and base, carefully position the fourth side, and drive home the nails.

8 Using a nail set and hammer, drive all the nail and tack heads below the surface of the wood and fill the holes with a suitable filler. When dry, sand the filler smooth with medium-grit sandpaper.

9 Cut a lid to fit over the box, and cut a handle hole as described in **2**. From blockboard, cut 3in square (7.5cm square) locating blocks. Glue them ¾in (19mm) from the corner of the lid and ⅟₃₂in (1mm) from the corners of the base panel.

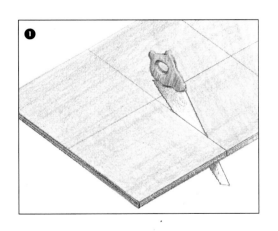

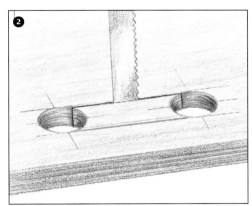

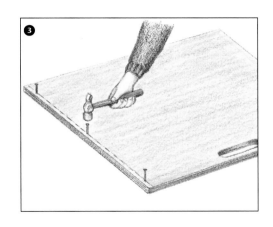

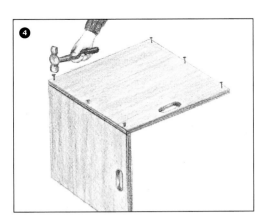

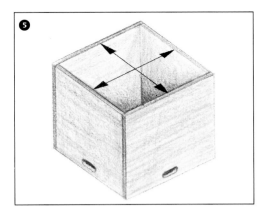

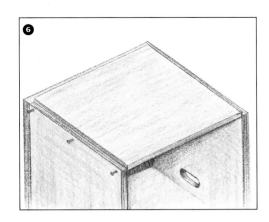

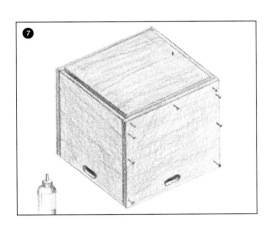

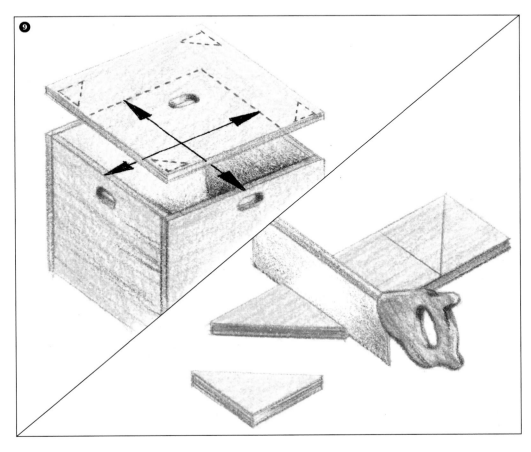

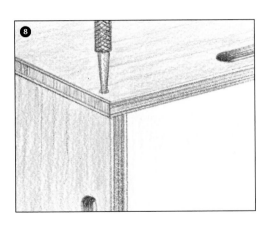

Unusual storage spaces

Practically every house has some area of under-utilized space that could potentially be used for extra storage; it is just a matter of looking properly. Older houses tend to be better endowed in this respect because they are likely to have more of the recesses, higher ceilings, and the types of nooks and crannies you find only rarely in modern, formula-built houses and apartments.

Over the years, houses are often added to and adapted to suit the needs of the current generation, and each change brings about its own potential for extra storage space. Look at the storage areas currently in use to see whether you could change the way the doors open or rearrange the internal divisions or shelving. You may find that you can make better use of them.

Below *The free space beneath this staircase has been utilized to the full. Racks of shelves running the full depth of the stairs can be pulled out to provide access and, when closed, they produce a flush finish.*

The modern home

In the contemporary house or apartment, rooms can be of such meager dimensions that your imaginations needs to work overtime to find space for the most modest amount of day-to-day clutter. In such a situation, the best solution may be to devote one room, perhaps a spare bedroom or an accessible attic, to storage. Clothes can be hung on a series of open rods, of the type used in stores, and one wall could be taken up with a series of modular storage boxes, stacked as high as necessary, to accommodate less-used objects. Where this is not possible, then look for unusual ways of utilizing what space is available – walls, for example, especially in little-used corridors, can often be pressed into service, as can the usually wasted space found underneath beds.

Left Any area of flat wall, even the tiny space seen here sandwiched between a doorway and staircase, can be fitted out with shelves for books. The supporting upright then makes a convenient surface on which to hand pictures.

Below left This unusual storage space surrounding the fireplace is turned into a feature by filling it with piles of logs.

Above In true Shaker tradition, the lengths of pegboard running around the walls of this room have been used to support a plain set of shelves hung on stout cords.

Left Older and traditionally built houses have interesting nooks and crannies that can be pressed into service as unusual storage areas.

The Shaker tradition

The Shakers were one of a number of Utopian sects that migrated to the New World in the 18th century. The interiors of Shakers' houses were kept light, plain, and simple. Storage was often built in, and their clever designs for walls of cupboards and smoothly fitted drawers have never been bettered. In fact, copies of traditional Shaker designs are on sale today and are still immensely popular. Because Shaker rooms were also often used as meeting places, any objects that might clutter the room – hats, cloaks, tools, chairs, clocks, and so on – were hung on pegboards high on the walls out of the way. Their storage boxes, which tended to be made in sets that fitted inside one another, were also coded in cheerful colors depending on their contents. Many of the practicalities that shaped these traditions are just as relevant now, especially where space is limited in modern homes.

Cabinets

Many houses have alcoves and recesses that are often wasted spaces. Built-in cabinets, of the type shown here, not only provide useful storage space for a range of items, but may also enhance the appearance of the room.

The recesses on each side of a chimney are obvious places to build in. But since the sides of an alcove are rarely flat and true, even in a new building, it is essential to construct each cabinet as a freestanding unit, fractionally smaller than the alcove. To fit it neatly into the recess, join it to a fascia frame. Make the frame very slightly oversized and then plane it to fit snugly into the opening with the top and bottom rails perfectly horizontal.

Materials and equipment

- Wood, blockboard, and plywood for fascias, frames, top and bottom boards, sides, shelves, and doors

- Ready-made doors, if preferred

- Marking gauge

- Try square

- Profile gauge

- Tenon saw

- Clamp

- Smoothing plane

- Powered jigsaw or hand coping saw

- Wood saw

- Adhesive

- Tacks, screws, and anchors

- Screwdriver and hammer

- Steel corner brackets

- Power drill and masonry bit

- Carpenter's level

- Iron-on veneer

- Hinges

- Handles

- Magnetic catches

1 Measure and cut 1 x 3in (2.5 x 7.5cm) softwood for the upper and lower fascia frames. Mark out lapped joints at the corners of the frames, using a try square and marking gauge, to half the depth of the wood and the width of the adjoining piece. Cut down the shoulder to the center line with a tenon saw, then remove the waste wood by cutting down from the end.

2 Check the joint for fit and then apply adhesive to the shoulder and face of both parts. Clamp loosely, check the corner with the try square, and tighten the clamp. Trim all

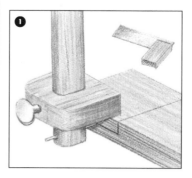

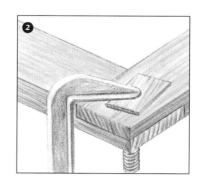

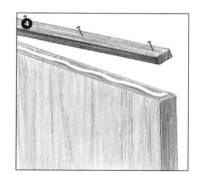

faces of the joint neatly with a smoothing plane and trim the upper frame to fit the alcove.

3 Set a profile gauge to the shape of the baseboard at the height of the lower frame, and then transfer the outline to the wood. Carefully cut out and smooth the baseboard shape.

4 Measure and cut ¾in (18mm) blockboard for shelves, top board, doors, and foot board. The top should overlap the finish flush with the lower cabinet fascia. Glue and tack a strip of hardwood to the front edge of the top board of the lower cabinet.

5 Use 1 x 1in (2.5 x 2.5cm) battens to join the cabinet components. Cut to length and drill for inserting screws.

6 Glue the screw battens to the outer edges of the top and bottom panels, and to the front edges of end panels. Join the cabinet and fascia frames by gluing and screwing through the battens on the outside.

7 The cabinet backs are ⅙in (4mm) plywood, glued and tacked into position.

8 Fit brackets into corners of cabinets. Drill the back through the hole in each one.

9 Cut the foot board from 1in (2.5cm) thick wood to fit between the baseboards and to reach from the floor to the underside of the bottom panel. Drill and screw to the back of the fascia.

10 Before anchoring the cabinets in position, finish the outside with paint or varnish. When dry, position each side and check that it is horizontal using a level. Mark through the brackets, remove the cabinets, and drill the wall with a masonry bit. Insert wall anchors and screw the cabinets securely into place.

11 Exposed edges of block-board on shelves and doors should be edged by applying a matching iron-on veneer.

12 Make doors to fit, or buy doors, and adjust them to suit your cabinet dimensions. Screw flush hinges to the backs of the doors and hang them by screwing the flaps of the hinges to the fascia frames.

13 Drill the doors (with scrap wood behind to prevent bursting through) and place the handles in convenient positions. Finally, install magnetic catches to hold the doors closed.

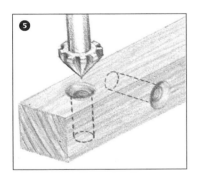

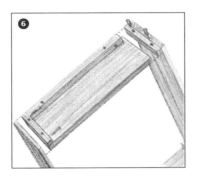

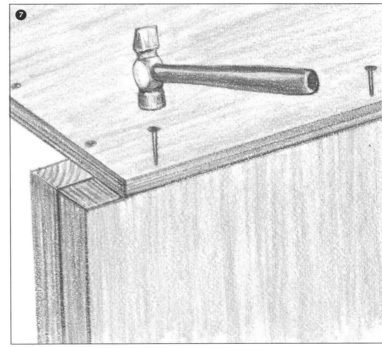

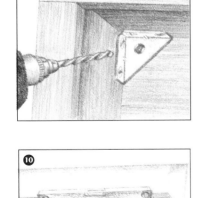

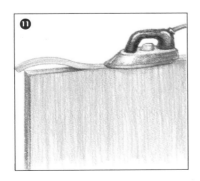

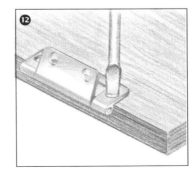

Closets

The major advantage of a built-in closet is that it makes best use of any available space – you can take it right up to the ceiling and wall, sometimes to both walls, to produce wall-to-wall storage. This, too, is often the most attractive option.

With built-in furniture there is the potential problem of uneven ceilings and out-of-true corners. To overcome this, first mount a framework to the walls, using masonite or plywood scraps to level out the undulations.

Below By building the closet out more from the wall, a chimney breast can be incorporated.

Bottom This closet fills out the alcoves, leaving the chimney breast intact.

Closet hardware

Built-in closets help you make the best possible use of space, but they must be fitted out carefully inside or you will end up with a disorderly jumble.

Interior fittings

It is a good idea to fit an intermediate shelf to the width of the closet just above hanging rail height, with a clearance of 1¾–2½in (4.5–6.5cm) to allow space for hangers to be hooked over the rod. Where the closet is not deep enough for a side-to-side rod, there are various front-to-back rods that will allow you to organize your clothes efficiently.

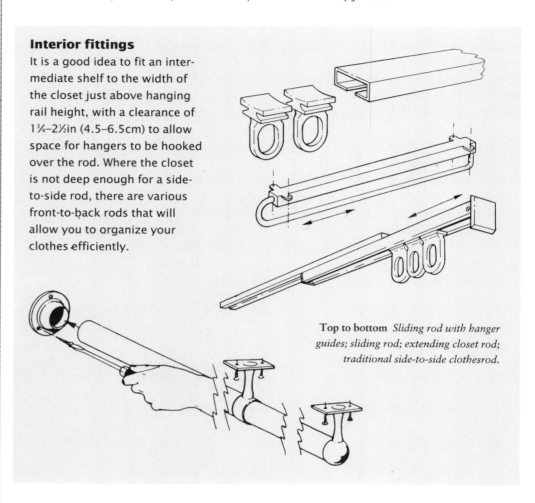

Top to bottom Sliding rod with hanger guides; sliding rod; extending closet rod; traditional side-to-side clothesrod.

Hinges

There is a good choice of different types of hinge designed to be used by those with little or no carpentry skills.

Lay-on – screwed to inside surface of door and cabinet side. Concealed when closed

Flush – does not need a recess in either the door or the door frame

Concealed cabinet – requires a hole to be bored on the inside surface of the door

Easy hang – this cranked hinge does not need a recess in either the frame or the door

Butt – made of pressed steel, this is useful for internal and external doors

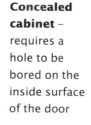

Simple woodworking joints

A well-made joint will increase the strength of the piece as well as ensuring that it is completely square. There are many different woodworking joints and their variations, but the ones most useful for the storage projects in this chapter are described here.

Butt joint This is a simple joint but it needs to be carefully prepared in order to be strong and look professional. The square-ended butt joint involves joining two pieces of wood or board together, usually end to side, to form a right-angled corner, or a T-joint. To be successful, a butt joint must be cut squarely and accurately. Trim the cut ends with a plane if necessary and then glue and pin or screw.

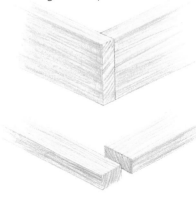

Dowel joint Dowels (hardwood pegs) are an effective means of strengthening a butt joint without resorting to screws or nails, both of which are visible on the surface. Use precut, fluted dowels with chamfered ends, which make a strong joint by allowing glue to escape from the dowel hole, coating the surface of the dowel as the joint is assembled.

Hardwood dowels are an excellent form of invisible

strengthening for a butt joint. Center points help to align holes.

Corner-lapped joints
Lapped joints are ideal for joining wood of the same thickness. This joint is formed by measuring and cutting each piece to half its thickness.

To make a corner-lapped joint, first saw down to the shoulder line on each side.

Hardware
The choice of simple-to-use ready-made joints now available makes many building projects very straight-forward. These joints require no woodworking skill to use, and all are invisible once the doors are closed.

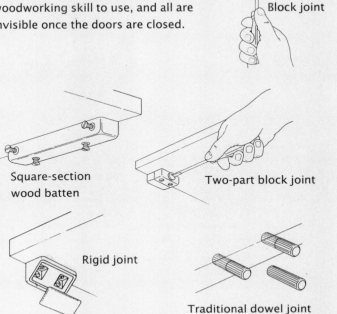

Block joint

Square-section wood batten

Two-part block joint

Rigid joint

Traditional dowel joint

Then saw square to the shoulder, and then finally across.

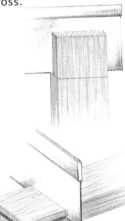

T-joints Like the corner-lapped joint, this type of joint is also used for joining wood of the same thickness, but this time to form cross rails. Again, you need to measure and cut each piece to half its original thickness.

To make the T-joint, saw down to the shoulder line using a series of cuts and then chisel out the waste wood.

Above *Wall-mounted shelves are an obvious storage solution when floor space is limited, but even a space too small for a traditional closet can be adapted by using freestanding racks of the type shown here.*

Materials and equipment

- Wood, blockboard, and plywood for fascias, battens, shelves, and doors

- Ready-made doors, if preferred

- Molding

- Wood saw

- Tenon saw

- Electric jigsaw

- Carpenter's level

- Try square

- Marking gauge

- Smoothing plane

- Power drill and masonry bit

- Clamps

- PVA woodworking glue

- Tacks, brads, screws, and wall anchors

- Hammer and screwdriver

- Chisel

- Angle brackets

- Iron-on veneer

- Hinges, handles, and magnetic catches

- Paint or varnish and brushes

Construction

The best way to approach a recess comprising a chimney and alcoves is to construct cupboards as identical units. An ideal width for doors is 24in (60cm) – this allows you to cut them from a 4ft (1.2m) sheet of blockboard without wastage (or use ready-made doors). If this width of door is not convenient for the space you have, determine the number and size of doors by measuring the distance from wall to wall and then calculating the number of same-size doors that fit, allowing space for them to open.

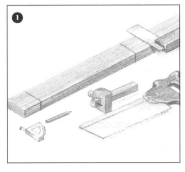

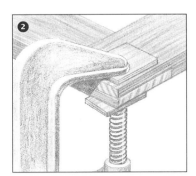

1 Cut to length 3 x 1in (7.5 x 2.5cm) softwood for the fascia framework. Mark and cut T- and corner-lapped joints using a tenon saw and chisel.

2 Use PVA woodworking glue and clamps to complete and secure the joints. Check with a try square before final tightening. When the glue has set, trim the joints neatly using a smoothing plane.

3 Mark and then cut out 6 x 1in (15 x 2.5cm) softwood for the footboard. Screw it to the rear of the bottom frame, ½in (12mm) below the top edge.

4 Cut ½in (12mm) plywood shelves. Screw 1 x 1in (2.5 x 2.5cm) battens to the wall and check they are level. Screw battens to the side and rear walls and then fix plywood to the battens with brads. Punch the brads below the surface. Install a batten at the rear of the frame on the horizontal member. Try the

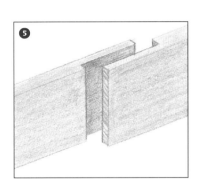

frame out. Tack the top shelf to the batten and the lower to the footboard.

5 Cut out the top inner fascia board from 6 x 1in (15 x 2.5cm) softwood, using a jigsaw or tenon saw. You may have to join two pieces.

6 Screw angle brackets to the rear of the fascia board and screw it to the ceiling – use the right hardware for your ceiling. Attach the inner fascia board to the rear of the side frames.

7 Make the central frame from 3 x 1in (7.5 x 2.5cm) softwood. Install it in between the side frames using brackets. Then screw it to the inner fascia.

8 Screw 1 x 1in (2.5 x 2.5cm) battens to the chimney wall, with inner edges aligning with those of the fascia.

9 Cut and fit ¾in (18mm)

blockboard to enclose each cupboard. Tack side panels using brads.

10 If required, cut the dresser top from ¾in (18mm) blockboard. Fit 1 x 1in (2.5 x 2.5cm) battens to the sides of the cupboards and rear wall.

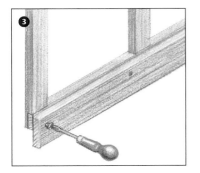

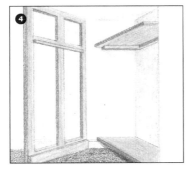

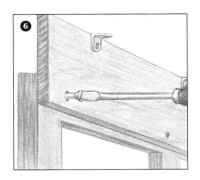

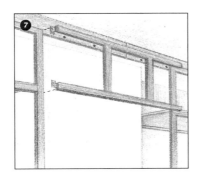

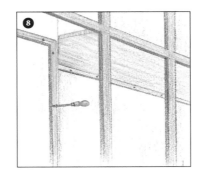

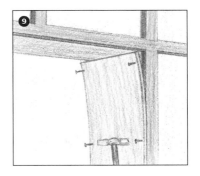

Attach a 2 x 1in (5 x 2.5cm) batten to the front. Screw the top to the battens.

11 Install clothesrod brackets on the end wall and the side of the chimney. Slot the pole into one bracket before installing the other.

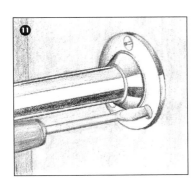

12 Cut the doors to size from ¾in (18mm) blockboard and add a decorative molding to give a panelled effect – or use ready-made doors adjusted to fit. If using blockboard, cover all exposed edges with veneer. Screw three 3in (7.5cm) flush hinges to each door, then fit to the frame. Install door handles and magnetic catches. Sand the complete structure ready for painting or varnishing.

Commissioning professionals

Having decided on a repair or improvement project for the home, the next decision is whether to do the job yourself or to call in a professional. Complicated or long projects may require expertise or time which the homeowner may not have, but that does not mean that the whole job has to be turned over to a contractor. A compromise could be to do most of the groundwork yourself and hire specialists, such as plasterers, plumbers or electricians, where necessary. Working much faster than an amateur is able to, skilled professionals can save a lot of time and worry. If you decide that hiring a professional is the answer, be it an architect, general builder or specialist, going about it in a businesslike manner will help you get what you want and avoid potential pitfalls.

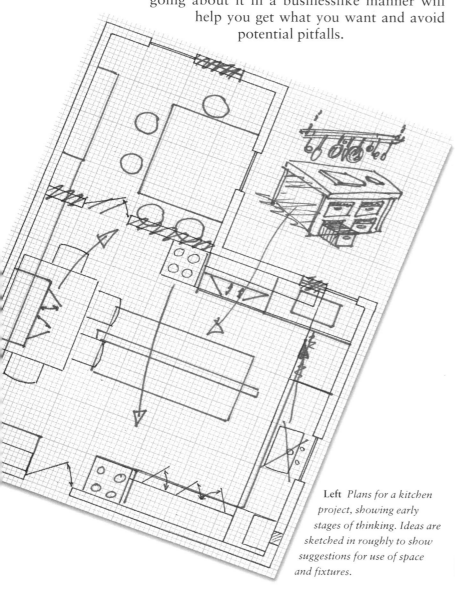

Left Plans for a kitchen project, showing early stages of thinking. Ideas are sketched in roughly to show suggestions for use of space and fixtures.

Choosing the right professional for the job

For large-scale projects, such as major structural alteration or building an extension, it is wise to consult an architect. An architect will discuss your plans with you, be able to make constructive suggestions you had not considered, and produce structurally sound designs that also look good. In addition, he or she can submit the necessary planning applications and, if desired, hire the building contractor and supervise the work to make sure it meets the specifications.

When hiring a builder yourself, it is essential to choose a reliable and reputable person who understands your requirements and can do the job competently within a specified time and according to your budget. Finding such a builder can be a daunting prospect but thankfully, and in spite of the many horror stories of shoddy work and unexplained absences, there are many reliable ones.

Personal recommendation is a good place to start. If you know someone who has recently used a builder, ask to see their work and ask how they conducted the job. Failing that, the names of builders can be found in telephone directories and newspapers. Not all builders do all kinds of work, however, so be prepared for some refusals. Look for contractors who are members of a trade association. Although membership does not necessarily guarantee the work, it usually is dependent on a having a sound reputation as well as bank and insurance references. A good craftsperson is proud of his or her work and will be pleased to supply you with references for you to follow up where you can inspect examples of workmanship.

Ask more than one contractor for an estimate so that you can compare costs. Estimates will be based on current prices, and may have to change if you do not decide to go ahead with the work immediately. Cost will not be the only criterion in deciding which builder to use. Their attitude and your confidence in their ability to do the job are equally important.

Establishing the brief

Disagreements between builder and client often arise from a misunderstanding as the result of inadequate briefing. The builder may be working to the best of his understanding which, unfortunately, is not what the client had intended. The best way to avoid this problem is to provide the builder with a written specification – a list of the work to be done, the materials to be used, and an indication of the required completion date. Many details will need to be revised, but this will give the builder a good idea of your requirements and can form the basis of an estimate for the cost. Before writing a specification, read the relevant chapter in this book to get an idea of the amount and type of work involved.

A quotation is a fixed price for a job. Before asking a builder to start work, ask for a firm quotation with a breakdown of the costs based on all the points you have discussed; provide a revised specification if necessary. There may be grey areas in the quotation, for example, estimated costs for sub-contractors such as plumbers or electricians; you can try to get these firmed up before the job begins or you must be prepared to accept the charges. Make sure that all rubble and debris are to be removed and the site left clean and neat. If you require any making good and decoration, make sure that these are included in the costs.

You also need to agree in advance how you will pay for the job. A small job can be paid for on or soon after completion. But if a job is going to last for several weeks or months, and involves the purchase of a large amount of materials, it is reasonable for the builder to ask for interim payments to cover delivered materials and completed work; never pay for anything in advance. You can arrange to hold back 5 to 10 per cent of the costs on completion for a specified amount of time until you are sure that there is no faulty workmanship, but you must agree this with the contractor before the work starts.

Dealing with the unexpected

One can never guarantee, especially with a large project, that there will not be any unforeseen problems as the work progresses. If something unexpected has to be dealt with in the course of the work, ask for an estimate before agreeing to do the work. The same applies if you change your mind during the job or you ask for extra work to be done.

For large jobs, it is a good idea to ask the builder to provide a schedule list; if an architect is overseeing the job, he or she will draw one up and ask the builder to fill it in. It sets out the stages of work such as building a blockwork wall, installing new wiring, plastering, putting in a sink, etc.

As well as his or her own work, the builder is responsible for the quality of workmanship provided by any specialists needed. If you have any concerns over the work supplied by a subcontractor, discuss them with the builder rather than the person concerned. To avoid confusion, a subcontractor should be directed by one person only – the person who employed him or her.

If you are hiring individual specialists yourself to help with specific jobs as and when you need them, brief them as carefully and precisely as you would a general builder, and also ask for estimates or quotations for the work. Again, personal recommendation is the best thing to go by and inspecting examples of their work will convince you of their ability.

Good relations always make for better results in all fields of work. Try to understand the builder's requirements and problems. Provide the builder with access to electricity and water, if required, and storage space for tools. Be prepared for a certain amount of mess where the work is being carried out; good workers will clean up as best they can each night before leaving for home. Without interrupting the work, monitor progress and inspect work at night after the workers have gone home. If you are unhappy about any aspect of workmanship or the progress of the job, discuss it with the builder in the morning. If you cannot be there, leave a note or telephone to discuss what is worrying you.

Finally, if you are around during working hours, an occasional cup of coffee, without holding up the proceedings, works wonders.

Right You can make a copy of this checklist and check off the tasks as they are completed.

Working Contract

Set out your requirements and know exactly what a builder intends to supply. This provides the basis of a workable contract between the parties concerned.

Finding a contractor	Approach several contractors, personally recommended if possible. Make sure they have good references and ask to see examples of their work.	✓
Specifications	Give prospective contractors a clear and precise outline of the job before asking for estimates and quotations.	
Estimates	Ask several contractors for an estimate. This will give you an idea of costs and help you narrow down your choice. An estimate may be written or verbal, and is only a guide to the envisaged costs; the job itself may cost more, or less.	
Quotations	A written quotation is a set price for the job and should detail how the job is to be done and the materials to be used; it may or may not include provision for unforeseen problems. It is usually recommended that you get quotations from three contractors.	
Schedule list	If a job is large, a schedule list sets out all the stages of work. It is a good way of keeping track of all the jobs to be done, especially where more than one contractor is involved.	
Access	You must provide the builder with reasonable access to electricity and water if these are required for the job.	
Payment	Before work starts, agree exactly when payment is to be made and whether there are any conditions that will apply.	

Glossary

Abrasive paper Paper coated with abrasive particles for smoothing wood. Graded by grit size and spacing.

Adhesive Powerful bonding agent. Many types available for specific materials.

Adjustable wrench Open-ended wrench with a movable jaw to adapt to a wide range of sizes.

Awl Small tool used to make starting holes for screws and nails and for piercing leather.

Bag graining A traditional paint finish created by dabbing the freshly painted surface with a bag full of old rags.

Ball valve Valve operated by a float that rises and falls with the water level in cisterns.

Basin wrench Long-handled wrench designed for working in awkward spaces.

Belt sander Machine for removing old paint or finishing wood and metal.

Bending spring Long spring that fits inside or over copper pipes so they can be bent without collapsing the walls.

Bevel-edge chisel Bevel-bladed chisel suitable for light woodworking.

Blockboard Board made from bonded softwood chips, sold in several grades.

Blowlamp Hand-held propane or butane gas canister with flame used for soldering work and softening old paint ready for stripping. Needs to be used with care.

Bolster Wide, spade-shaped cold chisel designed for cutting bricks, but often used for lifting floorboards.

Cable Thick insulated wire for the permanent wiring of electrical systems.

Carpenter's level Vial containing liquid and an air bubble fitted into a holder, which can be of a number of designs and sizes, for checking levels.

C-clamp C-shaped clamp with large screw for securing wood or metal to a workbench.

Chisel Sharp-tipped wood-cutting tool used with a mallet.

Circuit Complete pass of wiring through which electric current flows.

Circuit breaker Incorporated into the fuse box or added on, cuts electricity supply if an overload, fault or leakage of electricity occurs.

Cold chisel Steel tool with double-ground edge for rough-cutting cold metal.

Colorwashing Application of thin glaze washes over a ground coat to create subtle veils of color.

Compression joint Dismantlable joint made with a compression fitment on plastic or copper pipe.

Continuity (circuit) tester Device for testing faults on electrical circuits.

Cord Insulated wire used to connect plugs to appliances and hanging lights to ceilings.

Countersink attachment Power-drill bit for cutting recesses to take screw heads.

Coving Decorative plaster or styrofoam molding between walls and ceiling.

Craft knife Handle fitted with sharp replaceable blades useful for cutting sheet materials and other items.

Damp-proof membrane Layer of impervious material in concrete floors to prevent moisture from rising up.

Dowel Short lengths of dowelling (tubular-shaped wood, sometimes grooved) used for joining wood.

Dry brushing Process in which a glaze applied over a previously painted color is stippled with a dry brush and then lightly brushed with a dusting brush while still wet.

File Rough-bladed tool for smoothing metal and wood, removing burrs and irregularities.

Floor sander One of two types of machine used together for sanding floors: the large drum sander sands the main area and the smaller disk sander cleans the edges.

Fuse Rewirable or cartridge devices designed to interrupt a circuit if a fault, overload or leakage of electricity occurs.

Fuse box Wall-hung box housing fixed wiring fuses.

Glue gun Gun-shaped device loaded with glue sticks, which it heats. The glue dries instantly on application.

Hot air stripper Electric device for softening paint ready for stripping.

Jigsaw Power saw for making curved cuts in wood and man-made boards.

Joist Wooden or metal beam used to support a structure like a floor, ceiling, or wall.

Limewashing Dry-brushing technique used to create a mottled effect, traditionally achieved using authentic limewash.

Linoleum Flooring material made from natural fibers, linseed oil and resins, available in good colors.

Lump hammer Double-faced heavy hammer for driving steel chisels and demolishing masonry.

Mallet Wood or rubber-headed implement for driving sharp instruments that would be damaged by metal hammers.

Marking gauge Sliding device fitted with a pin for scratching lines parallel to edge of the workpiece.

Masonite Fiber building board generally used for covering framework. There are many different types.

Matting Woven natural fibers used as flooring materials.

Metal-detecting device Device for detecting hidden metal such as wiring or pipework.

Milk paint Traditional paint, made by mixing earth-colored pigments into buttermilk or skimmed milk and a little lime, which dries to a smooth, flat finish.

Mineral spirits Colorless liquid derived from petroleum used as a thinner for oil paints.

Nail set Pointed steel shaft used with hammer for driving nail heads just below surface of wood without damaging it.

Newel post Post at top and bottom of staircase supporting the handrail.

Oak graining Technique for painting woodwork to give it the appearance of high-quality wood.

Orbital sander Power sander that makes a series of tiny high-speed cuts to finely smooth wood surfaces.

Padsaw Tapered narrow bladed saw for cutting openings; a small starting hole must be drilled first.

Paint bucket Metal container with handle for holding paint.

Pasting table Lightweight folding table for laying wallpaper on to paste it.

Pickling Process of whitening the grain of hardwood using a paste or matte latex instead of the original lime.

Pincers Jawed tool for extracting nails and tacks.

Plasterboard Ready-plastered sheet with a different surface on each side: also called wallboard.

Plumb line Weight centrally attached to a line for checking verticals.

Plywood Strong sheet material made from bonded layers of veneer, available in a number of grades and thicknesses.

Portable workbench Fold-up lighweight bench with a central grip feature that can be moved to site of work.

Power drill Designed for drilling holes, the many available accessories and attachments turn this versatile instrument into any number of useful tools.

Preservative Chemical formulation painted or sprayed onto wood to prevent decay.

Profile gauge Tightly packed sliding needles held together by a center bar which take on the outline of any object they are pressed against.

PVA adhesive General-purpose liquid adhesive that makes a good primer and sealer when diluted.

Rag rolling Glazed finish resembling fine taffeta or watered silk, achieved by applying a glaze over a base color, then rolling a wet cotton rag over it.

Roller Fabric sleeve on a frame for applying paint. Can be made from a number of different materials.

Rose Ornamental plasterwork ceiling centerpiece or fixture through which a hanging light is wired to a cable in the ceiling.

Safety glasses or goggles Protective eyewear should be worn for any work that produces dust or particles at high speed.

Sanding block Shape for holding abrasive paper during sanding.

Scaffold tower Sectional scaffold frames built up to provide a stable working platform.

Scraper Tool designed for removing unwanted finishes or coverings on wood or walls. Narrow-bladed scrapers are for paint, wide-bladed ones for wallpaper.

Screed Thin layer of mortar spread over solid floor to give a smooth, level finish.

Sealant Paste squeezed into crevices to form a waterproof seal, such as around a bath.

Self-grip wrench Also known as a mole grip, this has jaws controlled by an adjuster to exert great force on objects.

Shavehook A scraper shaped for removing old paint from moldings. The head can be triangular, pear-shaped or a combination of the two.

Skarsten scraper Tool for smoothing wood surfaces or removing paint, available in long- and short-handled versions with a selection of blades.

Solid floor Concrete slab laid over a bed of compacted rubble. Modern solid floors incorporate a damp-proof membrane.

Spattering Speckled effect achieved by spattering one or more colors onto a previously painted surface.

Sponging Process of dabbing a sponge onto wet paint to create an effect.

Steel ruler Accurate tool for measuring and laying out. Can also be used as a straightedge.

Steel wool Matted steel strands used as an abrasive for smoothing metal and wood.

Stencilling Process of painting a design through a cutout which allows the shape to be repeated in any pattern.

Stillson wrench Heavy-duty wrench with a moving jaw operated by a nut, for gripping round objects.

Stippling Aged effect achieved by applying a stippling brush to a wet top coat of paint to break it up into a mass of tiny dots.

Stopcock Brass faucet fitted on a main pipe to allow a water supply to be switched off.

Straightedge Parallel-sided steel strip, up to 6ft (2m) long, used for scribing against and checking surfaces are level.

Stringer Board running at each side of staircase to hold the treads and risers.

Tenon saw Straight-edged saw with reinforced back for rigidity, used for cutting joints.

Transparent oil glaze Also known as "scumble" glaze, this is thinned with mineral spirits before being brushed over the surface. It can be tinted with stain or an oil-based paint.

Try square Parallel-sided metal blade set at a right angle in a stock for accurate marking and checking of 90-degree angles.

Varnish Clear protective coating for wood. Those made with polyurethane give a waterproof, heat- and scratch-resistant finish.

Vinyl Hardwearing all-purpose material used for sheet flooring and tiles. Available in a multitude of designs.

Wire brush Hand brush with steel wire bristles for removing paint and rust particles from metal.

Index

Acknowledgments

ACKNOWLEDGMENTS

The publishers would like to thank all those who supplied photographs for use in this book. We are particularly grateful to Kerry Davis from Sage Interiors, Gale Carlill, Claire Gouldstone, Lois Charlton, Maxime McCaghy for their help with this project.

The Alternative Flooring Company, 186 bottom. **Arc Linea**, Flower kitchen 174 top. **Artisan Furniture & Accessories**, 5 GF3 top, 5 GF1(below+2 details), 147 top inset, 152 top. **Laura Ashley**, 14 /15, 15 bottom right, 22 top, 124/5. **B&Q plc**, Brookland Kitchen 192. **Blanc de Bierges**, 93 bottom. **The Blinds Company**, 156 top. **Coloroll**, 129. **Cotteswood of Oxfordshire** Victorian painted kitchen 135 left. **Crown**, 1 GF1, 24 bottom, 32 bottom, 110, 111, 133, 187 centre, 56 shade.no 9 222, Anaglypta pattern no. RD383 123 centre left, Henrietta from Capri 27 bottom right, 29 top right, wall painted in pale Chamois A1-80 with pink check in Cherub D2-80, Expressions range 171 top left inset, walls & ceiling ivory cream vinyl matt 78 right. **Crabtree Kitchens**, 22 bottom, Shaker kitchen 204 bottom left, Shaker Natural Oak 209 top. **Crucial Trading Ltd**, Cottontop (beige) 180 top, Spice range 179 right. **Crowson Fabrics**, Mandaley roomset/Landscape collection 168 top, Mara & Calypso from Serendipity 31 top. **Czech and Speake of Jermyn Stree**, 78 centre, 78 top, 78 right, 78 bottom, 78 left. **Thomas Dare**, 2 GF3 bottom right, 7 GF3 centre left, blue plaid drapes designed by Christopher Davies 5 GF3 (bottom left), Kottnr/Tanur check/Chitor stripe 7 GF3 top left. **Designers Guild**, 2 GF3 centre right, 7 GF1(right+2 details), 165 bottom. **Dulux**, Walls in Natural Bamboo from Naturals range 3/4 GF1, wall in Ready-to-Use range/picture rail in Tutti Frutti gloss 10 top, 11 bottom, walls in Spice Island from Inspirations range 14 top, walls in Honey Bee/Flamenco from Inspirations range 17 top left, walls in Sorbet & Mint Julep vinyl matt 17 right, ceiling & walls in Surfspray from Kitchens & Bathrooms range 19 centre left, walls colour wahed with Sunshine Days & Pure White from Kitchens & Bathrooms range and Cockle vinyl matt from Definitions 21 top, walls in Naturals range 31 bottom, walls in Mountain Spring & Surfspray from Kitchens & Bathrooms range 32 top, Spanish Bathroom 109, French Kitchen 112/13 top left, 113 top right, walls striped with Pistachio from Inspirations range & Mint Julep vinyl matt from Ready-to-Use range 113 bottom, Scandinavian Living Room 115, Russian Sitting Room115 right, stencil paints from Inspirations/Natural Hints/Finishing Touches (Russian Sitting Room) 115 bottom left, walls in Barley Twist from Kitchens & Bathrooms range 141, 224, 181 bottom, walls in Definitions/Natural Hints range 183 top, 189 centre . **Fired Earth plc**, 20, 65 bottom inset, 93 top left/"Quashgai" Gabbeh rug 173 bottom left. **Anna French Ltd**, 2 GF3 top right, 7 GF3 top right,99 right. **GE Lighting/Mazda**, 172 top, 173 bottom right, 173 top. **Grange Furniture**, Morphee bed & bedside cabinet 30 top. **Habitat**, 13 top right, 21 bottom, 33 bottom, 94 right, 199 bottom left, 200 bottom left. **Hamlyn**, John Bouchier 102/John Cook 97 top, 100 centre right, 100 bottom right, 100 centre left, 100 top left, 100 bottom left/Simon de Courcy Wheeler 53 top/Paul Forrester 5 /6, 7 top left, 12 /3, 16 left, 30 /1, 34 /35, 34 /35, 36, 37, 38, 39, 40/1, 42, 43, 48, 49, 50/1, 51 right, 56, 59, 64/5, 65 right, 67 bottom right, 68 left, 78 left, 79, 85 left, 85 right, 88, 89, 96/7, 98/9, 106, 107, 117 bottom right, 122 top, 122/3, 123 right, 125 above right, 125 bottom left, 125 bottom right, 132 left, 134 bottom, 135 right, 138, 139 left, 139 right, 146/7, 147 right, 148 right, 148 top right, 148 left, 149, 154, 155 bottom, 155 top, 155 centre, 155/6, 156 bottom left, 157 below centre right, 157 above centre right, 157 bottom right, 157 right, 157 centre left, 161 top left, 166/7,169 top right, 169 centre, 169 top left, 170 top right, 171 centre, 177 top,177 centre, 178/9, 187 inset top, 187 inset bottom, 189 inset top,189 inset bottom,194 bottom,194 centre, 195 centre bottom, 195 top left, 195 above left, 195 below left, 195 top right, 195 bottom left, 195 bottom right,196/7, 197 right, 202 top right, 202 bottom right /Mark Gatehouse 117 centre right, 117 bottom left, 117 centre left, 117 top left, 117 top right, 118 bottom left, 118 top right, 118 below right, 119 centre right, 119 top left, 119 top right, 119 bottom left, 119 centre left, 121 above centre right, 121 bottom right, 121 top right, 121 below centre right/Bill McLaughlin 202 left/Vernon Morgan 161 bottom right /Kevin Murray 1 1/2 title/Andrew Twort 8, 9/Simon Wheeler 203 top, 203 bottom, 203 centre/Paul Forrester/Laura Wickenden 120 centre right, 120 bottom right, 120 top right, 120 left/Paul Williams 7 right, 7 bottom. **Robert Harding Picture Library**, 114 bottom 3 pics, 165 centre/Jan Baldwin/IPC Magazines 2 GF1 (top+2 details), 158 top, 158 bottom/Henry Bourne/IPC Magazines 112 bottom/Christopher Drake/IPC Magazines 7 GF3 bottom left/Andreas Von Einsiedel/IPC Magazines 5 GF3 bottom right/Peo Eriksson 159/Brian Harrison 23/IPC Magazines 2 GF3 top left/Tom Leighton/IPC Magazines 2 GF3 bottom left, Mann & Man/IPC Magazines 204 top right/John Miller/IPC Magazines 2 GF1 (left+2 details)/Trevor Richards/IPC Magazines 1 GF3 /M. Robertson/IPC Magazines 8 GF3/Brad Simmons Photography/O'Neill Home NJ USA 170 centre. **Harlequin Fabrics**, 161 top right/Casablanca collection 10 bottom right/Floraganza collection 151 bottom left, /Hullabaloo range 29 top left/Santa Fe collection 19 bottom/Sante Fe collection 151 bottom right. **Heuga**, 186 top/Bistro Buckwheat/Rug effect - Salt & Pepper Rivoli 14 centre right. **The Holding Company**, 201 top right, 205 top centre. **Ideal Standard Ltd**, Meadow 140 bottom. **IKEA Ltd**, Norrskar bathroom furniture 12/13 top, Natura range 30 bottom, Mammut children's furniture 114 top, Buuik bedframe 176 left, Silur 177 bottom, Haparanda seating 199 right, Tore desk, bookcase and bed frame 201 top left. **Junckers**, Standard Beech floorboards 180 bottom. **Liberty Furnishings**, 162 bottom. **Liberon Waxes Ltd**, 183 bottom 4 pictures. **London's Georgian Houses**, 86. **Marie Claire /Gilles de Chabaneix**, 200. **Material World**, 7 GF3 bottom right. **Mitchell Beazley**, Bill Batten 152 bottom, 165 top, 2 /3 title, 4 /5 GF3/13 bottom right, 147 bottom inset, 151 centre, 157 top right, 162 top, 162 top, 163 bottom right, 163 top right, 163 centre right, 163 bottom right, 163 top right, 163 top left, 163 top left, 163 centre right/Peter Marshall 24 top, 28 bottom/James Merrell 9 right. **Next Retail Ltd**, 11 top, 19 top, 26 right, 66, 73 bottom, 51 top 3 pictures. **Osborne & Little plc**, Lalezar designed by Victoria Waymouth 2 GF3 left. **The Pier**, 205 bottom centre, 205 bottom left. **Pilkington Glass Ltd**, Texture Glass 73 top. **Price's Patent Candle Company Ltd**, 171 centre inset pics, 171 right inset, 171 bottom left inset. **Reed Consumer Books Picture Library**, Robert Glover 52. **Arthur Sanderson & Sons Ltd**, Jardiniere from Manuscript 27 top right, Bangalore/Manuscript 29 bottom left, Canton/Manuscript 122 centre. **Sharps Bedrooms**, 24 centre, 212 top, /Prima in Pure White 16 right, /Savoy 28 top. **Shand Kydd**, April Showers from Mansfield Park 25, Coromandel from Mansfield Park 26 left,. Storeys/Rolatile 134 right. **Warner Fabrics plc**, Conversationals collection 2 GF3 top right/detail, 93 top right, Conversationals collection 150 bottom right. **Wellington Tile Company**, Rustic Rose Slate 181 top. **John Wilman Fabrics & Wallpapers**, Coral (Grey) from the Definitions Collection 105, La Rochelle collection 199 top, Regent Pink from the Floral Home Collection 27 left, Georgian House Collection 150/1. **Elizabeth Whiting & Associates**, 15 top right, 17 centre left, 80, 87, 143 top, 169 bottom, 174 bottom, 182 right, 182 left, 198, 200 top/Michael Dunne 91, 170 left, 175 top right, 209 bottom/Andreas V. Einsiedel 70, 130/31, 208 bottom left/EMAP 8 GF1/Brian Harrison 94 left, 205 top left, 208 top /Clive Helm 175 bottom left/Rodney Hyett 19 centre right, 77 left, 82 bottom, 119 bottom,143 bottom, 145, 172 bottom, 175 bottom right, 185 bottom, 201 bottom, 205 top right/Ed Ironside 140 top/Di Lewis 6, 18, 116 top, 175 top left/Neil Lorimer 17 bottom left, 176 bottom/ Nadia MacKenzie 10 bottom left, 184/Neil Lorimer156 bottom right, /Michael Nicholson 185 top, 214/Spike Powell 74 top, 150 left, 205 bottom right/SIP/B.Touillon 90,108 top/Dennis Stone 176 right/Tim Street-Porter.77 right,168 bottom, 208 bottom right/Ron Sutherland 82 top left/Friedhelm Thomas 142 top, /Jerry Tubby 143 bottom, 212 bottom/Simon Upton 12 bottom, 108 bottom/Nedra Westwater 74 bottom/Peter Woloszynski 33 top, 82 top right. **Brian Yates Interiors Ltd**, 204 left.

The publishers would also like to thank Laura Bangert for her tireless prop hunting and styling.

Thanks is also due to all those companies and individuals who supplied props for photography and in particular:

Brent Carpet Company Ltd, Bryon & Bryon Ltd, Sean Galpin of **The Decorative Fabrics Gallery, Foxell & James Ltd, Hamiltons Acorns Ltd, LG Harris & Co Ltd, Ikea, The London Lighting Company, Olympic Tiles CTD, Plastercraft, Simeon Oliver,The Stencil Store Company Ltd** and **A Touch of Brass.**